MAKING RECORDS

MAKING RECORDS

The Scenes Behind the Music

Phil Ramone

& Charles L. Granata

HYPERION
NEW YORK

Printed in the United States of America.

For information address Hyperion,
77 West 66th Street, New York, New York 10023-6298.

Library of Congress Cataloging-in-Publication Data
has been applied for.

ISBN: 978-0-7868-6859-9

Hyperion books are available for special promotions,
premiums, or corporate training. For details contact
Michael Rentas, Assistant Director, Inventory
Operations, Hyperion, 77 West 66th Street, 12th floor.
New York, New York 10023, or call 212-456-0133.

Design by Karen Minster

FIRST EDITION

10 9 8 7 6 5 4 3 2 1

Dedicated to Min, for mentoring Doreen and me.

*The mentoring continues with Karen, Matt,
Simon, BJ, Ann, Maxwell, Andi, Rick, Kelly, Seth,
Elizabeth, Joe, Suzie, Doug, Melissa, Kim,
Neal, Stacy, and Julie.*

IN MEMORY OF DAVID SMITH
1951–2006

Receiving the Grammy for *Genius Loves Company* from Bonnie Raitt, 2003
Courtesy of Michael Caulfield/WireImage

Courtesy of Larry Busaca

The greatest interaction in the world is the creativity involved in making music.

I wish everyone could experience the birth of a record the way I do, from the time a songwriter hits on a brilliant idea through the long hours spent getting it down on tape.

What makes for a great record? A fantastic song, convincing performance, and superb sound.

There's a craft to making records, and behind every recording lie dozens of details that are invisible to someone listening on the radio, CD player, or iPod.

Wherever I go, I'm amazed by the curiosity that both casual and serious music lovers express for the marginalia surrounding the records they love.

Who wrote the song, and why did the artist choose to perform it? Why was it done in a particular style? When, where, and how was it recorded? What decisions went into building the mix? What was happening in the world, the artist's life, and the studio on the day the record was made, and how did those things affect the performance?

The answers to these questions are what I live for, and I'm grateful that people are fascinated by the magic behind what we as engineers and producers do. And so, this book is about making records: the way we made them when I started in the late 1950s, the way we make them now, and everything in between.

Like mixing a record, condensing the decades of one's working life into the finite pages of a book necessitates many reductive decisions.

While it touches on numerous areas of my life and work, this volume is not an autobiography or technical manual, nor does it pretend to be a definitive study of any one topic related to record production. Instead, I've painted a broad picture, using personal anecdotes and vignettes to help illustrate the complex road traveled by songwriters, artists, engineers, and producers who contribute to the art of making records.

As an engineer and producer, I've strived to give singers and musicians the confidence to develop their ideas, find their best performance, and use the latest technology to share it with the world. I'm pleased to offer a glimpse behind the scenes, with hopes that the next time you hear one of your favorite records you'll be able to say, "Aha! *That's* how they did it."

Phil Ramone
New York City
April 2007

MAKING RECORDS

Frank Sinatra *Duets*

With Frank Sinatra, A&R Recording Studios NYC, 1967
Phil Ramone Collection

June 28, 1993.

Capitol Records Studio A, Hollywood and Vine Streets, Los Angeles.

The short walk from the main studio to the control room takes what seems to be an eternity. My heart thumps in my chest.

As I enter the booth, its thick door seals behind me with a sturdy *whoosh*. Trying to hide my disappointment, I look at the crew.

"That's it, gentlemen. He's gone."

At the end of any other night, these words might bring a collective sigh of relief, a funny comment, or a round of applause—all tension breakers meant to relax. Tonight they come at the start, and their implication is ominous.

Frank Sinatra, uncharacteristically full of self-doubt, has left the first session for his eagerly anticipated *Duets* album, and we have nothing to show for it.

While the notion of undertaking such a project is a gamble, I'm confident that pairing Sinatra with a variety of legendary artists will make for an attention-grabbing record. There's timelessness to Sinatra's music, and though his voice might be showing signs of age, he can still wring every nuance from a lyric.

I feel more prepared for this album than for any other of my career; I've worked with Frank before, and understand his musical shorthand.

Whether you're a musician or a producer, you always know where you stand with Sinatra. Since some of the younger guys aren't familiar with the singer's recording jargon or my cryptic signals, I warn them to listen carefully, and to watch my hands.

I realize that when the musical sparks start to fly we might have only one shot at getting it on tape, so I've assembled a top-notch team to work alongside of me: arranger-conductor Patrick Williams, engineer Al Schmitt, coproducer Hank Cattaneo (Sinatra's longtime production manager), and Don Rubin, head of Capitol's A&R department.

Patrick has lovingly reworked many of Sinatra's classic arrangements, the sassy swing and the tender ballad charts written by Nelson Riddle, Billy May, Don Costa, Billy Byers, and Quincy Jones. As I watch Patrick greet Frank for the first time, I recall what he said after the original scores arrived from the Sinatra library.

"Phil," he explained, "I opened the package and put them on the desk, and right on top was a chart marked, 'I've Got You Under My Skin—arranged by Nelson Riddle.' Nelson's copyist, Vern Yocum, had scrupulously handwritten every part. When I saw that I started to cry. It was one song after another, right there on my desk—all of these great Sinatra songs that had been such an important part of my life."

Sinatra's music represents the apotheosis of American popular music. The original charts—some yellowed and dog-eared—are the same ones that sat on the musicians' stands in this very room on the balmy nights when Frank first recorded his classic interpretations of the songs nearly forty years ago. For a musician or arranger, the chance to make a tactile connection such as this—to touch and reinterpret such well-respected music—is a humbling experience.

For a project such as *Duets,* a first-class engineer is a must and at my side is Al Schmitt. In addition to having recorded some of the best-sounding records of the past thirty years, Al is the last person to fold under pressure.

Ditto Hank Cattaneo, who has toured with Frank as his personal soundman for almost twenty years. Other than Quincy Jones, few people understand the complexities of a Sinatra performance—or the man's temperament—better than Hank does.

Don Rubin, a veteran EMI artist & repertoire executive and close associate of Capitol Records chairman Charles Koppelman, has tended to the dozens of business issues that accompany such an ambitious project.

Desiring to make Frank's return to Capitol Records special, we've lavished lots of attention on the details.

In a small passageway between Studios A and B (an area that is occasionally used as a vocal or drum booth), we've created a lounge with a couch, table, and bar stocked with Frank's favorite snacks and beverages. Knowing that he might want to warm up privately with pianist Bill Miller, we've placed a small piano in there, too.

We have also peppered the orchestra with familiar faces from Frank's past, extraordinary musicians such as George Roberts (bass trombone) and Gerald Vinci (violin)—musicians who played on the original records decades before. Joining them are the guys who've been backing Frank on tour: Chuck Berghoffer (bass), Ron Anthony (guitar), and Gregg Field (drums). Tying it all together is Sinatra's pianist of more than forty years, Bill Miller.

Tonight marks the first time the entire cast and crew is together.

Hank, Al, and I have been at the studio for hours, checking the mixing boards, digital recorders, and microphone cables. The orchestra has been rehearsing all afternoon, and we've gotten our preliminary balances.

All we need now is Mr. Sinatra.

Patrick has set a six o'clock call for the musicians; they begin trickling in early.

Frank arrives at seven, immaculately dressed in a sport coat, slacks, and tie. He greets me with a firm handshake and a broad smile. "Hi kid—good to see you again."

Besides being his first recording session in years, this is Frank's first visit to the Capitol Tower—the birthplace of his most acclaimed records—since he left the label under tense circumstances in 1962. He hasn't forgotten. "I know this joint," he deadpans as he walks down the hall leading to Studio A. "I've been here before!"

Sinatra's comment is a positive sign. He's in a great mood, and as we enter the studio he makes it a point to chat briefly with some of the old friends he sees sprinkled throughout the room.

The orchestra tunes up and runs down the first song. They sound fabulous. Patrick signals that he's ready to start. Looking at Frank, I point toward the vocal booth. "Should we try one?"

Sinatra glances nervously at the booth; he takes his time walking toward the three-sided structure. After a few minutes of halfhearted singing, he comes out. "This isn't for me," he says, looking at the booth disapprovingly. "I'm not singing in there. Why don't you just get some tracks with the band, and I'll come back later to sing over them?"

My heart sinks.

With Frank you've got to read between the lines. The subtext is, "Forget it. If I'm not comfortable, I'm not doing it." I know that if we tape the orchestra tracks without him, he'll find some excuse to avoid coming back to do the overdubs. It's a familiar scene, and one I've hoped to avoid. The words of a well-intentioned friend at Reprise Records pop into my mind. "Good luck," he'd said. "We've been trying to get him into the studio for years."

We've reached the moment of truth, and Sinatra is begging off. Pushing him would be pointless. "I understand," I explain, hoping to hide my disappointment. "We'll rehearse the band, and you can come back and try again tomorrow night." He agrees.

When Sinatra is out of earshot, his manager, Eliot Weisman,

complains of a nervous stomach. "We've blown it—he won't be back," Weisman says. Don Rubin is also perplexed; no one knows what the next step should be. Sinatra says his good nights, and as quickly as he came, disappears into the night.

I head for the control room, and the inevitable postsession analysis with my colleagues. I'm crestfallen. This session—and the success or failure of the entire project—rests with me.

The path leading to this session has been long and arduous. Convincing Sinatra to record again hasn't been easy.

When Eliot Weisman, Don Rubin, and I visited him a year earlier in Palm Beach, Florida, we explained why we felt Frank should do an album, and what I thought the approach should be.

The most intimate part of a Sinatra concert (and the one I loved most) was when he shunned the orchestra and sang with a jazz combo and strings, so my first suggestion was to book a week at New York's Rainbow Room and record Frank doing live supper-club-style shows. I thought it would be nice to surround Frank with a quintet, twelve strings, and four soloists. The intimate late-night jazz setting would allow him to stretch out a bit, and to tape some of the tunes he'd never officially recorded—chestnuts like "Lover, Come Back to Me," "I Remember You," and " 'S'wonderful."

As original as it was, Frank rejected the idea.

My second suggestion was pairing him with other artists to revisit the songs he'd made famous: "I've Got You Under My Skin," "Come Fly with Me," "Guess I'll Hang My Tears Out to Dry," "Where or When," and "New York, New York." While he didn't dismiss this option completely, Frank had reservations. "I recorded those songs forty years ago," he protested. "Why would I want to rerecord them now?"

I persisted. "Yes, you've sung those songs before, and the originals are models of their kind," I offered. "But the way you do 'One For My Baby' now is unlike the way you did it in 1958."

I reminded Frank that while Laurence Olivier had performed

Shakespeare while in his twenties, the readings he did when he was in his sixties gave them new meaning. I spoke with conviction. "Don't my children—and your grandchildren—deserve to hear the way you're interpreting your classic songs now?"

Deep down I knew that *Duets* was the right thing for Frank to do, while he still had that voice, and while audiences around the world were still honoring him nightly with standing ovations.

"Who would you like to invite to the party?" I asked. "Ella," he said, without hesitation.

I knew that Ella Fitzgerald wasn't well, and that she couldn't participate. Neither could Dean Martin or Peggy Lee.

"How about some of the younger people, like Luther Vandross?" I suggested.

To appeal to as wide an audience as possible we extended the invite to artists from many genres: Barbra Streisand, Aretha Franklin, Gloria Estefan, Julio Iglesias, Anita Baker, Natalie Cole, Liza Minnelli, Tony Bennett, Charles Aznavour, and Bono.

As expected, everyone clamored to sing with Mr. Sinatra.

But Frank's agreement came with a proviso. "If I do it, I can't have anyone sing in the studio with me," he said.

I appreciated his candor and reasoning. Frank was seventy-six years old, and he hadn't been in the studio for almost ten years. He was a perfectionist who was too impatient to record duets the way he'd done them years before with Ella, Dean, Rosemary Clooney, Bing Crosby, Sammy Davis Jr., and so many others. At that point in his life he was hard enough on himself. Why add the stress of extra rehearsals and repeated takes?

After whittling Frank's core repertoire down to twenty songs, we circulated it among his duet partners. "Give us the names of a few songs you'd like to sing with him," I asked. "And please be flexible."

The assignment of specific songs—and how the lines will be split—won't be finalized until after Frank records complete solo versions of the songs.

Adding to the excitement of making duets is the opportunity to use some cutting-edge technology. Since several of Frank's duet partners can't record in Los Angeles, we've planned to tape their parts using EDNet fiber-optic lines from whatever city they're in: Charles Aznavour in Paris, Bono in Dublin, Liza Minnelli in Rio de Janeiro, Gloria Estefan and Julio Iglesias in Miami, and Aretha Franklin and Anita Baker in Detroit.

But on this first night, all of these points are moot. We've stumbled, and as the producer I have a lot to consider.

Besides the artistic loss we'll suffer if Sinatra doesn't do the album, there'll be financial repercussions. Although my first concern is for Frank's satisfaction and the artistic integrity of the record we're making (or, at the moment, not making), I still have to justify the cost of underwriting the complicated production to Charles Koppelman.

To date, a fair amount has been spent adjusting the vintage charts to suit Sinatra's mature voice, rehearsing the fifty-five-piece orchestra, and setting up for the sessions. "How much are we in for?" Koppelman asks. "About three hundred and fifty thousand," I reply, knowing that the figure will surely increase by week's end, whether Sinatra records anything or not.

Koppelman's next question hangs in the air. *"Is there a chance . . . ?"*

I've got a lot on my mind as I head for the control room on this first unproductive night.

In the booth, Hank Cattaneo and I replay the night's events in our minds, trying to figure out why Sinatra's confidence had changed so suddenly. "Maybe the lighting wasn't right," Hank says. "Or his jacket and tie were too confining." I make a mental note to remind Sinatra to dress casually the next night.

Then it hits us: Frank had looked uncomfortable when he went into the vocal booth.

From the start, Al Schmitt and I had assumed that Frank would sing in the small area we'd partitioned off to separate his voice from the other instruments. But tonight's session proved that we've miscalculated. At this stage in the game, Sinatra isn't accustomed to being separated from his musicians; he's most comfortable when he can see and hear the band in front of him.

We think about how to tailor the recording environment to better suit Frank's needs. "Let's arrange it so that he's closer to the rhythm section," Hank suggests. "If he feels like he's singing on-stage it might help him relax." It's an excellent idea, and because there's a movable partition between Studios A and B, we're able to open up the room and spread things out.

Al, Hank, and I scramble to rearrange the studio and build a small platform between the two rooms. On it we place a chair, small teleprompter, and two monitor speakers so Frank will be able to hear the rhythm section and strings. While we'd originally hung three mikes in the vocal booth, we now place a single boom-mounted microphone on the stage.

For insurance, we prepare a wireless hand mike like the one Frank uses on stage for live performances. Al is apprehensive about using the handheld microphone. "It's a stage mike, Phil— and it's wireless." His concern is understandable. As anyone who has used a cell phone knows, wireless equipment can cut out while you're using it, and it's prone to radio-wave interference. I consider the risks and rewards. "We've got to move forward," I say. "I don't care what kind of microphone he sings into, he's still *Frank Sinatra*."

Drained, I go to my hotel. I barely sleep.

The next night Sinatra shows up at seven, this time wearing a nice jogging suit. He looks tired. Is he as nervous about the sessions as we are?

There's some small talk. Frank sips a bit of water and picks up the hand mike. He tries a tune.

Then, strike two.

Without fanfare, Frank quietly announces that he's not feeling well. "The reed's not working," he explains, tapping his Adam's apple. "Sore throat. I'm going home to rest. I'll see you guys tomorrow." He leaves, and disappointment turns to fear.

We're far from the finish line, and there's nothing to do but wait. If the sessions don't work out, it's not for a lack of trying, I remind myself. There are no guarantees when you embark on a project like this; there are many risks, and the artist, producer, and record label share responsibility for those risks.

"We've set the stage for something extraordinary, and I still feel that this will work," I tell everyone before leaving. "Get some rest— I'll see you all tomorrow."

The next day, Hank and I arrive at Capitol early to test the equipment. The musicians have rehearsed so much they've practically memorized their parts. Despite this, we hold a two o'clock rehearsal.

At four, the calls to the studio begin. "He's dressed and preparing for the session," comes the report from Beverly Hills. A few hours later, a second call from the car: "We're on Hollywood Boulevard—he'll be there in a few minutes." Suddenly, Frank— wearing an immaculately tailored business suit and tie—breezes into the studio, looking rested and years younger than the previous two nights.

Again, pleasantries are exchanged as Frank makes his way into the studio. I say a silent prayer, and escort him to the platform where he'll sing. In that moment, something that I've rarely seen before happens: although fifty-five seasoned musicians are preparing to play, there's a disconcerting silence in the room. A hundred and ten eyes follow as Frank and I traverse the floor. When we get to his spot on the stage, he turns to me.

FS: So kid, tell me—why am I recording these songs again?
      I did a lot of them years ago, right here.

ME: These renditions will be different—we're going to

arrange them as duets. We'll rework your solo recordings
and add your singing partners later.

FS: But the girls sing in different keys than the guys.
How's that going to work?

ME: That's why Patrick is here. If there are any inconsistencies
with the keys, he can adjust them right away.

FS: I'm sure you'll figure it out. I trust you.

ME: If you're unhappy with what we do, I'll personally erase
the tapes. No one will ever hear them. Don't worry—
this will be great!

I turn to walk toward the booth when Sinatra—sotto voce—
offers a final thought:

"It better be."

I signal the control room to roll tape, and two recorders—a
forty-eight-track digital and a twenty-four-track analog backup—
are started. I look out and give Patrick the thumbs-up. He kicks off
the band, and the booth is filled with the buoyant sound of the first
song's sweeping introduction. Then, the rich, burnished tone of the
most familiar singing voice in the world:

> Come fly with me,
> Let's fly, let's fly away
> If you can use some exotic booze
> There's a bar in far Bombay . . .

When Frank's first notes boom from the monitors, huge grins
break out in the booth. The voice is clear, confident, and command-
ing. Sinatra is still *Sinatra*. He's in the studio, and he's swinging. The
Duets album is finally under way.

By the end of "Come Fly with Me," I know that we've got one
solid take in the bank. I rewind the tape and play it back. Frank
beams, and without missing a beat asks, "What's next?" Before we

can get the tapes rolling, the band launches into the opening of the next song, catching everyone off guard. I make a mad dash for the tape machines. *"Get those tapes going!"* I shout.

From here on out it's one song after another, for nearly five hours, until we have nine songs in the can.

After the first few numbers I see some of the brass players pointing to their mouths. Their lips are tired. "Let's take a break," I suggest. "How long?" Sinatra asks.

"Ten minutes."

"Give 'em five," he jokes.

We come back from the break, and Frank offers a glimpse of the intuitive sense that has made him a studio legend. As the band starts the intro to "A Foggy Day," he motions for them to stop. "The tempo's a shade too bright, and there's a problem in the woodwinds," he proclaims.

Patrick scans the chart, consults with the musicians, and discovers that Frank is right. He makes the correction, and says, "Okay—we've got it." Without another word, Sinatra gently taps a finger on his leg to define the tempo. The gesture is barely visible—so subtle that Patrick strains to see Sinatra's hand. This time, the tempo is right where it belongs, and the mistake in the woodwind part is nowhere to be found.

Once Frank has settled into a groove and everyone has relaxed, I sit back and absorb the energy coming from the studio. I feel a glow, realizing that my dream for one last Sinatra album is finally coming true. As I tap my foot to the beat of the music, Al Schmitt looks at me inquisitively, the strain of the week evident on his face. He cocks his head. "Why do you do this?" he asks. "Why do you put yourself under this kind of pressure?"

It's a fair question, and gazing out at the studio I think about it.

We're at Capitol Records in Hollywood, recording Frank Sinatra. The walls in this studio have absorbed as much seminal music as any place on Earth. The singer and the songs being sung have been part of my life since I was a child. The performances are uplifting and invigorating.

Has it been stressful? You bet. But whether it was playing the violin, mixing a record, or working as a producer, I've lived my life for moments like this. "He's the reason I'm here," I say, nodding toward the studio. "He's what makes it all worthwhile."

Artists and their music are my lifeblood—my reason for being. While projects like *Duets* are challenging, the pressure, risks, and rewards are all part of making records. And, there's nothing in the world I'd rather do.

With Terry Woodson and Al Schmitt, Sinatra *Duets* session, 1993
Phil Ramone Collection

Courtesy of Sam Emerson/Redbox

The Producer

I'm not a screamer.

I've seen producers yell, badger, bully, and throw tantrums to get results, but that approach has never worked for me.

Recently, an artist with whom I was working for the first time amused me by expressing surprise at the tranquility of our inaugural session. "I was expecting all kinds of gestures and running and stamping," she said. "Yet, you direct so quietly."

As she spoke, I wondered what had shaped her image of a producer. "It's not about hysterics," I explained. "What's important is for you and I to communicate, and for me to calmly relay information and directions to the people that we're collaborating with."

During the drive home, it dawned on me that if a seasoned performer was confused about the role of the producer, then the general public probably was, too. Why don't more people understand who the record producer is, and what he or she is supposed to do? I thought.

To help explain how the producer influences what we hear, I'll answer some of the questions I'm frequently asked about record producers and their role in the recording process.

The record producer is the music world's equivalent of a film director. But, unlike a director (who is visible, and often a celebrity in his own right), the record producer toils in anonymity. We ply our craft deep into the night, behind locked doors. And with few exceptions, the fruit of our labor is seldom launched with the glitzy fanfare of a Hollywood premiere.

Just as a successful film director helps to inspire an actor and draw out an exquisite performance, the producer serves as an objective filter and helps the artist bring life to their records. As a producer, my primary goals are to create a stimulating environment, help the artist develop their ideas, and ensure that the performance is recorded and mixed properly.

There are three basic parts to making a record, and the producer is directly involved in each of them:

1. *Recording*—the "session" when the music is played and recorded
2. *Mixing*—when all of the individual sections recorded at the session (or sessions) are blended together
3. *Mastering*—when the final sound is tweaked and polished

But there's much more to making a record than recording, mixing, and mastering. There are dozens of things that happen behind the scenes before one note is played or sung. The artist has to write or choose the songs, and orchestrations must be written. Studio time must be scheduled, an engineer chosen, and a budget developed. A producer deals with all of these issues.

But the responsibilities don't end there.

What happens when an artist asks you to pull together a band at the last minute? Or when, in the middle of a session, the electrical system plunges the studio into darkness? Or, a creative block affects the deadline on a record the label has been hounding you for?

Someone's got to think fast and move things ahead, and those tasks fall to the producer. Because he or she is involved in nearly every aspect of a production, the producer serves as friend, cheerleader, psychologist, taskmaster, court jester, troubleshooter, secretary, traffic cop, judge, and jury rolled into one.

Through the years, the role of the producer and their relationships with artists has changed dramatically.

Forty years ago, singers and musicians who were intimately involved in the creation of their records (such as Frank Sinatra and Brian Wilson) were exceptions. Most artists would come to a session and sing whatever their record company's staff producer put in front of them. Artists & repertoire executives at the record labels crafted every facet of an artist's work, from their look to their sound.

Today, artists are extremely independent—and more involved in the production of their music than ever before. Many performers have formal musical training, and in addition to writing and orchestrating their own songs, immerse themselves in the process of recording them. More often than not, singers and musicians have small home- or computer-based studio setups that they use for rehearsing, making demos, and at times producing their own records.

So, why do even the brightest artists seek the services of a producer when they can do it all themselves? For the experience and objectivity a record producer brings to a project.

It can be daunting for a performer—especially a singer-songwriter—to edit their own work, and that's when the services of a producer can be extremely useful. As Elton John recently explained, "A producer knows when a song should be changed or a vocal isn't good, because he isn't as close to it as the artist is. The knowledge and experience that a producer brings to the control room when a musician is playing and singing on the other side of the glass is very reassuring."

While it's professional, the bond between an artist and their producer is personal and complex, too.

A producer can be closer to the artist than anyone else in his or her life during the weeks or months they spend together making a record. The intimacy they share is largely unspoken; it touches raw nerves, and if the producer is especially good at what he does, helps peel back the anxiety and fear that dwells within every performer.

An artist's anxieties and fears are, by the way, very real. They're normal, too. Although the best performers make it seem effortless, putting oneself in front of an audience, TV or motion picture camera, or recording studio microphone requires extraordinary confidence. The normal insecurities that most of us experience from time to time are magnified a hundredfold for an artist who is making a record or rehearsing a show, and I've spent countless hours reassuring artists during late-night telephone conversations—much to the consternation of my wife, I'm sure.

But the investment of such intense, heart-to-heart time usually results in a handsome creative payoff.

I've had times when I've called an artist at two in the morning and said, "I hate to wake you, but I'm driving in my car and I've been thinking about what we're having trouble with. Maybe you should come and meet me right now. I've made a few notes . . ."

When you spend a lot of time in the studio, you savor the times when things go well. If we've had smooth sailing one day, and things seem to be dragging the next, I'll turn to the artist and say, "Remember last night? It was so cool. Why doesn't that happen every day?"

The most successful artist-producer relationships are based on honesty and trust, and respecting the trust and confidence of the performers I work with has always been my top priority.

Of all the artists I've known, few appreciate a producer's honesty and trust more than Barbra Streisand.

I first met Barbra at a political event in Washington, D.C., in 1963. She was twenty-two years old, and already a star. Like most, I was impressed with the tonal quality and range of Barbra's voice, and the stunning way she performed.

By mid-'63, Barbra had made major appearances on *The Tonight Show* (with both Jack Paar and Johnny Carson), *The Ed Sullivan Show,* and *The Judy Garland Show.* She had recorded two albums for Columbia Records: the Grammy-winning *The Barbra Streisand Album,* and *The Second Barbra Streisand Album*; both records went gold. Barbra's coup de grace, though, was her showstopping performance as Miss Marmelstein in Broadway's *I Can Get It for You Wholesale.*

That was just the beginning.

In early 1964, Barbra was again on Broadway, this time winning acclaim for her portrayal of Fanny Brice in *Funny Girl.* With the show came two quintessential Streisand classics: "Don't Rain on My Parade," and "People."

The first time Barbra and I worked together was 1967, when I designed the sound system for her groundbreaking Central Park concert. Knowing my penchant for tackling complicated projects, she called on me again in 1975 to ask if I would supervise the

With Barbra Streisand, circa 1985
Phil Ramone Collection

recording of *A Star Is Born* in Hollywood. Our collaboration on that film illustrates the value of mutual trust and the importance of an artist and producer trusting their own instincts.

In the Hollywood film studios, every production is scripted before work on a picture begins. If the film is a musical, all of the vocal and instrumental parts are recorded before the actors shoot their scenes. The actors then lip-synch to those tracks when filming a scene where singing is involved. The dialogue, music, and sound effects will all be mixed in postproduction to create the final soundtrack.

The challenge with *A Star Is Born* was that Barbra wanted to break tradition and record all of the film's music live, as each scene was being performed. Why did she want to do this?

Anyone who's familiar with Barbra's work knows that she feels and interprets a song differently each time she sings it. Capturing every nuance of her voice—and her look while singing—was essential to authentically conveying the premise of *A Star Is Born*. Barbra knew that prerecording days or months before shooting began would compromise the spontaneity of her performance.

Recording audio in sync with film intrigued me. But, since almost everything was being shot on location, recording this way required painstaking organization. Once you leave the confines of the soundstage you're at the mercy of the less-than-perfect acoustics and ambient noise of whatever area you're working in; the controls that help insure consistency are lost.

To accommodate our needs on *A Star Is Born*, I rented a mobile recording truck from Enactron in Canada, outfitting it with a small vocal booth so Barbra could make vocal corrections on the spot. Knowing that she'd want to see her performances immediately after shooting them, I also arranged for the crew to run a video camera alongside the master film camera.

In the film, Barbra plays a singer (Esther Hoffman) who falls in love with rock star John Norman Howard (Kris Kristofferson). As the plot develops, Howard's wild partying causes his career to crash, while Esther's begins to soar.

Our first test was filming a nightclub scene at a small club in Pasadena.

All of the action—including a fight scene between John Norman Howard and a club patron—occurred in real time, meaning it wasn't patched together from multiple takes. Recording it live as it happened—Barbra singing while two men argued and fought in front of her—was surreal. We felt confident that what we'd captured would quell the uneasiness of the executives at Warner Bros.

When the studio bosses saw the footage the next day, they applauded. While they marveled at our success and approved the concept of recording live-to-film, they insisted that Barbra prerecord everything too—for insurance.

Much of the film was shot on location in Arizona, and a setting for one of the movie's key scenes, a rock concert, was Arizona State University's Sun Devil Stadium. Instead of mocking up the set and using extras for the audience shots, film producer Jon Peters hired legendary concert promoter Bill Graham to stage a genuine rock-and-roll fest featuring five acts, including Peter Frampton and Carlos Santana.

The audience consisted of students and others from the surrounding area, each of whom paid $3.50 for admission. The plan was for each of the rock groups to play their sets, with Barbra and Kris Kristofferson filming their songs in between.

Bill Graham was a savvy stage producer, and he paced the show brilliantly. He also covered all of the ancillary bases. He knew that at large-scale events kids get sick, people become overheated, and drugs are consumed. To minimize problems, he set up medical stations, placed showers along the sidelines, and warned the audience about the possibility of some bad acid being passed around.

At midnight, a crowd of university students began streaming into the stadium. The weather was perfect; at dawn I played the Beatles' "Here Comes the Sun," and the patrons—anticipating an eventful day—cheered.

By seven a.m., the first band—the L.A. Jets—hit the stage and juiced everyone up. Then came Graham Central Station. Around nine, Barbra appeared and kibitzed with the crowd. "We're gonna rock and roll today," she yelled. "And we're gonna be in a movie!"

Barbra wanted the audience to understand the technicalities behind filmmaking, so she sang "The Way We Were" to a taped instrumental track. "That's the way it's usually done in Hollywood," she said. "But I don't want to lip-synch—I want to sing live, to you." She proceeded by belting out an electrifying version of "Woman in the Moon," backed by her band.

When it came time to shoot Barbra's first scene, the crew was nervous. Could recording everything live work in this situation? Would the audience behave, despite the long hours and the heat? Would we get the sound and picture quality we needed? The set was prepared; the audience in place; the crew ready to roll.

Everyone was intensely focused. Some of us were on pins and needles, knowing that singing in front of large crowds wasn't easy for Barbra. We watched carefully for last-minute jitters. We needn't have worried; the performance of "Woman in the Moon" she gave for the cameras was a triumph.

Anyone who'd been skeptical of Barbra's professionalism was won over after that. The cast and crew admired the way she handled the concert and the audience, and told her so.

After the second break, she came out and again spoke to the crowd. "In this film I speak the language of rock and roll," she explained. *"Aren't you having a great fucking time?"* They went nuts.

To lead into Kristofferson's first scene, Barbra offered the audience some direction. "This is a concert where you've been waiting two hours for him to show up. When he comes onstage, you should boo him. But when he starts singing, settle down and become the fans who've always loved him." When Kris came onstage, they booed the hell out of him. When they calmed down, he performed "Watch Closely Now."

After noon, Santana played their set and Barbra previewed "Evergreen," a ballad she'd written with Paul Williams. "I'll be crushed if you don't like it," she said. The crowd ate it up, and shooting continued until well after six p.m. Montrose and a new sensation from England named Peter Frampton closed the show.

Five days of work culminated with a massive concert that went off far more smoothly than anticipated.

Our next stop was the setting for the film's seven-minute, twenty-second climax: the university's Grady Grammage Memorial Auditorium, a historic building designed by Frank Lloyd Wright. As before, there would be an audience. After the concert shoot, this will be a snap, I thought.

As the plot evolves, John Howard becomes so depressed that he commits suicide, and in the final scene, Esther sings for the first time in public since his death. She begins with a ballad ("With One More Look at You") then segues into "Watch Closely Now"— one of Howard's songs that she discovered on a cassette tape after he died.

The finale was a long scene by any standard; where most actors would balk at a director wanting to shoot one continuous take, Barbra insisted on it. The way she handled Esther's transformation from grieving lover to confident star was inspired. Still, I felt unsettled about the take we had in the can.

Before leaving the Grammage, I watched the videotape of Barbra's finale. As wonderful as it was, it lacked the scintillating spark that I'd seen before in her acting. While I doubted she would consider reshooting the scene, I decided to let her know what I thought after she'd had the chance to relax.

At nine that night I saw her at the dailies—the cast and crew's preview of the footage shot the day before—and seized the opportunity. Here's where honesty and trust come into play.

"How are you doing, Phil?" Barbra asked. "What did you think about today's scene?"

"Well," I began, choosing my words carefully. "I thought it was fine. But something's missing. I think there's a better one in you."

I wasn't lying. I knew that if Barbra dug a bit deeper, she could *really* show the character's reach for strength. "The set's still there for tomorrow morning's pickup and cutaway shots," I offered.

As I expected, Barbra disagreed.

"Are you out of your mind?" she asked. "The take worked—we're done." I couldn't argue—the take *had* worked. But seven minutes is a long stretch for any performer, and I didn't want to forego our last chance at getting a truly gut-wrenching performance.

Barbra and I knew each other well, and on some level I knew she must have understood what I meant. Although I didn't belabor the point, I implored her to think about redoing the scene.

Sure enough, a little while later there was a knock at my door. A production assistant had come with a message from Ms. Streisand. "You have an eight o'clock call on the theater set—we're shooting the ending again." I smiled. Barbra just couldn't ignore the possibility that she could do it better.

And she did.

The next morning's performance had the gutsy confidence that Barbra is known for; the scene delivers everything one desires of the ultimate moment in a dramatic film.

What gives a producer the freedom to trust him- or herself, and to convince an artist like Frank Sinatra or Barbra Streisand that they should trust him too?

There are many qualities and skills that successful producers share: musical, technical, and performing experience; a knack for working with people; diplomacy; and above all, a passion for music and the recording arts.

Although it sounds cliché, there's no substitute for experience.

When I began my career in the studio, I listened and watched more than I talked. My training came from engineers such as Bill Putnam and Bill Schwartau, and producers such as John Hammond, Jerry Wexler, Tom Dowd, Ahmet Ertegun, and Milt Okun. As mentors, they taught me to engineer and produce the same way that they'd learned—by doing.

The men who influenced me were masters of their craft. Their work ethic, attention to detail, and high standards affected me deeply. What I saw in them became the blueprint for the way I work.

While I became familiar with the ins and outs of recording, the most valuable lessons I learned as an apprentice related to the social aspects of engineering and producing: respecting an artist's opinion, making suggestions and disagreeing in a tactful way, and resolving emotional and technical crises in the studio swiftly and effectively.

Whether dealing with an artist or a business associate, conscientiously tending to the personal details goes a long way toward engendering trust. A case in point was my professional relationship with the late Morris Levy, the rough-around-the-edges owner of Roulette Records.

It was the early 1960s, and my studio (A&R Recording) was fairly new and scraping to make ends meet. Roulette, a small label that made explosive rock-and-roll and jazz records, was one of our clients. I particularly loved the Count Basie and Sarah Vaughan sessions I engineered for them.

The gag around town was that Morris Levy never paid list price for anything, nor did he pay on time. One afternoon my business partners called me in. "Hey—we've got to collect from Roulette. Go over to Morris's office and ask for a check." With all of my youthful innocence I strolled into Morris's office, sat down, and politely explained to him that A&R really needed the twelve thousand bucks that Roulette owed us so we could pay our bills.

Morris was affable and relaxed; we conversed and had a good laugh about the business. Then, Morris called for his secretary. "Bring me the A&R invoice and the checkbook," he asked. He glanced at the invoice, wrote the check, and said, "You do good work—thanks."

On my way back to the studio I unfolded the check, and to my chagrin saw that Morris had created his own discount. He'd only paid us eight thousand dollars! When I got back, everyone applauded my courage. What's the big deal? I thought. Our meeting was unremarkable; we were simply two adults treating each other with respect.

Dealing with Morris was never dull, but he was always cordial to me. After that meeting he'd drop by the studio whenever there was a Roulette session, and compliment my work. And the studio always got paid *something*—even if it took a while to collect.

Because I was young and inexperienced, my one-on-one with Morris Levy didn't unnerve me. But, my heart was in my throat during a session at which Atlantic Records producer Tom Dowd modeled the way to calmly handle an impending disaster in another area of my life—the control room.

We were recording the double jazz quartets of Ornette Coleman and Eric Dolphy, and Tom arranged the two groups facing each other, placing the microphones in between. I cued up a four-track tape machine, and we began recording.

As any music fan knows, jazz is all about improvisation—and beboppers like Coleman and Dolphy were renowned for their abstract, impressionistic approach to a melody. Well, the first piece the group played just went on and on. Ten minutes, eleven minutes, twelve minutes. We were all getting lost in the endless barrage of solos when I realized that we only had three minutes left on the reel of four-track tape.

If the solos continued unabated, the tape would surely run out before the band was finished. I was contemplating how to reload without losing too much of the performance when Tom looked toward the tape machines. I didn't have to explain; Tom's intuition and experience made him a quick study. His eyes darted around the room, and he spotted the two-track Ampex recorder that I used for mixdowns sitting off to the side. Luckily, there was a fresh reel of tape on the machine. "Get that two-track going!" he said.

As the second recorder started, Tom nimbly fed the mix from the four-track to the two-track. It wasn't the ideal way to make a transition, but since Tom's live mix was so good there was no loss of quality, and we captured the entire performance without interruption.

I was embarrassed that I hadn't caught the problem sooner, and the smooth, proactive way that Tom Dowd responded—to the problem, and to me—became part of my modus operandi.

I didn't think much about the Coleman-Dolphy date until years later, when an assistant engineer fumbled during a session I was doing with Guns 'n Roses guitarist Slash. It was an error I still shudder over.

We were taping a segment for a tribute to Les Paul in Studio B at Electric Lady, the New York studio designed and built for Jimi Hendrix in 1970. Slash was in a jovial mood, his fingers blazing over the strings of the Les Paul Standard under his command.

The guitarist's playfulness was contagious; drummer Kenny Aronoff's ferocity behind his kit pushed the rhythm of the song to a whole different level. Sensing that we were headed for a peak moment, I asked the assistant to change tapes. It should have taken a minute—or less.

Like the musicians on the other side of the glass, I was lost in the music. I turned to my left, gazing at the spools of tape rewinding at top speed. I froze.

The tape shouldn't be rewinding like that, I thought.

To my dismay, the assistant had taken it upon himself to rewind before reloading the machine with fresh tape, and we'd lost some of the performance.

"What are you doing?" I asked. "I told you to change reels!"

The assistant's face flushed. "Oh, I'm sorry—we rewind before changing tapes here," he mumbled. "It's our studio's policy."

Anyone who works with me regularly knows that rewinding tape before you change reels is not the thing to do.

One can't predict when inspiration will arrive, and those few minutes might have represented Slash's finest playing ever on that song. The hot guitar licks, lightning-fast drum fills, and unbridled energy I heard in the first take had passed, and we hadn't captured it.

When he heard what had happened, Slash was beside himself. Like us, he knew that we'd lost something elusive and magical.

Moments like this are terrifying. There's nothing more humbling than having to tell a musician that they've got to do a retake because you (or someone on your crew) was careless. In this case, I kicked myself for not being more explicit in my presession instructions; doing so would have reduced the tension and stress that those around me probably felt.

Ideally the producer, engineer, and crew should keep stress at a minimum, and away from the performer. Everything we do should be invisible to them.

Interrupting the flow of a session to say, "Excuse me—we've got to fix a microphone," or, "Sorry, the board hiccupped" is like blocking the path of a marathon runner in the last quarter-mile of a race. There were many times during sessions when I'd go out into the studio—while the band was playing, and the recorders rolling—to adjust a guitar amp, or upright a mike stand that had fallen over.

A bit of thoughtful, presession planning can go a long way toward avoiding embarrassment and give you the chance to recover from a sudden crisis. I learned the importance of preparation early on from two of the best teachers: Quincy Jones and Frank Sinatra.

Quincy and I became close in the late 1950s. He had played trumpet in Lionel Hampton's big band, written arrangements for Count Basie, and in the early 1960s became the director of artists and repertoire at Mercury Records—the first African American to hold such a position at a major label.

In recent years, "Q" has earned a reputation as a musical thoroughbred: a musician, composer, arranger, and producer. He's a splendid teacher who radiates warmth and spirituality that's rare, and I gleaned much of what I know about friendship, treating an artist well, and recording a big band from watching Quincy work in the studio.

In 1966, Quincy was arranging and conducting for Sinatra and the Count Basie band, and he invited me to see them perform at The Sands in Las Vegas. It was a classic event; everyone donned their best formal wear, but I had to fake it with a business suit 'cause the only tux I had was the one I shared with Quincy, and it was onstage with him.

Basie's orchestra opened the show and swung their asses off. After intermission, Sinatra's rhythm section joined them on stage.

With Quincy Jones and songwriter Tony Renis, Milan, Italy, 1964
Phil Ramone Collection

Quincy kicked off the band, and a deep voice boomed from the PA system. *"The Sands is proud to present a man and his music . . . the music of Count Basie and his great band . . . and the man is Frank Sinatra!"*

The epitome of cool, Frank swaggered onstage, picked up the mike, and began to sing. But the audience couldn't hear him; his microphone was dead.

When he realized it wasn't working, Frank dropped the mike onto the floor and left the stage. There was a strange silence in the showroom. A few minutes later the introduction was repeated, and Sinatra made his second entrance. This time the microphone worked.

Lesson number one, forever.

That evening at the Sands showed me that it wasn't enough to make sure that all of the microphones, recorders, and cables were working when I ran a session; I needed to have two vocal mikes, a backup recorder, and a technician on hand to instantly resolve any problems that came up. In my early years as an engineer I was so obsessed with having everything in order that I'd set up the night before and come in a few hours before a session to check and recheck the equipment. The last thing I ever want is for an artist to come to work and walk into chaos.

Am I fussy? You bet.

But I only demand of others what I demand of myself: dedication and attentiveness. I can laugh and enjoy myself, but when it comes time to make the record I expect everyone's full attention.

Until after I made *The Stranger* with Billy Joel in 1977, I engineered most of the records I produced. When my partnership with Billy flourished, I devoted myself to working closely with him on style and approach, and relinquished the recording duties to engineers whom I trusted, like Jim Boyer and Bradshaw Leigh (both of whom I trained). It was an excellent choice; being able to concentrate on the artist and their needs without worrying about things like Are we getting this on tape? made producing far more enjoyable.

Preparation, however, doesn't guarantee that once we begin recording there won't be tension in the air.

There are times when making records is tough: the recording console might be giving us hell, or the instruments might not sound right (pianos and string instruments are particularly affected by temperature and humidity).

Maybe the singer is having an off day and can't find his or her groove, or we spend hours working on a guitar overdub that should take thirty minutes.

And it's almost guaranteed that every album you make will have at least one song that says, "If you think I'm gonna give up my lyric and melody to you so easily, you've got another thing coming!"

Minor annoyances such as these affect every artist from time to time, regardless of stature or experience. The key to overcoming them is persistence.

While rehearsing "Still Crazy After All These Years" in New York with pianist Barry Beckett in 1975, Paul Simon experimented with many different keys. For Beckett, it was bewildering.

"Try C," Paul suggested.

Barry played the song; Paul shook his head.

"No, no—how about C-sharp?"

Barry tried another run-through; Paul mused.

"Nope. I've got it—D."

The deliberation continued as the pair tested E-flat, A-flat— every key that Paul could think of.

As a founding member of the esteemed Muscle Shoals Rhythm Section (based in Muscle Shoals, Alabama), Beckett was accustomed to nailing down a part in thirty minutes or less. He adored Paul and wanted to please him, but after three or four hours of concentrated effort on "Still Crazy After All These Years," his exasperation spilled over.

"Paul, this isn't going to work," he said. "I will *never* get this song—*ever.*"

I was amused.

What Barry underestimated was Paul's resolve, and his perfectionism. I've seen Paul toil for hours on an instrumental track, only to come back the next day and scrap everything because he'd made changes he thought would improve the song.

With "Still Crazy After All These Years," Barry ended up being inspired by Paul's tenacity. They kept at it, and after a bit more work they agreed on an appropriate key.

The bonus was that by the end of the day, Barry knew the tune so well he could anticipate Paul's phrasing. When the band came in to record it, they went straight to it without rehearsing. It didn't take long at all to cut the record.

Nothing was more ironic than the weeks it took for Billy Joel's band to perfect "Get It Right the First Time," a song we recorded for *The Stranger* in 1977. The tune has a complex rhythm, and it took a while to coalesce.

As I recall, we would start a date by trying "Get It Right the First Time," and, when it didn't click, put it aside to work on another song such as "She's Always A Woman To Me," or "Movin' Out." We'd come back to "Get It Right the First Time" later in the session, and when it *still* didn't click, we'd turn to yet another tune—"Only the Good Die Young," perhaps.

At the end of each of *The Stranger* sessions I'd say, "How about trying 'Get It Right the First Time'?" It got to where the guys would anticipate coming back to it, and when we did, they'd moan. *"Come on, we're not doing it again, are we? Fucking song doesn't wanna be born!"* This went on for more than a couple of weeks.

Then, Billy and I decided to give the tune a rest—we didn't even mention it to the band for a few days. Then, one afternoon, we were putting another song through its paces when Billy stopped abruptly and said, "Let's do 'Get It Right the First Time'—*right now.*"

It was impulsive—maybe even instinctive. He counted it off, and miraculously, the groove slipped right into place. We had it down in a few takes; afterward, we cracked open a bottle of wine and said, "Amen!"

The Music That Makes Me Dance

At the Palace Theatre, New York City, late 1950s
Phil Ramone Collection

I'll always be a musician at heart.

Music has been part of my life since I was three, when I saw a gypsy fiddler playing for tips in a restaurant. Something about him fascinated me, and I went so crazy that my parents ran out and bought me a toy violin. I found the violin enchanting, and by the time I was four, I was playing the real thing and studying classical music with the conductor of a symphony orchestra.

The restaurant violinist of my youth was simply a catalyst.

No one can master an instrument unless they have some aptitude, and I was lucky to have been born with a latent affinity for music—an unwavering passion that, once ignited, couldn't be repressed. Thankfully, my love for music was recognized early on and nurtured in innumerable ways.

There's a strict discipline that comes with playing serious music, and that discipline is ingrained in me. It's guided my life and helped me accomplish everything I've done. Discipline, and a strong sense of purpose, came from my parents. Mom and Dad's encouragement fostered our creativity and helped bring out the best in my sister, Doreen, and me.

While most ten-year-olds were outside playing ball, I was inside playing the violin. My teacher was a gifted man named Ivan Galamian, and whenever we were home, my sister and I were usually practicing. Once in a while, people would knock on the door and say, "Keep practicing—it sounds good." Then, you might hear, "Shut up!" It paid off, though: I ended up at Juilliard, and Doreen went on to study opera and dance.

Although I had little time to myself, studying music on that level gave me a solid foundation. I probably absorbed more music as a teenager by going to Juilliard and knocking around the city than most people do in a lifetime.

But I wasn't just playing the violin—I was listening, too.

I loved tinkering with electronics kits and phonographs, and a big delight for me was discovering the link between music and sound recording. Captivated by my instrument's tonality, I spent hours trying to rig it up electronically so it would sound good on a recording. That curiosity helped me learn about the *sound* of music. While I studied hard and played the fiddle for years to come, it was the irresistible urge to make it sound better that drove me to become a recording engineer and producer.

A common question that hopeful producers often ask is, "Do I need to be a musician—or be able to read music—to become a record producer?"

While having formal musical training isn't required, it certainly helps. In fact, for me it's been invaluable.

My experience as a musician has a discernible effect on the way I approach production. It also enables me to follow a score, recognize errors in tuning and pitch, and explain what I hear in my head to artists, arrangers, and musicians.

The communication aspect is particularly important. Musicians are an eccentric lot, and speaking their language helps me tap into their needs more easily. A good example of this is what happened when Paul Simon recorded "Have A Good Time" for the album *Still Crazy After All These Years* in 1975.

The song has a jazzy feel, and to emphasize its leitmotif I asked saxophonist Phil Woods to play a wild, free-form jazz riff at the very end. Knowing how much Woods idolized saxophonist Charlie Parker, I snapped my fingers to set the tempo. "How about some bebop in B-flat right about here?" I asked. "Just give me thirty seconds of insanity."

Woods went right into the solo, and blew up a storm. After a minute of hot and heavy playing he stopped and took a deep breath. "Is that what you wanted?" he asked. "Yeah!" I said. "Perfect."

In addition to having a bit of musical ability and being able to converse fluently with musicians, having eclectic musical tastes—and a knowledge of different musical styles and genres—is a prerequisite for working with songwriters and recording artists.

Jazz, more than any other genre, has been a consistent theme in my life and work.

For a classical student, it was the forbidden fruit, but I was a rebel. Jazz became my musical nirvana: the ultimate confluence of melody, rhythm, and unrestrained musical expression. Although my classically trained professors discouraged it, I wanted to let my violin wander into the jazz world the way Stephan Grappelli and Django Reinhardt did. I began playing in small clubs on Fifty-second Street, which drew the ire of my Juilliard professors, who had no compunctions voicing their displeasure.

Contrary to their opinion, I found copious musicality in those jazz performances. I learned to speak the language of music because I was exposed to the best of both worlds—classical *and* jazz. The role model who drove the point home for me was Andre Previn, who could arrange, orchestrate, compose, conduct symphony orchestras, and play jazz piano. Andre's versatility was a real inspiration in my life as a budding musician, engineer, and producer—he helped me assimilate a generous array of music.

I'd spend hours listening to Art Tatum, Count Basie, Charlie Parker, Miles Davis, or John Coltrane play a solo, and then I'd dissect it. Sitting at the feet of the jazz masters—literally and figuratively—gave me a better education than a dozen classes in music theory ever could.

One of the greatest things I learned from the jazz players was how to edit. Not how to physically splice tape, but how to condense a musical thought without diluting its coherence or artistic intention. To that end, recording saxophonist John Coltrane's *Olé Coltrane* in mid-1961 taught me a great deal. The album came at a moment in Coltrane's life when the notion of self-editing was foremost in his mind.

Bebop hadn't seen a sax player with the emotive brilliance of Charlie Parker until John Coltrane came along. Although he could play sweetly (as albums such as *Lush Life, Ballads,* and *John Coltrane and Johnny Hartman* demonstrate), Coltrane's modern improvisations were ingenious. In the period that wrought *Olé Coltrane*, he attacked every phrase like a pit bull.

While the jaw-dropping ferocity of Coltrane's lengthy solos appealed to ardent beboppers, their depth was often lost on the casual jazz fan. Inspired by some patrons who walked out when he launched into one of his abstract meanderings, Coltrane decided to refine the way he collated and framed his thoughts while playing to an audience.

"Sometimes [I] would get up and play a twenty, maybe thirty minute solo," Coltrane explained. "Then, [my band] went into the Apollo, and the manager said 'You're playing for too long—you can only play for twenty minutes.' Well, we ended up playing *three songs* in twenty minutes. I played all the highlights of the solos that [individually] had taken me twenty or more minutes each to play. It made me think, 'What have I been doing all this time?' If I'm going to take twenty or thirty minutes to say something that I can say in ten minutes, maybe I'd better say it in ten minutes!"

Although I didn't fully comprehend their value at the time, Coltrane's comments—the way he acknowledged the problem, and his thoughts on brevity—definitely affected the way I helped prune and shape the records I was involved in making.

Another important thing I recognized during my early years was that jazz musicians weren't afraid to experiment, and part of the reason I was blessed with success as a producer is because I wouldn't hesitate to juxtapose a classical soloist with a rock-and-roll band, or a jazz player with a pop singer.

I started by doing it with Paul Simon (Michael Brecker playing on "Still Crazy After All These Years") and Billy Joel (Phil Woods on "Just the Way You Are" and Freddie Hubbard on "Zanzibar"), and found that it added a nice texture to their songs.

While a producer can suggest ideas such as these to an artist, they won't work unless the artist buys into the concept.

Paul Simon loves musical exploration, and was pleased when I suggested bringing in Bob James to do some arrangements for *Still Crazy After All These Years*. Paul also welcomed the freshness that drummer Steve Gadd and keyboardist Richard Tee brought to his solo records.

Billy Joel, however, was a bit apprehensive about featuring jazz players. He wanted to be accepted as a rock and roller, but critics insisted on branding him as "pop." Billy expressed genuine admiration for the players I suggested; he simply wasn't sure whether veering into jazz territory would help or hurt his cause.

Billy's lyrics had a distinct dramatic flair; his ideas, and the eloquent way he expressed them, were sophisticated. Songs such as "She's Always A Woman To Me," "Just the Way You Are," and "Everybody Has A Dream" allowed their stories to unfold effortlessly, and reflected sentiments that everyone could understand.

"Why shouldn't you experiment a bit, at least on a few songs, if not a whole album?" I asked. "It's okay to create a jazz kind of mood. You can do it credibly because you've written a song called 'Zanzibar,' and at the very end there are jazz riffs. Those phrases are a nod to all of the great jazz artists you heard while you were growing up."

I convinced him to chance the dramatic, and *52nd Street*—the second record that Billy and I made together, in 1978—took his music in a new direction.

The overarching flavor of *52nd Street* is sultry and cool, and to enhance its seductiveness we invited Freddie Hubbard and Jon Faddis (trumpet), Steve Khan, Dave Spinozza, Hugh McCracken, and Eric Gale (guitars), Mike Manieri (marimba and vibes), and Ralph MacDonald (percussion)—a group of prodigious contemporary jazz soloists—to make guest appearances. As it turned out, the all-stars we chose clicked so well with Billy's band that we took to calling them "The Lords of 52nd Street."

Both "Zanzibar" and "Stiletto" are momentous examples of Billy's versatility, and the polish that marks the best of his records.

"Zanzibar"—the story of a young man trying to make it with a nightclub waitress—embodies the suave, provocative tone of the chic dance clubs that sprang up around New York City in the late 1970s. The theme offered us an expansive forum for experimentation; what emerged was a solid pop tune adorned with tasteful elements of hot and cool jazz. A particular highlight is the song's bridge, where a dreamy interlude (featuring keyboards and vibes) erupts into an unexpected jazz trumpet solo by Freddie Hubbard. Underscoring the passage is a driving, ascending/descending bass line, which lends it an urgency that's irresistibly sexy.

"Stiletto" cuts fast and deep; tension plays a starring role. But the qualities that make "Stiletto" a standout took time to develop.

When we first recorded the track there were no funky bass lines, crackling finger snaps, or cliffhanger breaks. After auditioning the first playbacks, Billy decided that "Stiletto" needed a visceral hook, and incorporating the aforementioned bass lines, finger snaps, and breaks helped to create the tension that serves the song so well.

Memorable fills, phrases, and breaks—such as the ones heard on "Stiletto"—are what set the best records apart. These devices are especially effective when they're heard at the beginning of a song; if you can come up with something spicy and unique, you've got a better chance of getting (and holding) the audience's attention.

Think of a pop or rock song that gets your adrenaline flowing: one with such an exciting feel that once you hear it, the melody and the sound of the record become emblazoned in your memory. The Beatles' "Drive My Car," The Beach Boys' "Wouldn't It Be Nice," Queen's "We Will Rock You," Bruce Springsteen's "Hungry Heart," and Nirvana's "Smells Like Teen Spirit" are a few good examples.

One of the greatest thrills for a producer is helping the artist find a hook to define their record. Sometimes all that's needed is a simple twist of instrumentation, or a subtle effect to turn a lackluster opening into something extraordinary. Often, the intrinsic style of a special guest artist, or a top-flight session player can spur unexpected moments of greatness.

Remember the drum cadence at the beginning of Paul Simon's "50 Ways to Leave Your Lover"?

The way we stumbled upon it was a happy accident.

On the day we tracked the band track for "50 Ways" Paul was in the control room, strumming the melody on his guitar. He'd been playing around with a Rhythm Ace electronic drum machine, and had found a samba beat that he thought would work for the song.

Out in the studio, Steve Gadd was warming up. Following his usual pre-recording routine, he began playing a drum corps–style street beat, the precision of which was compelling. Paul heard the nagging rhythm through the open door, and stopped playing his guitar. He went out into the studio. "That's good, Steve," he said. "Play it again." As Gadd tapped away on the snare, Paul grabbed his guitar and began singing over the melody. It was a stunning combination, and Paul was delighted. "Phil, I think we just found a way to start the song!"

In that moment the personality of "50 Ways to Leave Your Lover" changed. Steve's happenstance contribution was a driving force that helped push the single to number one on *Billboard*'s Hot 100 chart; *Still Crazy After All These Years*—the record on which it appeared—won the Grammy for Album of the Year (1976).

As "50 Ways to Leave Your Lover" shows, you can't predict what will happen as you begin working on a tune, and I've found that the best performances often come during the first few minutes of a session while everyone is warming up.

Catching those serendipitous moments is easy if you follow one of my cardinal rules: Start rolling a tape the moment an artist walks through the door.

In the analog days I recorded more two-inch multitrack tape than most producers, and the record companies never understood

With Paul Simon in 1976, receiving the Grammy
for the album *Still Crazy After All These Years*
Phil Ramone Collection

why. I'd laugh when label executives were annoyed that I used ten rolls of tape instead of five. "Tape is the cheapest commodity on the date," I'd say.

At the very least, I would always keep a two-track stereo recorder running throughout a session. In recent years those tapes have become valuable; the labels now scramble to include the session chatter and alternate takes as bonus tracks on CDs and downloadable reissues.

I rarely stop a take when someone blunders; what might seem like a mistake to a musician playing in the studio could actually be a chance moment of brilliance. What I tell the artist is, "If you make a mistake, keep going—don't interrupt the flow." If the rest of the performance is incredible, we'll do another take and splice the best parts of each together.

Because they were recorded live and the songs went through many permutations as the band worked to define—and redefine—their design, many of Billy Joel's recordings contain small, fortuitous miscues. We often left such missteps in, as Billy and I both felt they reflected the spontaneity inherent in the band's sound.

As Billy remembers, one such error occurred during the recording of "A Room of Our Own" for *The Nylon Curtain*:

"In the part where I sing, 'Yes, we all need a room of our own' before I go into the final vamp, my drummer [Liberty DeVitto] got confused and started to play the beat backwards. He was still playing in time, but he suddenly turned the time signature inside out. There was a look of horror on Liberty's face, but we could see Phil in the control room waving his arms, telling us, 'Keep going! It sounds great!' "

Mistakes that work in your favor can be technical too, as Billy learned when he erased part of a tape during another session for *The Nylon Curtain*.

"On 'Pressure,' the noise that sounds like the horn of a French taxicab—that strange, breathless staccato *beep*—is actually a tape of me singing every note in my repertoire," Billy explained. "We recorded me singing the notes, and then loaded the tape into an effects gadget called an Emulator. Then, we overdubbed me hollering, *'PRESH-AR!'* with the same inflection that a Royal Air Force captain might use to bark out a command like *'TEN-HUT!'*

"While the master tape was running, I impulsively hit all the buttons on the tape machine to punch out everything but the section with the yelling. Phil was dumbstruck. *'God! What did you do? You erased part of the song!'* Phil was right: for that one segment everything stops dead but my voice, but it was just what the track needed."

In this instance, I agreed with Billy: the inadvertent error added an inexplicable dimension to an already stylized song. A different artist (or producer) might have disagreed and asked for a retake, but I believed then (as I do now) that a producer's role is to objectively guide the creation without stifling it.

Amongst musicians and engineers, I'm known for recording rehearsals.

Whenever possible, I arrange to hold rehearsals in the studio, where I can put up a few microphones and record it professionally. Portable digital recorders make it much easier to record a remote rehearsal; the best we could do outside of the studio twenty years ago was run a cassette, which wasn't optimal.

What's the advantage of recording a rehearsal?

Paul Simon's "Loves Me Like A Rock" is a prime example of how a rehearsal tape can be a lifesaver. Paul had made an acoustic-guitar-and-vocal demo of the song, and the next day we rehearsed with the Dixie Hummingbirds, a vocal group that was well versed in the gospel vernacular.

Among gospel quartets, the Hummingbirds were the most colorful—and versatile. While steeped in the tradition of jubilee gospel music of the 1920s, their sound was inflected with elements of hard gospel, blues, jazz, and pop. The secret to their distinctive style was "trickeration," an overlapping-note technique in which a member of the group would pick up a note just before lead singer Ira Tucker finished it. Tucker was a *physical* performer who would jump, shout, and fall to his knees in prayer; there was always a great interplay between the Hummingbirds and their audience.

In setting up the rehearsal I thought, how am I going to fit the group in the vocal booth? "Loves Me Like A Rock" is not a "booth" kind of song, nor are the Dixie Hummingbirds a group that's accustomed to being confined. To solve the problem I sat them in a circle (which helped them feed off one another) and dropped a single Neumann U47 microphone in their midst. I put a second mike in front of Paul.

The rehearsal was magnificent; everyone was clustered around the microphones, singing, shaking their heads, stomping their feet, and clapping while Paul played guitar and sang. It was the most unrestrained performance I'd heard in a long time: in the hands of that group—in that particular setting—the song was elevated to a whole other spiritual level. It was rollicking, earthy, and fun—jubilation personified. The groove was so infectious that I couldn't get the tune out of my head, and I had high hopes for the "real" session the following day.

The clincher is we *didn't* rerecord "Loves Me Like A Rock" the next day.

When we came back to lay it down, we just couldn't catch the right feel. Despite everyone's efforts, the formal attempts never came close to the exuberant "rocking-down-the-house" performance I'd heard the day before.

Looking to refresh everyone's memory, I pulled the rehearsal tape and called Paul and the Dixie Hummingbirds into the booth. They gathered around the console, and after listening, agreed that nothing they had done that day could touch the infectious groove of the rehearsal. "Why not use it, then?" I asked. All we needed to do was overdub the band (including Paul Simon on electric guitar,

David Hood on bass, and Roger Hawkins on drums), and the composite mix became *the* record.

Does it matter whether something that contributes to the appeal of a record is intentional or happenstance, or if the final record contains a minor flaw? Not to me. A record doesn't have to be musically or technically faultless to be good.

Some artists and producers spend months or years polishing every note until their record is perfect. I'm all for doing things right—just not at the expense of that spine-tingling moment when the music sounds spontaneous and real.

When it comes to making records, substance should outweigh perfection. Great records are all about *feel*, and if it comes down to making a choice, I'll go for a take that makes me dance over a bland one with better sound any day.

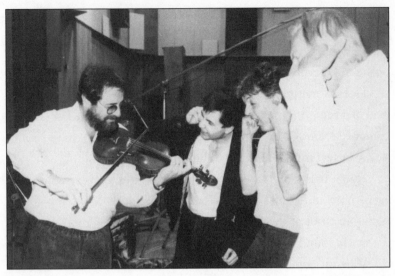

Fiddling around for violinist Nigel Kennedy,
Paul McCartney, and Beatles producer George Martin
Phil Ramone Collection

Music First!

Everybody wants a hit.

The songwriter, artist, engineer, and producer all pray for hits and the prizes that go along with them, such as a coveted spot on the *Billboard* charts or a Grammy Award.

I'll get back to the subject of hits in a few moments. But first, let me explain how *The Nylon Curtain,* the fourth (and most ambitious) record that Billy Joel and I made together, came about.

One day in 1982, Billy said, "I want to make a good 'head-phones album,' and use exotic instrumentation and layering the way the Beatles did." We were both in awe of the Beatles and what they and producer George Martin accomplished with *Rubber Soul, Revolver,* and *Sgt. Pepper's Lonely Hearts Club Band.*

"I'm Only Sleeping," "Within You, Without You," and "Norwegian Wood" were very different from earlier Beatles recordings such as "I Saw Her Standing There," "Twist and Shout," and "All My Loving."

The use of nontraditional instruments (often detuned), and

technical effects such as ADT (Artificial Double Tracking) and the Mellotron (an electromechanical keyboard using magnetic tape loops), brought unusual contrasts and textures to the band's experimental recordings of the mid-1960s.

The time for a departure from Billy's past work seemed right; there was little to lose with *The Nylon Curtain*.

Billy's previous three albums (*The Stranger, 52nd Street,* and *Glass Houses*) were extremely successful, and yielded a torrent of songs that were staples of Top 40 radio, including "Movin' Out (Anthony's Song)," "Scenes from an Italian Restaurant," "She's Always a Woman," "Only the Good Die Young," "Just the Way You Are," "Big Shot," "My Life," "You May Be Right," and "It's Still Rock and Roll to Me."

I saw Billy's suggestion as an opportunity to make a credible avant-garde statement. Our palette was vast, and I thought a lot about how to give *The Nylon Curtain* an unexpected dimension. After hearing a sample of the songs that Billy was considering for the album, I became very excited.

The Nylon Curtain marked Billy's maturation as a writer.

Some songs—like "Allentown" and "Goodnight Saigon"—had salient sociopolitical overtones. Others—"Laura," "Scandinavian Skies," and "Where's the Orchestra?"—were philosophical and dark. Production-wise, each song begged for an aggressive, unexpected approach.

To help create the rich aural experience that Billy had dreamed of we used vocal treatments and sound effects liberally on *The Nylon Curtain*, and imbued it with an abundance of odd instrumental textures. We broke our own mold with *The Nylon Curtain*; it was our form of musical expressionism, and the closest we came to approaching a concept album.

In concept and execution the album was smart and cohesive, and when it was finished we eagerly previewed it for the executives at Columbia Records.

Our enthusiasm was soon to evaporate.

The label proclaimed the album "too strange and impressionistic." A few people—including Billy's manager—took to calling it *The Nylon Schmata.*

What bugged me most was the audacious question posed by Columbia's promotion men: "Where's the 'Movin' Out' kind of song?"

The real question—the one they were afraid to ask—was, "Where's your hit?"

Forget that *The Nylon Curtain* contained "Allentown," "Pressure," and "Goodnight Saigon." At that moment, Columbia's perception was that the songs on the album weren't cast in the predictable Top 40–AM radio mold, and they all but dismissed it.

I can assure you that having a hit record is wonderful—it can truly change your life. But I can also tell you that it's risky for an artist or producer to go into the studio hell-bent on making one.

So, what do I tell an artist, manager, or record company executive who asks, "Could this [or will this] record be a hit?" I tell them the truth: Picking a hit from a batch of songs is nebulous at best. It's dangerous, too. As good as a record might sound while you're creating it, it's hard to predict whether radio—and the public—will embrace it.

"But isn't it your job as the producer to spot a potential hit?" you might ask. "Can't a producer hear when a song or performance has all the earmarks of a hit?"

The answers are "Yes, and yes." But it's not always that simple.

A seasoned producer knows when the right song or the right take is there. But being that close to the creation can be overwhelming, and it's difficult to objectively say, "This record is going to be a hit." You may *think* a particular record has the potential to hit it big, but you avoid saying it for fear of jinxing yourself.

How do I know when we've got something special brewing in the room? The skin on the back of my neck begins to tingle. The people around me know it when my body starts grooving to the music.

Occasionally I'll get "the feeling," only to learn that the artist disagrees with my assessment. When that happens, I'll explain my reasoning and encourage them to reconsider my opinion.

I'm mindful that it's the artist's name and picture on the album cover—not mine. But there are times when a songwriter or performer is so caught up in writing or polishing a song that they lose objectivity. If the artist and I disagree and I feel strongly about a song's potential, it's my obligation to defend my position to the end.

Here's an example that might surprise you.

One day I told Billy Joel that we could use another ballad for *The Stranger*. "Well, here's a song we'll never record," he said. "But you should hear it."

Billy prefaced his live demo of the song by explaining that he had performed it a few times in concert, but no one in the band— including him—was overjoyed with it. He then sat at the piano and halfheartedly played me a tune called "Just the Way You Are."

I liked the song—a lot—and despite Billy's trepidation, we agreed to run it down at the next session.

As Billy recalls:

"We originally played 'Just the Way You Are' as a cha-cha: *'Don't go changing (cha-cha-cha) . . . just to please me (cha-cha-cha). . . .'* Well, Liberty DeVitto got so pissed that he threw his drum sticks at me. 'I'm no goddamned sissy drummer,' he said. It was a chick song, and we really weren't sure about it from the start. But Phil lobbied hard to include it on *The Stranger*. He never said, 'That's a hit,' because it wouldn't have sat well with us. All Phil kept saying was, 'That's a song you definitely want on the album.'"

The band *did* seem unwilling to give the song a proper chance, but I felt their resistance was less about the song and more about the way it was being presented. A big concern was that it was too schmaltzy, and that it would brand Billy a "wedding singer." After hearing the first few takes, I was inclined to agree.

Part of the problem was that some people were comparing Billy to Elton John. Originally, the beat that the band was using on "Just the Way You Are" sounded much like Elton's "Daniel," or Stevie Wonder's "You Are the Sunshine of My Life." But I saw the possibilities of the song, and felt that if we found the right groove it could work.

Liberty DeVitto clearly remembers the controversy, and the moment that "Just the Way You Are"'s fate was decided: "We all said, 'We're not playing that song.' We were *adamant* about it. But Phil knew that it had something, and that all it needed was a tougher groove.

"I was in the control room arguing—and procrastinating—because I didn't want to do the song. Phil—who never raised his voice or gave us a hard time—just listened. After a while he simply looked at me and said, 'Enough of this bullshit. You guys can play whatever you want later, but I'm telling you to get out there and play this song, *now!*' He said it jokingly, but I knew that he meant business.

"The cha-cha thing didn't work, so when we started recording 'Just the Way You Are,' I played the loose bossa nova rhythm that I'd been playing all along. After a run-through, Phil came out of the booth. He walked over to me and quietly said, 'Lib, I think I know what the problem is. That rhythm isn't cutting it. This song needs a more sensuous feel.'

"Phil suggested trying a South American Byonne rhythm, and tapped out the pattern to show me what he meant. We tried it again, and this time I began dropping the bass drum out in certain places, and playing the tom-tom on the 'and' of four. The slight rest, and a little extra pressure on each kick of the bass drum pedal gave it extra emphasis. Using brushes on the snare gave it a very sexy sound.

"I always knew that Phil liked what I was doing when he started to move. From my perch behind the drums, I could see him in the control room, and when we started playing 'Just the Way You Are' with that sexy rhythm, he began swinging his arms and grooving to the beat. That was my indicator that 'Just the Way You Are' was headed in the right direction," DeVitto concluded.

The new rhythmic pattern made a tremendous difference, and once the song began settling in, Billy and I realized that the sound of the piano in the first few bars sounded cold when juxtaposed with the melody's exotic beat. Trading the standard piano for a Fender Rhodes keyboard with a Small Stone phaser gave the opening a warm, cozy touch.

But after making a rough mix, Billy and I sensed that something was still missing. The song needed more dimension, and my next suggestion unwittingly caused the first scrape between the band and me as their producer.

Although Richie Cannata's tenor sax playing on "Scenes from an Italian Restaurant" and "Only the Good Die Young" was dazzling, I felt that the solo in the bridge of "Just the Way You Are" needed the throaty texture of an alto sax.

When I think of alto saxophone I immediately think of Phil Woods—one of the top jazz session men in New York. And so I called on him, and his exceptional solo lent "Just the Way You Are" a sublimity that was greater than anything I had imagined.

My suggestion to use Phil Woods wasn't meant to offend Richie Cannata or his playing. In this instance, I believed that we needed a specific sound that only a specialist such as Phil could provide, and as the final arbiter, I followed my instinct.

I've found that if you can justify the merits of doing something that will help make a stronger musical statement, everyone usually understands. I knew that Richie would understand—and he did.

As Richie recalls:

"Phil had made an album with Phoebe Snow just before *The*

Stranger, and he had used Phil Woods on her record. All of us (Michael Brecker, David Sanborn, and I) looked up to Phil Woods; he was the Charlie Parker of our era. If Phil (Ramone) had asked Michael Brecker or David Sanborn to play on 'Just the Way You Are,' I would have felt hurt. But it was a real honor to have Phil Woods play on our record. Since I had to play the part on the road, 'Just the Way You Are' forced me to learn to play alto sax."

Despite all of the time we spent tweaking "Just the Way You Are," Billy still wasn't sure that he wanted it on the album—until the night Linda Ronstadt and Phoebe Snow visited the studio.

We were talking about the album, and I played "Just the Way You Are" for them. They were floored, and when Billy mentioned that he wanted to eliminate it, neither Linda nor Phoebe withheld their opinions. "Are you crazy?" they asked. "That's the hit! You're out of your minds if you don't put it on the album." Thank God we listened: "Just the Way You Are" won a Grammy for Song of the Year (1978). Next to "Piano Man" it's Billy's most requested tune, and at many a wedding it's been played, I'm sure.

Two questions I'm frequently asked are, "Is there a secret to making a hit?" and "Do you follow a formula when making a record?"

There are no fail-safe recipes for creating a hit. And, the closest thing to a formula that I follow is making sure the artist's voice— vocally or instrumentally—is recognized within the first fifteen seconds. Establishing their identity right up front is critical.

There are, however, three ingredients that all great records share: a good song, a talented artist, and distinctive production.

A song that touches you as a producer is liable to touch others, too, and if you're blessed with having an artist who can put a magical spin on that song's melody or lyric, you're on the road to making a record that people will want to hear again and again.

Production style has more to do with the sound and feel of a record than anything else, and it varies from producer to producer.

Like film directors, record producers bring an individual aesthetic to their work. Few things compare with the grainy distortion of an early Stones record, the euphoric tone of a Burt Bacharach production, or the irresistible funk of a Motown single. Each has a sound or feel that's unlike any other, because of the techniques used to record and mix them. Originality is crucial.

Although some people say that my records have a signature sound, I don't hear it. The goal for me is to bring clarity and simplicity to every record I make, and they *shouldn't* sound alike.

In designing a sound for a record, every element must have a purpose. I love using musical color, texture, and shading to enhance a record, and using those tools to emphasize a song's inner rhythms helps the artist and me direct its emotionality. If the music is loud and bombastic, I want whoever hears it to feel like it's a celebration. If it's soft and tender, I want them to linger over the sentimentality of the moment.

Keeping my sound transparent (chameleonic, really) has enabled me to work with a wide variety of artists in many different genres.

I used to buy things in electronics stores and guitar shops—effects pedals and gizmos—and say, "Man, that's cool!" Once in a while I'd take one of those contraptions into the studio and use it as an effect on a song. Then I'd wrap it up and say, "I'm really glad that I had that, 'cause it worked well for this song and the record did very well." But I'd rarely (if ever) use that effect or pedal again. I didn't want people to say, "That's a Phil Ramone production" every time they heard a certain effect.

It's easy for artists and producers to get lulled into complacency and rely on what's been successful in the past, but I've found that it's inaccurate to say, "This (or that) *always* works." Nothing in this business is a slam dunk; each record has to stand on its own. I'm forever cautioning young artists and producers to avoid repeating themselves or copying whatever's in vogue.

Yet some producers pigeonhole themselves by only making rock, jazz, or hip-hop records—or by working with just one artist for fear that they'll lose their momentum. I understand why a producer who's become known for a specific style or particular sound might be afraid to do a Broadway album or a film soundtrack; there's comfort in security. But that kind of thinking is precisely what leads to predictable, formulaic records.

George Martin is a good example of a producer who has been successful because of his willingness to grow. The reason that groups like the Beatles endured is because neither they nor their producers were afraid to experiment. Early Beatles albums like *With the Beatles* and *Please Please Me* are as far removed from *The Beatles* (aka *The White Album*) or *Abbey Road* as Mozart is from Stravinsky.

Take Rod Stewart, a rocker whose renaissance came via the classic pop standards written during the 1930s and '40s.

Rod's a singer who's constantly reinventing his image, and after many years in the limelight he has attracted a broad fan base. When Clive Davis asked me if I would work with Rod on his first two *Great American Songbook* albums, I was intrigued. Could it work? I thought so. Were we guaranteed success because it involved Rod Stewart? No. Just because an artist has had success in one genre doesn't mean that a crossover project will work, or that their record will be a hit.

Luckily, the *Great American Songbook* concept came at a time when Rod and his faithful audience were open to something new. As a result, Rod's versions of gems like "It Had to Be You," "These Foolish Things," and a couple dozen other standards have endeared him to a more mature audience who may never have heard "Maggie May" or "Do Ya Think I'm Sexy?" The album also exposed his younger fans to the classic songs of the 1940s. Best of all, Rod did it all without sacrificing his foothold in the rock and pop world, which proves that meaningful interpretations of quality songs never go out of style.

While having a hit record and garnering accolades is thrilling, the rewards should never come at the expense of artistic integrity. If there's one single artist I know who has bridged the gap between old and new songs and audiences—and done so without relinquishing his commitment to quality—it's Tony Bennett.

Tony began his career in the late 1940s as a singer in the Army, and became a sensation in the early 1950s with hits such as "The Boulevard of Broken Dreams," "Because of You," and "Cold, Cold Heart." But while he became famous for the catchy pop numbers of the day, Tony was always a jazz singer at heart.

"When I began my career at Columbia Records in 1950, I wanted to sing the great songs by Duke Ellington, Johnny Mercer, and the Gershwins," Tony explained. "But, producer Mitch Miller insisted that I sing novelty tunes, which he had a hand in popularizing at the time. We had vehement disagreements, and the only way I could stomach recording some of the tunes that Mitch wanted me to do was to compromise: For every two novelty records I recorded, I'd get to make one jazz record, using the musicians and songs that I preferred."

The standards have always been sacred to Tony; he once told me that his mom, a seamstress who was widowed at a young age, inspired his predilection for singing and recording top-quality songs.

"My mother would become frustrated when she was given an inferior dress to tailor," he said. "You could see the exasperation on her face as she ripped out the poorly sewn stitches. She would become agitated and mumble, 'Don't give me junk; give me a good dress, one that I can work with.' From the moment I heard my mother say that, it became the principle that guided me."

Tony's adherence to that philosophy has served him well. Along with scores of hits, Tony has won accolades for the landmark albums he's made with Count Basie, Bill Evans, and the Ralph Sharon Trio; he has also won an impressive number of Grammy Awards (eleven in the last fifteen years alone), and has attracted a retinue of rockers such as the Red Hot Chili Peppers to the graceful elegance of his music.

The consistently high standards set by the Tony Bennetts of the world are a testament to the importance of being faithful to one's convictions. As I've told many students, the mantra that should guide every songwriter, singer, musician, and producer who cares about what they do is, "Music first."

With Billy Joel, New York City, 1986
Courtesy of Sam Emerson/Redbox

The Song

Songs are the nucleus of my world.

While I grew up with the classic American standards written by George and Ira Gershwin, Jerome Kern, Irving Berlin, Richard Rodgers, Lorenz Hart and Oscar Hammerstein II, Cole Porter, and Johnny Mercer, my career as an engineer and producer coincided with one of the most profound periods in pop music history: that of the contemporary singer-songwriter.

In the late 1950s, the Brill Building at 1619 Broadway was a magnet for young musicians and songwriters. Carole King, Gerry Goffin, Howard Greenfield, Ellie Greenwich, Jeff Barry, Burt Bacharach, Lieber and Stoller, and two Neils—Sedaka and Diamond—all got their start writing teenage love songs inside tiny cubicles in the famed building.

It was a revolutionary time for contemporary pop music: an extension of the Tin Pan Alley era, and the last major epoch for the American song plugger. Since producers, arrangers, music publishers, agents, and managers also had offices in the Brill Building it was the ultimate place to write, sell, and plan the production of a song from start to finish.

While the standards of the forties were written to advance the plots of stage shows and films, the goal of the Brill Building writers was to write two-and-a-half-minute hit singles destined for radio. Their success was unparalleled.

The upheaval that America saw in the mid to late sixties—the Vietnam War, race riots, civil rights protests, psychedelic drug use, and overt rebellion—offered a springboard for young pied pipers to profess their political, social, and emotional views in song. Bob Dylan and a handful of other assertive singer-songwriter-activists entered the fray and revamped the way that songs were conceived, performed, and heard.

Soon the Brill Building gang realized that singing their own songs was more satisfying—and lucrative—than selling them off, and started performing careers of their own. By the early seventies the singer-songwriter era had hit America full-force, and artists such as Paul Simon, James Taylor, Jim Croce, and Billy Joel were on the threshold of stardom.

Songs are deceptively complex; their structural variations vast. Arranging thirty-two bars of melody and lyrics to coherently express a thought or emotion isn't easy.

The late Sammy Cahn (Frank Sinatra's personal lyricist) once said that, "Writing a song can be agony or ecstasy; it can take half an hour, or half a year." Cahn weathered the storm well. The songs he wrote with composers Jule Styne and Jimmy Van Heusen are among the most beloved of the last sixty years: "Love and Marriage," "Three Coins in the Fountain," "Time After Time," "Be My Love," "Let It Snow! Let It Snow! Let It Snow!" "All the Way," "High Hopes," "Call Me Irresponsible," and "My Kind of Town (Chicago Is)."

And Jimmy Webb—the author of such hits as "Up, Up and

Away," "By the Time I Get to Phoenix," "Wichita Lineman," "MacArthur Park," "Didn't We," "Adios," and dozens of others—characterized songwriting as "Hell on Earth."

Why would Cahn and Webb—both highly accomplished songwriters—make such harsh statements?

Because as smooth as they seem when you hear them on record, great songs don't always come easy. Behind many three- or four-minute masterpieces are days, months, or years of effort.

Yes—believe it or not—years.

It took ten years and seven albums for Billy Joel to complete the lyrics to "And So It Goes," and he tried to finish it for nearly every album we did together.

This is how it happened:

We would come to a session, and Billy would start to play the song.

The melody was fine, but at the end of the phrase "And so it goes, and so it goes . . ." his lyrical thoughts stopped cold. When it reached that point he'd begin to joke around, singing it several ways in rapid succession, varying his emphasis on the word *goes* each time:

"And so it goes . . . and so it *goes* . . . and so it GOES!"

I finally figured out that Billy had written the punch line for something he hadn't yet defined, and I told him so. "I've painted myself into a corner with a line like 'And so it goes,'" he admitted. "What does that mean? So *what* goes? What can I write to lead up to it? 'I jumped off a bridge and fell in the water—and so it goes?' It sounds like the end of a news program: 'I'm Walter Cronkite, and so it goes . . . '"

Billy's frustration with the song became a running gag. Whenever we'd start a new album, I'd ask:

ME: Have you finished "And So It Goes" yet?

BILLY: Naw, I'm stuck.

ME: And so it goes . . . !

Billy finished the song—finally—and included it on *Storm Front* (an album I did not produce) in 1989. The song and the recording are resplendent in their simplicity; "And So It Goes" is a staple in Billy's repertoire, and one of his most moving ballads.

Not every songwriter finds songwriting a chore. Elton John, for example, wakes up inspired.

Elton might start his day to find that two or three sets of lyrics from Bernie Taupin have arrived, and when he does he will walk over to the piano and begin improvising a melody. The ease and speed with which Elton writes is unrivaled; he is exceptionally disciplined. Sometimes Elton and I will talk and he'll say, "I wrote seven new songs for a show this week." That's one song a day! Of those seven songs, three are probably finished.

While most singer-songwriters pen both words and music, Elton enjoys letting others write the lyrics. His primary collaborator for the last forty years has been Taupin, who has helped Elton write most of his greatest hits, including "Crocodile Rock," "Honky Cat," "Daniel," "Rocket Man," "Saturday Night's Alright for Fighting," "Goodbye Yellow Brick Road," "Someone Saved My Life Tonight," and "Candle in the Wind."

The way Elton and his lyricists write—correspond would be a better description—is bewildering. I was privileged to witness such an exchange while Elton finished up the songs for *Aida*. In that instance, Elton—who was in the States—e-mailed and faxed the melodies to Tim Rice, who was writing the lyrics in London.

Whether the songs come easily or not, I'm awed by the way a songwriter can take a wisp of an idea—a few notes or chords—and spin it into a full-fledged melody.

I've been at dinner with Burt Bacharach and seen him pull a scrap of paper from his pocket and scribble some notes that might later become the melody of a song.

Paul Simon would hum a melodic line in the studio, and it was a privilege to hear him develop it into a song. The most exciting part of the process for Paul was playing a new song for someone, and he and I would often sit in his study listening to new tunes.

"This is a guitar song," he would say, or, "This one's definitely piano." Paul's guitar songs have a palpable folk feel—a chunky rhythm. His piano songs are tinged with jazz and blues inflections, and he tends to experiment more with their rhythms. I loved being part of those moments.

My curiosity is aroused by the kind of on-the-spot creativity that some songwriters possess, and it invariably begs a host of questions: "Did that little melody just pop into your head? How long have you been thinking about it? What brought it to the surface? How will you go about finishing it? How long will it take?"

For songwriters who are blessed with "the gift," songs dwell somewhere within; they're germinating all the time.

Paul Simon once explained how a musical idea embeds itself in his mind, and how he follows its lead:

"I write from instinct, from an inexplicable sparkle. I don't know why I'm writing what I'm writing. Usually, I sit and let my hands wander on my guitar. I sing anything [and I] play anything. When I come across a surprising accident I start to develop it. Once you take a piece of musical information, there are certain implications that it automatically contains: the implication of that phrase elongated, contracted, inverted, or in other time signatures. You start with an impulse and go with what your ear likes."

For Paul Simon and Billy Joel, the process of writing and recording are intertwined. Each of them writes and rehearses their songs in the studio, although their approaches are vastly different.

Paul is precise; he nurtures his music in an organized, cerebral way. Generally, each of his songs is polished before he records them.

Because he often coproduces his sessions, Paul listens critically in the studio. He prefers to make the instrumental tracks first and over-dub the vocals later. Whether he's making music tracks or laying down a vocal, Paul pays careful attention to the phrasing, tweaking every note and word.

Billy's approach is just the opposite. He always has plenty of ideas brewing, but nearly all of his songs are born in the studio.

Billy treats a session like it's a live performance: writing, rewriting, arranging, and rehearsing with his band, relying on the lively interaction between everyone to push things along. Perfection isn't the goal; Billy doesn't obsess over small mistakes if the feeling is there.

When Paul and I make an album, he starts with a few of the songs fully written. His studio time is spent working on the arrangements until he gets exactly what he wants. *Still Crazy After All These Years* took nine months to make.

Once he begins writing and recording an album, Billy works rather quickly. From rehearsal to completion, our first album together—*The Stranger*—took only six weeks to finish, because Billy had a number of songs written before we began recording and the band was already playing them onstage. Subsequent albums took a bit longer—nine or ten weeks—because Billy wrote everything for them from scratch.

For Paul, the process of writing and recording merged—but in an analytical way.

In Paul Zollo's book *Songwriters on Songwriting*, Paul Simon offered some thoughts, and what he said neatly coincides with my theory that understanding the nature of writing is 90 percent of making a record better:

"My writing has always been connected to record-making, and one of the characteristics of my work is that I have very good aural recall—I remember sounds of a lot of things," Paul explained. "I remember how records I grew up with went—and I remember obscure records, and what part of the record I liked. 'Did I like the drum sound?' These were thoughts that I had when I was fourteen. I've kept that, and I'm still recapitulating those early sounds in records today.

"When I'm in the studio I'll say, 'I want this color and this sound, and I want it to be contrasted with this [other] sound.' What I'm doing is working by orchestration. I'm working with musicians who are really gifted and, for the most part, supple enough that they can adapt to what I'm saying. Or, if they play exactly the right thing, I'll say, 'That's it—that's exactly the right thing.' "

A well-crafted song offers infinite possibilities for the arranger, musician, and producer, who can use a melody's inner rhythms—and the syncopation of the lyric—to emphasize its emotionality.

I marvel at Paul's persistence. He can work on an arrangement for hours, take it home and rethink it overnight, and have it ready for everyone to hear in the studio on the following morning. The band members will say, "But we did such a good job on this yesterday," to which Paul will reply, "It wasn't quite what I was looking for."

Billy doesn't have the same patience. And unlike Paul, he loves having the band around him while he's hammering out melodies and lyrics.

The birth of a Billy Joel song is organic: He filters and homogenizes his ideas, the producer's ideas, and the band's ideas as

Recording with Paul Simon, late 1970s
Phil Ramone Collection

he writes and records. Here's how Billy explained his predilection for working this way:

"I love having written a 'hit' catalog, but I hate the writing process. I don't want to waste any of my creative energy if the band isn't going to like the songs, so I take them into the studio for a reading.

"I write for the way the band plays; they were there when I was nothing—we all grew up together, personally and musically," Billy continues. "Their presence gives me a sensible perspective about my work that's invaluable. If they really like it (which is rare), they'll go, 'Yeah, yeah! That's solid!' and I'll finish inserting the bridge. Writing this way is like torture for me, because they'll be standing there all the while, watching me like a jury, and they can be a really nasty bunch of guys. They really nudge me with their 'show-us, Billy' routine, and they do it to spur me on," Billy concludes.

Although I never fancied myself a songwriter, I used my understanding of song form and structure to help Billy organize his thoughts when we were in the throes of making an album.

Billy and I would work together for a month before the first session. For these casual meetings we would work in a hotel room or at Billy's New York apartment. Once in a while we would go to his home on Long Island, or into the studio. I'd put together a mini recording setup that sat on the piano so that if Billy was toying with an idea he could record it for reference.

During that presession month, Billy and I would often work alone: he sitting at the piano, and me standing alongside him while he played and sang.

Sometimes Liberty DeVitto would join us, and he and Billy would experiment with tempos and grooves. When they had a couple of ideas worked out, they'd start polishing them—but not enough to stop the process of allowing the whole band to work out a spontaneous arrangement later. Every once in a while, Billy and Liberty would lay down a demo with piano, drums, and vocals.

During our prep session, Billy would occasionally stumble upon a chord progression or simple melodic phrase that he thought had potential. When that happened, he would try to develop it further, right then and there. If for some reason the idea didn't seem to be going anywhere, he would say, "I'm going to let this simmer for a few days."

Then, when he and I met again a day or so later, Billy might say, "You know that phrase I was trying to flesh out? It's a piece of garbage—it doesn't work."

I took comments like that to be a sign that Billy was too close to what he was writing to see the overall picture, so I'd offer an objective opinion. I'd make him sit and play it at the piano; many times, I found myself encouraging him to reconsider his decision to discard the song. The conversations went something like this:

ME: Wait a minute—I like this part.

BILLY: You do?

ME: Yeah—this section has an interesting texture. I agree that
        the chorus is commonplace, but I love the "B" section,
        where it moves into that weird bridge. I hear some cool
        things there. How about this: we'll let it have space, and
        instead of trying to make all the chord changes, you'll go to
        a pedal, and let the pedal build. One note, one note, one
        note—bigger, bigger, bigger—BOOM! Then, let's go to
        something really simple: two guitars, your voice, a bass,
        and a kick drum. It'll be more dramatic that way.

After this dialogue Billy would say, "Okay, what should we do?"

"Let's start recording," I'd suggest. "Do you want me to book the band?"

Frequently, the ideas that Billy laid down on cassette felt uncomfortable when he got to the studio and the band started playing them. If after giving them a fair shot Billy deemed a tune unacceptable, it was set aside. Since I recorded virtually every note of Billy's sessions, we would relegate unused songs that had potential to what I called the "spare parts reel," and file it for future reference.

I can't tell you how many times we went back to those tapes. "Remember a few weeks ago when you played that great riff, and you couldn't come up with a chorus?" I'd ask Billy. "There was definitely something there. Let's go back to that session's work reel."

One such instance was a demo song called "The Prime of Your Life," which Billy and the band recorded at the end of 1981.

Billy finished most of the melody and a good portion of the lyric, but for reasons I've since forgotten, it was never completed.

Not long after the demo was made, Billy was searching for ideas. He vaguely remembered the demo of "The Prime of Your Life," and we rummaged through the work tapes until we found it. Eventually, the opening chords of the demo became the main melody for "Don't Ask Me Why" (*Glass Houses*), and its chorus turned into "The Longest Time" (*An Innocent Man*).

Frequently, songwriters are asked about what they do when their ideas run dry.

It's daunting for a songwriter to confront his or her emotions and share them with the world. The reluctance to share, however deep in the subconscious, can be paralyzing. At some point, fear hits every songwriter, regardless of stature.

With every new album, Paul Simon fears that he'll hit a wall, but he doesn't beat himself up. He rationalizes his fear by saying, "It'll come when it comes." Paul tries to motivate himself: "Try a little harder . . . maybe you'll get something, and then a little more."

I've watched writers like Paul, Billy Joel, and dozens of others grapple with a melody or lyric, so I can assure you that writer's block is real, and that it perpetuates a vicious cycle of fear. When the mind is focused on writing it can stump you, and once stumped, you can't write a blessed thing.

Here's how Paul described being blocked: "Your mind says, 'I have nothing to say.' [It's more likely] that you've had a thought that you'd prefer *not* to have, and you're not going to reveal that thought. Your mind is protecting itself. Once you find a less negative way of dealing with the thought, you can probably deal with the subject matter you're trying to write about."

Every writer struggles to find a way to address his or her impediment.

For some, confronting the fear head-on does the trick. For others, it's physically moving to a different environment that refreshes their thinking.

To help stimulate his writing, Billy Joel retreated to small writing nooks: a loft in the Puck Building in SoHo, a place on Long Island, a studio at his house. We called these places Billy's "think tanks."

During the making of *The Bridge,* Billy explained how his downtown getaway helped inspire "Big Man on Mulberry Street": "If I was writing at my studio in the Puck Building and I got stuck, I'd pace the room—it had big windows and a nice view. Sometimes I'd leave the building; I'd go down to Little Italy to get a little food, a little wine, and some espresso. The walk I took on this one night was on Mulberry Street, and I just kind of invented this character that was like 'Mr. Cool.' The character is a nebbish, but in his own mind he's the 'King of Mulberry Street.' When he walks by, the old ladies sitting on the stoop wave to him. It's just one of those things I invented."

Billy's song "Baby Grand" also didn't come without suffering. The agony, however, resulted in pure musical ecstasy.

I knew the profound influence that Ray Charles and his R&B roots had had on Billy's style, and one day Billy confessed that he'd written "New York State of Mind" with Ray in mind. Paying homage to Ray was one of Billy's goals, and when we were making *The Bridge* in 1986, "Baby Grand" became their shining hour.

Billy and Ray had never met, but Billy idolized Ray so much that he named his daughter (Alexa Rae) in Ray's honor. When he asked me if I thought Ray might consider doing a song with him, I called Quincy Jones and got Ray's private number.

Billy was nervous the first time he spoke with Ray.

Getting Ray Charles on the phone was one kind of thrill; Billy's telling Ray that he wanted to write a song for them to sing together was another. It amused me that Billy was so anxious. "This is what musicians do," I reminded him. "Remember: You and Ray are both on a playing field that few people get to play on."

"Yeah, but Phil—what do I say to *Ray Charles?*" he asked.

"Well, you can start by telling Ray how much you admire him," I suggested. "If you want to say something about how you wrote 'New York State of Mind' with him in mind, say it."

I couldn't imagine Billy *not* telling Ray about it—I knew he'd be thrilled—and when they spoke, I was happy to hear Billy sharing his secret with Ray. He then said something titillating, and it caught me by surprise. "Ray, I'd like to write a song for us to do together." Ray was receptive, and asked Billy to send him a demo. With the phone call over and the big question out of the way, the only thing left for Billy to do was sit down to write the song.

Billy went on his way, and called me a short time later. "I've got the basic premise for a song, but I'm still not sure how to develop it. I just want to write it, and get a tape out to Ray right away," he said.

I don't recall exactly how much time elapsed, but it wasn't long. The night before we were scheduled to make the demo, Billy was still searching for a way to corral his thoughts. The pressure on him was tremendous.

"I've got to get this right—I've got one shot," he said.

He headed down to his retreat in the Puck Building, but nothing came. Billy took a break. He ambled around the city, and grabbed a bite to eat. Then, he went back to the apartment.

When he arrived at the studio the next morning he looked exhausted. I offered him some coffee and asked, "Have you got a song?" Billy pulled a few sheets of paper from his jacket pocket and showed me the chords and lyrics he'd hastily scribbled only hours before. The name of the song was "Baby Grand," and it blew me away.

I scanned it. "When did this come to you?" I asked. "About two o'clock in the morning," he said. "I just went over to the piano and wrote it. It came to me all in one shot."

In a promotional interview for *The Bridge* in 1986, Billy spoke at length about writing "Baby Grand":

"I was sitting in my house and I said, 'Jeez, I have an opportunity to make a record with Ray Charles. If I write the right song and Ray likes it, he'll actually be singing on my record.'

"[When I was looking for inspiration for the Ray Charles song], I began looking around at things that have been consistent in my life, and in this age of synthesizers and electronic keyboards the piano has almost become an old-fashioned instrument," Billy continued. "I glanced at the baby grand piano and realized that I had a lot of love for that thing. The piano has provided me with a nice living, a career, and happiness. It's gotten me women, and it's gotten me through some strange times.

"Sometimes at night I'd sit down and give myself a concert, and it's almost like the piano did it—I didn't even have anything to do with it. When I was thinking about a theme for Ray and me, it seemed apropos: you know, Ray Charles, piano player. Billy Joel, piano player. Let's talk about a real love in our lives—the baby grand. 'Baby Grand' is really a love song to an instrument," Billy explained.

Building the song around something they had a mutual affinity for was masterful. Billy empathized with Ray Charles. As a celebrated musician, he'd suffered through many lonely hours, and believed that, despite his raucous life, Ray had probably had his share of loneliness, too.

When Billy was in a funk, he'd go to his hotel room—or to a quiet room backstage—and play the piano. When you're a songwriter and you're feeling down, you pray that a unique melodic line will emerge from the gloom. Billy imagined that like him, Ray found relief by releasing his angst behind the piano. It turned out that Billy was right.

I thought "Baby Grand" was brilliant, and we immediately made a demo and sent it to Ray in Los Angeles. Billy was brimming with anticipation—and I was, too. We were sure we'd get a call from Ray within a few days.

Two weeks went by, and we didn't hear a thing. Billy began second-guessing himself. "Does Ray not like it?" he wondered aloud.

The lack of a response from Ray was odd, and after the second agonizing week I said, "Let me call him to see if he received it." I dialed, and Ray picked up the phone. "Ray, it's Phil Ramone. Billy and I were wondering whether you received the cassette."

"Yeah," he said. "Clever!"

As he listened to my end of the conversation, Billy motioned furiously. "Is it thumbs-up, or thumbs-down?" I gave him a thumbs-up.

When I handed the phone to Billy, Ray was equally cryptic.

"Did you like it, Ray?" Billy asked.

"Very clever!" Ray said. After the call, Billy looked at me quizzically. "What does that mean, 'Clever'? Does he like the song or not?"

I smiled. "That response is typically Ray," I assured him. "He loves it."

When we finally got Billy and Ray into the studio to cut "Baby Grand" it was pure bliss. We recorded Billy, Ray, and the orchestra together, with Billy and Ray playing the two pianos and singing while Patrick Williams conducted the orchestra.

Billy was extremely grateful to be working with Ray, and went out of his way to make sure that Ray was comfortable, and that the session ran smoothly. But after they recorded the first take, Billy discovered that there was a misprint in Ray's Braille lyrics, and he became worried. He knew that the error needed to be corrected, but he felt awful about having to put Ray out.

"How do I explain an error like that to Ray Charles?" Billy

asked. "Now you're getting a taste of what it's like to be the producer!" I said. "Just apologize, and tell him that there was a mistake
in transposing the words."

Billy explained, and Ray seized the opportunity to kibitz with
us. "Yes—the mistake is right here," he said, as his fingers scanned
the page. "You wanna read it yourself?" Once the problem was
fixed, they did another set of vocals—this time in front of two stationary mikes.

You could see that Billy and Ray shared a warm bond, and the
reason that "Baby Grand" works is because it's heartfelt and simple.
It's just two giants who admire each other, singing and playing together.

As "Baby Grand" demonstrates, for songwriters with the gift,
inspiration—and the moment of unblocking—does come. It takes
time, patience, and faith.

Billy Joel and Ray Charles, "Baby Grand" session, 1986
Courtesy of Sam Emerson/Redbox

Call
Me

With Gloria and Emilio Estefan
Phil Ramone Collection

It all starts with a phone call.

The discussion and planning phase of a record project begins long before the artist and I meet in the studio, and the call can come from a manager, the record company, or the artist himself.

For example, I bumped into Tony Bennett backstage at the Grammys a year or so after we made *Playin' with My Friends* and he said, "I've been meaning to call you. I think it's time we did another album together." Not long after Tony *did* call, and we began work on his Grammy-winning *The Art of Romance*. We recently followed it up with Tony's eightieth-birthday celebration, *Duets: An American Classic*.

Sometimes, it's me who makes the call.

My introduction to Gloria and Emilio Estefan came in 1988 when I called to congratulate her after hearing Miami Sound Machine's "Conga" on the radio. Gloria's voice was prominent and strong, and the record had a pulsating energy that was out of this world.

My intent was to say hello, tell Gloria how much of a fan I was, and pay her a well-deserved compliment. She was delighted that I took the time to call and invited me to meet with her, Emilio, and the band when I was in Miami. I did, and that simple phone call—made from my car—turned into a productive, fulfilling association and an enduring friendship.

Emilio had always produced Gloria's records—with great success. But after we met he asked me to remix several of her singles, and called on me when he was looking for an objective producer to help Gloria make her holiday album, *Christmas Through Your Eyes*. Later, I produced her duets with both Frank Sinatra and Placido Domingo.

Regardless of how it comes, I love getting "the call." The ultimate compliment is having someone you respect ask you to collaborate. It's flattering to hear someone say, "We love the album you did with so-and-so, and this new project would be perfect for us to work on together."

But what happens after the artist and I hang up? How do we get the ball rolling?

The way I began working with Billy Joel is an excellent example of how an artist and producer meet and forge an alliance from the ground up. Between 1977 and 1986, Billy and I made seven albums together: *The Stranger, 52nd Street, Glass Houses, Songs in the Attic, An Innocent Man, The Nylon Curtain,* and *The Bridge.* Those records—and the close friendship we still enjoy—occupy a significant place in my life.

The first time I saw Billy perform was in the spring of 1976, at a Columbia Records convention in Toronto. Columbia's conventions were legendary: raucous, fun-filled, and occasionally bawdy. My favorite part of the annual event was the evening concert, which was a showcase for the label's new and established artists.

For the Toronto gig I was working with two acts: Paul Simon and Phoebe Snow. I was backstage when Billy opened the show and knocked the audience out. My former wife—who was in the audience—ran into the dressing room while we were waiting to go on and said, "I want you to see this." I went out front and sat with her through at least thirty minutes of Billy's encores and watched him energize the room. I had no idea who he was—I hadn't seen him perform, and I hadn't heard any of his records. Billy's performance that night was stupendous, and I was impressed.

A couple of months later, Mickey Eichner and Don DeVito from Columbia Records called and said that Billy was looking for a producer. They invited me to see him perform at Carnegie Hall. Before the show, I went to the sound truck to see what the engineers were doing, and then watched the concert. Again, he amazed me. He's a remarkable songwriter, I thought. I went home and listened to his first four albums.

What bothered me was that the power I'd seen twice onstage was missing from Billy's records. A lot of people perform well, but for some reason their dynamic stage presence doesn't carry over to the recordings. I could tell this was happening with Billy; I told Mickey and Don what I thought, and a lunch meeting was arranged.

During lunch I discovered that making *Turnstiles* (released in 1976) had been traumatic for Billy. Over his objection, Columbia had assigned Jimmy Guercio—the wunderkind who'd made a string of successful records with Chicago and Blood, Sweat & Tears—to produce the album. Billy was especially frustrated because Jimmy insisted on recording at Caribou Ranch in Colorado, with Elton John's band. While Billy adored Elton, he felt that by using Nigel Olsson and the others he was copying Elton's sound and forsaking his own. He was right.

After haggling with Columbia and rejecting the Caribou session tapes, Billy remade *Turnstiles* at Ultra-Sonic Studios in Long Island, producing it himself using the core musicians with whom he'd record and play for the next twenty years: Russell Javors (guitar), Richie Cannatta (saxophone), Doug Stegmeyer (bass), and Liberty DeVitto (drums).

Although it wasn't his most well-produced album (by his own

admission Billy doesn't have the inclination or patience to produce), *Turnstiles* contained some of his best songs, including "Say Good-bye to Hollywood," "I've Loved These Days," "Miami 2017," "Prelude / Angry Young Man," "Summer, Highland Falls," and "New York State of Mind."

I told Billy that I thought his songs were outstanding. Before I said that, I sensed that he was sizing me up to see whether I was bullshitting him or if I actually knew the music. By now I'd seen him perform twice, listened to his albums, and heard the frustrations he'd vented over lunch. I knew exactly what was missing from Billy's first four records: his band. Billy's musicians were a tight group, musically and personally. Until he remade *Turnstiles* he'd been forced to use studio musicians who lacked the intensity of what I'd seen the Billy Joel band do onstage.

Was Billy's group perfect? No—but that's what I loved. They were a real band that worked together night after night, playing his music with passion. As Liberty DeVitto has fondly said, "We were a garage band, arranging songs as we played them—on the spot."

It was the unconstrained energy of Billy's live gigs that had hit me between the eyes, and that's what I wanted his records to reflect. I knew we could keep him in a live studio setting and still make vital rock-and-roll records. He showed me some of the new songs he was writing, we committed to making an album together (*The Stranger*), and our partnership was born.

Here's the twist: although I didn't know it at the time, Billy was also auditioning *me*. Producer George Martin was also under consideration. Why was I chosen over the distinguished Sir George, better known as the "Fifth Beatle"? Years later Billy told me that like his previous producers, George wanted to use session musicians, and not the guys in Billy's band. Every so often, luck is on your side!

Getting
to
Know
You

With Julian Lennon
Phil Ramone Collection

My first meeting with an artist is like a blind date.

While the story of how my relationship with Billy Joel began summarizes how an artist woos a producer (or vice versa), it's worth explaining in detail what goes on behind the scenes during the first date—and beyond.

The first thing I do after receiving a call from a prospective artist is listen to their music. I'll ask for some demos, or go out and buy a bunch of their CDs. Listening doesn't just give me insight into the artist's musicianship; it can help me determine how serious they are about their work.

One artist whose demos proved his sincerity was Julian Lennon.

Ahmet Ertegun had signed him to an Atlantic Records contract, and Julian was looking for a producer. He'd been studying different records to figure out what he liked and disliked in their production. While driving home from an interview one day, he listened to Billy Joel's *The Nylon Curtain* and liked what he heard. The sound had the overall feel that Julian desired for his own recordings, and he asked Ahmet to arrange a meeting.

Julian wasn't even twenty years old, and he was carrying the immense burden of being adorable, and the son of a legendary musician—a Beatle, no less. The entire world eagerly anticipated his first album. No one knew what Julian could do yet, and he was incredibly hard on himself. He found songwriting—and figuring out where he fit in musically—to be difficult.

He struggled, but in the end *Valotte*—named for the French château where the fabulous demos I had heard were made—was very special. Julian was nominated for a Grammy in the Best New Artist category (1985), *Valotte* went gold and then platinum, and "Too Late for Goodbyes" spent two weeks in the number one position on the Adult Contemporary chart.

After familiarizing myself with their music, the artist and I will begin to chat.

When I was an engineer, the first time I'd meet the performer was ten minutes before the session began. As a producer, I try to spend as much time as possible planning a project with them, and we'll usually meet (or speak on the phone) three or four times before we get to the studio.

Our first meeting is like a film director's "table read," at which the cast members meet each other and read through the script page by page. This introduction allows the artist and me to quickly size each other up. I like to keep the setting informal: breakfast, lunch, dinner, or drinks. Sharing a meal is a nice way to break the ice and get to know each other. It's like dating, really.

Probing to learn the artist's range of interests helps me design a framework for their album. Asking them to name ten or twelve songs they love—whether they're songs they'd choose to record or not—is revealing. Later, we might burn a CD of those songs and listen to it together.

Artists are always eager to tell me who their influences are, and

I'm interested in hearing about them. I'm often taken by surprise. "My parents used to play Bing Crosby and Rosemary Clooney," they'll say, or, "I grew up listening to Broadway music, but I didn't pay attention to it until I was eighteen. I realized then that it wasn't as bad as I thought."

I once had a very young artist say, "What used to put me in a really good place was listening to Ravel." I thought, What would this kid know about Ravel? It turns out that his dad—a hardworking guy who operated a bulldozer—used to sit on the back porch, smoke his pipe, and play Ravel.

You'd be surprised at what comes out during these casual conversations.

When we first met to discuss the making of *Am I Not Your Girl?*, a set of pop standards, Sinéad O'Connor revealed that she'd long dreamed of doing such an album. Why? Because when Sinéad was young, one of her mother's favorite records was an album by Marilyn Monroe. When she began performing in small Irish pubs, those were the songs Sinéad sang.

As we reviewed songs for her project, Sinéad started rattling off songs that Marilyn Monroe had sung: "My Heart Belongs to Daddy," "Diamonds Are a Girl's Best Friend," and "She Acts Like a Woman Should."

In another case, singer Melissa Errico, arranger Michel Legrand, and I were discussing songs for an upcoming record. Michel brought in some of the classic recordings made by Shirley Horn and encouraged Melissa to listen to them. When she did, she discovered that while they were beautiful records the tempos were much slower than she had anticipated. The ultra-ballad approach was not what Melissa had in mind.

During the planning meetings, I listen more than I talk. Some producers walk in, take charge, and dictate what an artist should do. Nothing is more offensive than a producer who disregards the artist's ideas; it's presumptuous, and it usually leads to disappointment and failure.

Consider what happened to Aretha Franklin.

When she signed with Columbia Records in the early 1960s, Aretha was molded according to a formula devised years earlier by Columbia's A&R director, Mitch Miller. Although she was a sensational pianist, Aretha's instrumental prowess was largely ignored and her vocals emphasized. The music she was given to record was aimed at a middle-of-the-road white audience. While she made some very good records for the label, few of Aretha's Columbia recordings were big sellers because they didn't reflect who she really was: an incomparable rhythm and blues artist with a ton of soul.

Remember what I said about the danger of formulas?

While Mitch's ideas for turning neophytes into stars worked for vocalists of the early 1950s (Tony Bennett, Rosemary Clooney, Guy Mitchell, and Frankie Laine), they didn't work for the edgier artists (like Aretha Franklin) that Columbia signed a decade later.

It took Ahmet Ertegun, Jerry Wexler, and Tom Dowd at Atlantic Records to recognize who Aretha was, and where she belonged. When he signed her in 1967, the first thing Wexler told Aretha was, "I want you to feel free, and to record the music that's in your heart."

Planning session with Michel Legrand and Melissa Errico
Phil Ramone Collection

Wexler and Dowd listened to Aretha's ideas, and it made a difference in what she recorded. Singles like "I Never Loved a Man (The Way I Love You)" and "Respect" were the antithesis of what she'd done at Columbia. Recording them helped her build a wide audience and succeed the late Dinah Washington as the "Queen of R&B."

I spoke earlier about honesty and trust, and few things can shake an artist's faith in a producer faster than the perceived mishandling of a problem, no matter how minor.

Nearly every project hits a bump or two along the way, and I try to find a moment during our initial meeting to discuss in advance some strategies for coping with them.

What happens if we get to the session, and after listening to a playback of the day's work the artist decides they don't like the arrangement, or the way a particular soloist is playing? If we *haven't* thrashed out the details, the artist may not feel comfortable telling me they're dissatisfied until late in the session. If I've just let the band (or the offending soloist) leave the studio and there's not enough time or enough money in the budget to bring them back for a retake, no one will be happy.

Sharing our expectations up-front helps everyone understand their roles.

I'm easygoing, but I have a methodical way of working, and the first meeting is also a good time for me to set the ground rules so we can maximize our productivity once we get to the studio.

Don't misunderstand: I'm not a schoolmarm, or a strict disciplinarian by any stretch of the imagination! If the setting and mood are right, the sensitive topics I touch on at this first meeting are broached in a friendly, inoffensive way. Most of them are fundamental, commonsense social and emotional issues that are essential to any successful interaction, whether you're a performer or producer.

First and foremost, I strive for genuine, direct communication. In our business, phoniness rings outrageously loud. *"Oh,*

Sweetie! Baby! Cookie! Darling! How wonderful you are!" That sort of fawning is cloying and superfluous. A few genuine words of praise mean more to an artist than a string of sycophantic compliments. Simply saying, "It works" or "That's great" after a performance reassures an artist—and speaks volumes about your sincerity. Most of the time the artist will know how excited (or tepid) I feel about a take from the tone of voice I use. Subtlety speaks volumes.

Being at the helm and communicating effectively isn't always easy. How do you tell someone like Paul McCartney, "It can be better—let's do one more take!" I'm just as big a fan of Paul and the Beatles as the next guy. Working with a big-name artist—someone you respect as a songwriter, musician, and cultural icon—can be intimidating if you're not well grounded.

What if the performer is a fellow record producer?

I've partnered with many musicians who've had experience in the control room—artists whose writing ability and production sensibilities I admire and respect. If I can stretch my brain, heart, and soul to bring them something new, I'm doing my job—as a producer and friend. If another producer is kind enough to say, "Will you work with me?" I'm there.

The question I ask myself when producing a fellow producer is, "Can they be objective about their own work?"

In the control room with Paul McCartney, 1986
Phil Ramone Collection

Producing an artist is one thing; standing on the *other* side of the microphone and putting oneself in the hands of another producer like me, is another. In this situation I say, "You have the ability to produce yourself. But, you've got to trust that I can step back, look at the overall picture, and help you figure out where to go musically."

The years I spent with Paul Simon and Billy Joel taught me about how to work cooperatively with an artist who has the capability to produce, and where my own ego fits in. I might have a better idea, or come up with a more suitable chord or phrase than the artist I'm working with, but when the record's done it's the composite of all our input that makes it work.

Whether it's an especially gifted or famous artist or a fellow producer, taking a step back to remind yourself that all they want to do is make the best record possible is often helpful. Even the most celebrated musicians look to the producer for honest feedback, not false praise. The caveat is that if I tell Paul McCartney (or anyone else), "I think you can do a better take," I'd better be right.

Regardless of whom you're working with, rudeness is neither acceptable nor tolerable. In my work domain the doorman, receptionist, the assistant who does the grunt work, and the kid who brings us coffee are as sacred to me as the artist. Music provides the relief in life, and there's no reason why we can't be kind to each other and have a good time while we're making it.

At every step, humbleness and discretion should guide what we do.

Frank Sinatra, for instance, was able to walk into a recording studio anywhere in the world and command respect because of who he was as a musician. The public may have fawned over him because he was a star, but music people revered Sinatra for his professionalism and musical acumen. While fans might forgive celebrities who push their weight around, seasoned musicians aren't inclined to make such concessions.

Dealing with tantrums or other temperament issues—whether it involves an artist, musician, or member of my crew—isn't pleasant, and handling them sensitively is the secret to turning them around. While there's no specific technique I use to restore tranquility, speaking calmly and letting the other party know how I feel is always the starting point. Then, I probe to find out why they're frustrated.

If the issue concerns one of the assistants or engineers in the control room, I advise them to take a break, and not return until they feel they can maintain their composure and focus on the job at hand. I simply can't allow anyone to disrupt a session or distract the artist while they're working on the other side of the glass.

If an artist has an eruption, everything stops. I clear the control room so as to give them space and avoid embarrassment, and then sit with them to figure out what's wrong.

Is it the material that's bothering them, or the way it's coming to life? Are they unhappy with their voice? Are they physically uncomfortable? Is a certain player getting under their skin? Has someone inadvertently said something to offend them?

One of the most awkward moments I've ever had in the studio came during a session with actress Jodie Foster, who was doing some recording for the TV movie *Svengali*. It happened not long after John Hinckley—a deranged fan who was infatuated with Foster—shot President Ronald Reagan and bragged that he had done it to get the actress's attention.

At the start of our session, Jodie walked into the studio just as the engineers were testing the mikes. The drummer—in an isolated booth—didn't think anyone could hear him talking to another musician. "She [Foster] is alright, but I wouldn't shoot a president over her," he casually said. Because the microphones were open, everyone in the studio—including Ms. Foster—heard it loud and, unfortunately, *clear*.

My jaw dropped as the drummer's voice echoed in the control

room. This is one of those awkward moments when you'd rather do anything than have to walk out into the studio to face the artist. How are we going to get through the next three to five hours? I thought. What happens when it's time to introduce the musicians to Jodie and I get to the drummer?

In this instance, the artist had the grace and dignity to act as though she hadn't heard the comment, but all of us—the drummer especially—were mortified. I had to do something, so I used humor to help smooth it over. When I introduced the drummer to Jodie a bit later, I began by saying, "Out of the mouths of drummers come . . . *drumsticks.*" It was the best line I could think of under the circumstances, and fortunately, it helped us move on.

I knew that the drummer didn't intentionally offend our guest; often, comments such as his stem from nervousness.

Session players, nightclub performers, and pit musicians are a special breed. They live fast-paced lives filled with tremendous pressure. The top musicians must be more than proficient, and able to perform on demand. Playing a piece of music you've only run through once or twice—and making it sound as though you've been playing it with the other men and women in the orchestra for years—is far more difficult than it looks.

I rarely have problems with musicians, but every once in a while I'll come across a player who's full of him- or herself. When I do, I remind them of something that Quincy Jones said to Bruce Springsteen, Michael Jackson, Stevie Wonder, Cyndi Lauper, Bob Dylan, and a couple of dozen other stars when he produced "We Are the World" in 1984: "Check your ego at the door."

What can the producer do about an obstinate player? Get rid of him, as I once did with a violinist on a Paul McCartney date.

It was 1970, and Paul was recording *Ram,* his second solo album. He'd come to Studio A1 at A&R on Seventh Avenue to record string overdubs for "Uncle Albert/Admiral Halsey." When I first called the contractor to book the musicians, I specifically requested an all-star orchestra. "Fill it out with as many concertmasters as you can find," I instructed.

On the morning of the first session, I discovered that we had no conductor. Uh-oh, I thought. This could be a problem.

As a musician, I appreciated the skills of a competent conductor. The fact is, while the audience may believe that every member of the orchestra is in sync and playing off of each other, the appearance is deceiving. The reality is that once you're sitting among your fellow players, it's nearly impossible to hear what anyone else—let alone yourself—is playing. The conductor, however theatrical his or her appearance might seem, is really the glue that holds the orchestra together.

At the first *Ram* string overdub session, the lack of direction caused by the absentee conductor was telling. "Why don't *you* conduct?" I suggested to Paul. "I'm not trained," he replied. "You're Paul McCartney!" I shot back. "You wrote the song. Who would know better than you how to conduct it?" He accepted the challenge.

When Paul and I spoke about what he wanted to accomplish with the string overdubs, I wasn't sure how much time we'd need so I booked a "double" session—a situation that then, as now, earns the musicians handsome dividends. Then, I told everyone who came through the door that there was the distinct possibility that we'd go *beyond* the double session. Even handsomer dividends!

Everyone was okay with the long but lucrative workday, except one lone violinist who ignored the possibility of a triple session and booked himself for another job at five thirty. He then pestered me all afternoon. "Will we be done by five? Do you think we'll be going into overtime? I have another date to get to." I dreaded taking a break, knowing the musician would besiege me.

When I had a minute I ducked into the bathroom, where I

found Paul washing his hands. The player's anxiety was driving Paul batty, too. "That guy is really distracting," he said. "Can we make do with thirty-nine strings?"

I apologized to Paul for the man's rudeness, and quietly asked the offending player to leave. Despite my discretion, the word soon spread: *"Ramone has a reputation for being tough on fiddle players!"*

With Tony Bennett during the sessions for *Playin' with My Friends,*
Capitol Studios, Los Angeles, 2001
Courtesy of RPM Productions

Spare the Rod
and Spoil the Artist

People say I spoil my artists, and it's true.

I coddle and cajole them, and constantly reassure them that
they're the focus of what we're doing every step of the way.

I'll do almost anything to please a client: bring in comfortable
furniture, put up special lighting, make sure that we have yellow jelly
beans, or brown M&Ms. Indulging an artist's fancy is a sound investment in the final product. Giving the artist every opportunity to put
him- or herself in the right place mentally is extremely important.

At some point during the first couple of meetings, I'll ask questions to ascertain the artist's preferences.

How (and where) do they like to rehearse?

Formulating a schedule for rehearsals is vital, and when it comes
to rehearsing, everyone has a different style.

Frank Sinatra rehearsed in private. He preferred to set his vocal keys with his pianist in advance, and then stand next to the orchestra to hum or sing softly as they ran down the chart for him moments before he recorded it.

Bob Dylan didn't rehearse before he came in to make *Blood on the Tracks*. His rehearsals were the actual studio sessions.

Peter, Paul and Mary were musical architects who designed sound, shaped songs, and disseminated messages that resonate as powerfully today as when they stood at the center of the folk music world in the late 1960s. They rehearsed face-to-face for hours on end until every note of every song blended seamlessly. Then, they'd obsess over it again when they got to the studio.

When Barbra Streisand runs through songs for a new album, she'll usually ask an arranger/pianist such as Dave Grusin or Mike Melvoin to come to her house, where they'll work together at the piano. Songwriters Alan and Marilyn Bergman will often attend too. Barbra has a hundred suggestions for melodic counter lines, tempo, and instrumentation, so I record every second of her rehearsals whenever we collaborate.

Because a lone piano can't impart the depth of an arrangement, I'll sometimes recommend that the artist rehearse in the recording studio, where we can have a synthesizer play the string lines and other parts. Hearing a fuller sound offers a better idea of how the music will sound with an orchestra and gives the artist the freedom to make changes before the session.

Choosing the right setting is important for two reasons: comfort, and sound.

A productive rehearsal should be inviting—and private. If you were a singer or musician, would you rather rehearse in a gym with fluorescent lighting and harsh, reflective floors or in an air-conditioned room that makes you feel at home?

I like to put the "No Visitors" rule into effect for rehearsals, because once the friends and assistants start popping in, the negative temperament invariably comes out. And since I usually record the rehearsal, it keeps things quiet, too.

At what time does the artist prefer to work?

Some singers think their voice sounds better during the day, while others feel it's more open at night. It makes no difference to me what time we work; I'll show up at two o'clock in the morning if it makes an artist happy. Knowing that he or she prefers to work between midnight and eight o'clock in the morning is necessary, because I'll need a crew that's used to staying late and working long hours.

Would the artist rather "track" (sing to a prerecorded instrumental), or record their vocal "on the floor" (live in the studio with a rhythm section)? Should we consider doing an old-school session, with everyone—the rhythm section, brass, strings, and singer—all performing at once?

This question speaks to the biggest difference between the way records were made when I started out in the business and the way they're made today.

The days of recording a vocalist and big band or orchestra together in the same room began waning when isolation and multitrack recording entered the picture in the late 1960s. By the 1990s, truly "live" studio recording was all but unheard of. Perfectionism has become part of the recording arts, and vocalists and musicians are eager to embrace the tools that allow them to make better records. A producer has nothing to gain and everything to lose if he stands on ceremony and allows a musician to walk away feeling that he hasn't given a record his very best.

I recently did a session with Etta James, and after Etta finished singing, the guitar player came up to me. "May I redo a line or two on my part? After hearing the vocal I thought of something that would sound better against what Etta sang," he asked. I was more than willing to help. All I had to do was put him back in the studio, play back the song, and punch in (rerecord) his guitar track at the point where he wanted to make the correction.

Occasionally, an artist's request will surprise me.

Before one of our many sessions together, Natalie Cole asked if she could sing out in the studio with the band surrounding her, the way she saw her dad record when she was young. "Would you mind if I did that?" Natalie asked. "Would I mind?" I replied. "You're the artist—of course you can sing out there!"

Everything boils down to assessing each artist's comfort level and determining how I can help them relax in the recording environment.

When Tony Bennett and I were discussing the upcoming sessions for *Playin' with My Friends: Bennett Sings the Blues* in 2001, he told me that he felt restricted by the stationary microphone he'd been forced to use at most of his vocal sessions. "I can take care of that," I said.

To make Tony feel at ease, I arranged the studio as if he were giving an intimate concert, and set him up with a handheld mike. After the session, he thanked me. "You know, for more than fifty years I've made records in some of the best studios in the world, and no one ever let me sing on a hand mike and made me feel so comfortable."

Trading glasses with Bono, 2003
Phil Ramone Collection

Bono used a handheld mike—and stood on a couch in the control room—when he overdubbed his part on "I've Got You Under My Skin" for Frank Sinatra's *Duets*. We were in the small but tastefully appointed room at STS Studios in Dublin where U2 had made most of their records, and Bono wanted to be as spiritually close to Frank as he possibly could. He wanted volume, and I cranked the monitors up until they were *frighteningly* loud.

Several years later, when Bono taped his bluesy solo rendition of Sinatra's "That's Life" for the film *The Good Thief* at Right Track Studios (now Legacy Recording) in New York, he did virtually the same thing.

When he arrived, Bono saw that the studio had been stocked with all sorts of food and beverages. He peeked in, shook his head, and shocked the film's producer by coming back into the control room and saying, "Phil, I think I'd rather sit next to you and track it right here at the board." He plopped down in the chair beside me, asked for a handheld mike, put his feet up on the console, and sang his ass off.

Bono later explained why he'd chosen to do it this way. "The scene in the film is gritty—the character is out on the street. Standing in the studio isn't something I could imagine the character doing—it just didn't seem like the best way for me to find the character's voice." To me, Bono's reasoning made perfect sense.

There are times, though, when having an artist record in a way that they're unaccustomed can bring vibrancy to a record.

When Danny Bennett proposed doing a duets record for Tony's eightieth birthday in 2006, we invited everyone to sing live, face-to-face with Tony and the rhythm section. For some (Bono, James Taylor, Billy Joel, Paul McCartney, and Elvis Costello) it was tradition; for others (such as the Dixie Chicks, Juanes, and Michael Bublé) it was a brand-new experience.

"I was surprised when several of the artists commented that they had never made any of their records live in the studio," Tony remarked. "Back in the day, you had to have a song memorized. You had one full take—maybe two or three—to make the cut. When the Dixie Chicks came in to record 'Lullaby of Broadway' with me, I couldn't believe that they had never sung a swing tune, or that they had never recorded the way I do. Afterward, they said they loved it! Maybe I turned a few kids on to the 'old' way of making music."

Michael Bublé—a student of Sinatra and Bennett—knew that Frank and Tony recorded live; he came to the studio expecting that he and Tony would cut their vocal to a prerecorded track. "When I arrived, I saw Tony standing there," Bublé explained. "But I also saw the musicians setting up in the other room. I looked at Tony and asked, 'Is there another session going on?' He looked at me and said, 'No—they're here for you and me!' "

Although Michael has had tremendous success with his own albums, he was like a kid in a toy shop. He kept saying, "This can't be real. I'm recording with Tony Bennett. Am I done yet? Tell me it's not over!" He and Tony did only a few takes; when they were finished I said, "There's your moment, Michael. It's now a part of your history."

"We entered Tony's world when we entered the studio," explained Elvis Costello. "He has this way of making you feel relaxed—totally like yourself. He's so comfortable with the material—even when it's a tune like 'Are You Havin' Any Fun,' which is what we sang together. Tony is very serious about respecting a songwriter's intentions: He'll let you take a few liberties with a song, but not many. All of these things rub off on you so that your game is pulled up to his level—without you even realizing it.

"I have rarely approached recording any other way," Costello continued. "But I was really surprised that many of the other artists had never recorded live in the studio—with the musicians right there in the room. They were not used to working without a net."

The examples cited above deal with the technical aspects of recording. But what does a producer do if the artist is *physically* uncomfortable in the studio?

I've turned off the lights and let vocalists face the corner of the room when they're singing, and I've set up microphones in the control room so they could stand behind me if they were intimidated by the immensity of the vacant studio.

To help Paul Simon and Art Garfunkel find the right mood when they tracked their vocals for "My Little Town," I put blue gels over the lights in Studio A at 799 Seventh Avenue so that all you could see was their silhouette in the room: two friends singing side by side into their microphones. It was eerie, but the atmosphere mirrored the subtle darkness of the song.

Some discomforts, though, aren't as easily alleviated as others.

Not long ago, I did a session with singer Melissa Errico and composer-arranger Michel Legrand. At the time, Melissa was pregnant. She had some very high notes to reach for, and I could tell that something was wrong. Melissa didn't say anything at first, but her body language screamed, *"I just want to be anywhere but in front of this microphone!"*

When we took a break and I asked about how she was feeling, Melissa started to cry. She simply couldn't get comfortable. "It's not fair to me, it's not fair to the baby . . ." she said. "Listen, you don't have to do this right now—it can wait until after the baby arrives," I reminded her. "Why don't you go home and relax? Come back when you're ready. We'll figure something out."

The solution was to make the setting more inviting, and the fifteen or so hours between sessions made a huge difference. When she came in the next day, we lowered the lights in the studio, repositioned the microphone, lit some candles, and put a big pillow against a ladder so Melissa could lean back and take the pressure off her diaphragm when she sang. I'll never forget how Melissa, who is a wonderful cook, brought in homemade vegetable soup, which made us all feel cozy and warm. Instead of tackling the numbers that required tremendous effort, Melissa started off by singing some easier tunes. Because of the inviting atmosphere, she was relaxed, and that helped her work through some very taxing material. I'm pleased to report that despite the session's tenuous start, Melissa, baby Victoria, and record are all doing fine.

While Melissa Errico's situation was serious, there have been many lighthearted moments when fulfilling an artist's wishes has been downright fun.

Most creative folks have eccentricities that others simply don't appreciate. Engineers, producers, musicians, and singers all have a ritual or lucky object that they swear affects their work. I've succumbed to the lure of placing faith in a talisman or two myself (usually an article of clothing), so I understand where they are coming from.

Dionne Warwick would never go for a take unless she'd smoked a cigarette, followed by a Luden's wild cherry cough drop. "Here's a drop for my voice," she'd say. I used to joke with her about it. "Let me get this formula straight: you ravage your throat with cigarette smoke, and *then* soothe it with a cough drop?"

One of the most memorable nights of my life was spent with French chanteuse Patricia Kaas. She called me one night and said, "Do you know the song where I want to sound sultry? I need for you to drink and smoke with me until four or five in the morning before we record it."

What a challenge! I could think of worse ways to spend an evening.

Patricia and I repaired to a bar near the studio, where she drank brandy and smoked cigars. After a couple of hours—when her voice had taken on the measure of huskiness that Patricia desired—we went back to the studio and she rendered the song with a sensuously smoky hue.

In a healthier vein, Paul Simon took to jogging before tracking a vocal because it opened up his lungs and relaxed his breathing. The exercise loosened his diaphragm, helped the air pass to his vocal cords, and relieved some of the physical stress of having to concentrate on singing. It all started during a session when Paul was recording "American Tune" in 1973.

For some reason, the vocal wasn't coming easily to Paul; he sang the song eight or nine times, and sounded forced on every take. "Why don't you give it a break?" I suggested. "Go take a run around the block while I finish these edits."

I was half-joking.

I thought that maybe going out into the fresh air to walk around or get a bite to eat would help ease Paul's distress. But Paul took my advice literally. He jogged from Seventh to Ninth Avenue and back again. When he got back to the studio he said, "Oh, fuck it—let me just try the song again."

Paul did another take, and for the first time that day, his vocal on "American Tune" sounded comfortable. "Should I include that in your schedule? Run a couple laps before every session?" I quipped.

Nothing, though, compared to the couple whose prelude to recording a song was having sex—in the booth. "Kill the lights," they'd say. After the engineer left the room they'd proceed to fornicate with an immodesty that was impressive, even for our business. Afterward, the man would go out into the studio and sing his lead. "The poor girl," I said. "We've got five songs to do tonight! How the hell is she gonna make it?"

On the Record

With Natalie Cole
Phil Ramone Collection

What is an album?

Fifteen or twenty years ago, an album was a vinyl record containing five or six songs (eighteen to twenty-five minutes) per side. In the rock and pop worlds, the collection often had a loose concept, with songs that were—to some degree—related to the theme. Each album was conscientiously programmed to have a discernible ebb and flow; we'd often fret as much over placing the right song in the right place on the album as we did over recording them.

At that time, listening to music was part of socializing, and when people partied, they listened to album *sides*. Friends would gather, put an album on, drink, and have fun. When the album side was finished, they'd either flip it over and listen to the other side, or move on to dinner, dancing, or a movie.

The compact disc reinvented the way records were made and how we listened to them. For better or worse, a CD treats the listener to one long, uninterrupted helping of high-fidelity music. While today's technology offers unprecedented sound quality and convenience, it poses a serious dilemma for the artist and producer.

Does the artist have to fill the entire seventy-seven minutes of available time on a CD? Is an artist who is compelled to fill a CD to capacity really giving the listener their best efforts?

Not long ago, Paul Simon and I reminisced about the days we spent making LPs.

When Paul wrote twenty-two minutes of music for one side of an album, it was pure: He refined every note until each song stood up on its own. There's a big difference between conceiving, writing, and recording a fifty-minute album (our limit during the vinyl LP era), and an eighty-minute album (the capacity of a compact disc).

For singer-songwriters, the prospect of writing enough songs to fill a CD can be overwhelming.

The shuffle mode on CD players—and portable music devices such as the iPod—has further refined the concept of programmed albums. While I love the convenience and variety that shuffling offers, it has killed the art of assembling a cohesive hour of music that brings the listener through a thoughtfully designed musical arc.

In a sense, things have come full circle: We're back to condensing music into singles the way we did in the 1960s.

I consider these factors when the artist and I begin developing ideas, and during the second meeting I'll ask several questions to help us hone in on what they'd like to achieve:

1. What is the concept?
2. Will the album feature old songs, new songs, or a combination of both?
3. What kind of audience will it appeal to?
4. Will the record present you in a way that your fans are unaccustomed to?

Karen Carpenter and I spent hours talking about these things in 1979 when I produced *Karen Carpenter,* her first (and only) solo album. The last two were points we dwelled on, given Karen's close identification with the Carpenters.

The *Karen Carpenter* album holds bittersweet memories for me, and in the course of explaining how it came about I'll share some very personal thoughts. My involvement with Karen and the record not only illustrates the planning process; it underscores the fragility of the relationship the artist and producer share with the omnipotent record label.

I'd known Karen and Richard Carpenter for years, and like everyone else, loved the sound of their records. The opportunity to work with Karen came at the request of her manager, concert promoter and filmmaker Jerry Weintraub, who explained that Richard was taking a year off and that he (Jerry) thought it would be the right time for Karen to do a solo album. Not long after, I received a call from Herb Alpert, asking if I would produce the record.

When Karen and I first sat down to talk about the project, I had no idea that the record we were about to make would stir up considerable controversy and lie in the vault for sixteen years.

Richard Carpenter wasn't overjoyed about his sister going solo, and I understood his concern. Her voice and wholesome image was the Carpenters' trademark, and Richard was afraid that a solo album might alienate their loyal fans or lead to speculation of a breakup. To Karen and me, that was preposterous. She loved Richard and the music they made together, but she also yearned to express herself as an individual. Karen had no plans to abandon Richard or the Carpenters.

To truly appreciate the love and adventure that accompanied the making of her solo album, you should know that Karen made a conscientious decision to experiment with songs and styles that differed from the Carpenters' records.

Karen loved disco, and asked me to find a song with a good dance beat ("Lovelines") to open the album; she also entertained recording songs that included adult overtones—those that spoke more provocatively about love and relationships.

Presenting her in a new context became the focus of our prerecording discussions, and Karen insisted that whatever we did should express her love for all music, while appealing to Carpenter fans *and* a new audience alike.

While she was in New York, Karen stayed with my family in Pound Ridge, and we drove back and forth to the studio together. The laughs and silliness we shared on those trips forever made us friends. While we were driving, Karen would be the DJ, playing all the songs that had been submitted for her consideration. She'd sit with a legal pad, listen intently, and rate them. "Should this be on the A list, or the B?" she'd ask.

Karen liked the energy on Billy Joel's records, so we decided to use his band (Russell Javors, Doug Stegmeyer, and Liberty DeVitto). They gave Karen love, support, and reassurance, and validated her artistic decisions. Russell—a fine songwriter—wrote two memorable tunes that were included on the album: "All Because of You," and "Still in Love with You."

To add a bit more texture, we brought in Peter Cetera (who wrote and sang a duet with Karen), Rod Temperton (who wrote several songs and did vocal arrangements), Richard Tee (a first-rate keyboardist who also played on Paul Simon's records), Bob James (who wrote orchestrations), and all-star jazz musicians Michael Brecker (saxophone), Steve Gadd (drums), and Airto Moreira (percussion).

We recorded at A&R in New York, and during the sessions I saw Karen blossom. It was wonderful to see her relax and let loose, joking with the crew and the guys in the band. You could see the sparkle in her eyes, and you can hear her smile on the record.

But everything wasn't perfect.

Karen's lingering sadness was evident to me, and it sometimes came out in unexpected ways. At one point during the sessions she

sang the word *love* and it cracked. I said, "Karen, it sounds con-
trived." She did it again and I said, "Not quite." She tried it a third
time, and I noticed tears in her eyes. I felt guilty. "Did I do that?" I
asked. "No," she said. As much as she was enjoying what we were
doing, she was under a lot of pressure. It was as if she sensed the inevitable hassles she'd face for taking this leap of faith.

The reception that Karen's album received from her brother
Richard and the executives at A&M Records was cooler than expected. The pessimism of the executives won out, and Karen decided to shelve the album.

A year or so after we finished her solo album, Karen called me
at home.

She and Richard had signed a new deal with A&M Records earlier in the day, and she was happy about going back to work. "We'll
be making a new Carpenters album," she said, "And I just wanted
to tell you how much I love you." Then she lowered her voice. "I
hope you don't mind if I curse. I still love our *fucking* record!"

In the morning she was dead.

Although Karen didn't live to see her solo record in the hands
of her fans, it was issued on CD in the mid-1990s when Richard
agreed that enough time had passed. By then, it had become a curio
more famous for the rumor surrounding its nonrelease than for its
musical significance.

As the aforementioned story shows, an album's concept—and
the songs an artist and producer selects—can make or break a
record.

Singer-songwriters commonly write songs custom-tailored to fit
their album's concept. But what if the artist is not a songwriter?
How does he or she sift through thousands of potential songs to arrive at the twelve or thirteen that will end up on the album?

Usually, I'll start by creating a list of songs that I think fit the
kind of album we're making. When Tony Bennett started talking
about doing an album of blues standards, I compiled a CD of songs

that I felt would both fit the blues mold *and* work as duets. This made narrowing our choices much easier.

I've produced several albums for Natalie Cole, and one of the things I love about Natalie is her keen sense of balance when it comes to choosing songs. When she was picking songs for the album *Snowfall on the Sahara*, we mulled over scads of them.

For *Snowfall*, Natalie wanted to bring an edge to some classic R&B songs, but she didn't reject the idea of singing contemporary tunes, either.

To start, I asked Natalie to select twenty or thirty of her favorite R&B songs, and told her that I would do the same.

I then combed the archive for some of the classic tunes recorded by Sam Cooke and the Soul Stirrers, and the songs that Al Green made in Memphis during the 1960s. Frank Military at Warner-Chappell Music sent over a CD full of possible choices. Friends called both Natalie and me to suggest Motown songs; a few mentioned the duets that had been done by Marvin Gaye and Tami Terrell.

TONY BENNETT

"Bennett Sings The Blues" – Duet Suggestions

1. Why Don't You Haul Off And Love Me- (Female Duet)
2. Done Somebody Wrong- (Sting Duet?)
3. Baby What You Want Me To Do- (Female Duet)
4. After You've Gone- (Female Duet)
5. Let The Good Times Roll- (BB Duet?)
6. Careless Love- (Female Duet)
7. Well Alright OK You Win- (Ray Charles Duet?)

Additional Suggestions
8. 'Til The Well Runs Dry
9. Got My Mo- Jo Working
10. Hop, Skip And Jump
11. Jumpin' At The Jubilee
12. Morning Glories

March 27, 2001

Rough song choices for *Playin' with My Friends,* 2001
Phil Ramone Collection

After a week, we compared notes, and found that our ideas were similar. During phone calls between Los Angeles and New York, Natalie and I whittled the list down to twenty-five candidates, which I burned onto two CDs. After repeated listening, some clear favorites emerged. We spoke almost daily, and through the process of elimination, distilled the remaining songs into a "must do" list.

One of the unexpected songs to top the list was Bob Dylan's "Gotta Serve Somebody," which Natalie's sister suggested. Natalie loved the song, but after running it down at a rehearsal, she voiced a concern. "The message is powerful, but Dylan makes reference to guns in one of the verses, and I'm not comfortable with it," she explained.

"Gotta Serve Somebody" was a very strong choice, and I knew that Natalie would be disappointed if we didn't include it. So I decided to ask Bob Dylan if he'd consider changing the verse in question for Natalie's recording.

I sent Bob a message through his manager (Jeff Kramer), and Bob quickly sent back two new verses written especially for Natalie. They worked beautifully, and Natalie wrote Bob a note to thank him and to let him know how much of a musical influence he had been. Until then, I had no idea that she was a fan of his work.

Sampler CD of potential songs for
Natalie Cole's *Snowfall on the Sahara*
Phil Ramone Collection

On a par with the selection of songs is the selection of musicians.

Some artists leave the choice of musicians to me, while others
travel with their own band and use them on their records, too. But
as I explained earlier, I have a list of session players—many of them
noteworthy jazz players—whom I use frequently, and if I feel that
one of my regulars would bring something special to a particular
record I'll suggest using him. Ninety-nine percent of the time the
artist agrees with my recommendation, as Paul Simon did on *Still
Crazy After All These Years* and Billy Joel did on *52nd Street.*

But what happens if an artist insists on using one of their players, and that person isn't the best choice for the job?

It's not the end of the world—we'll adjust to emphasize that
player's attributes. I've had situations where the musician in question has approached me and said, "I don't think this is working for
me. Maybe one of your experts—one of the better-known guys—
would be better suited for this song." If someone is a pro, they
know their limitations.

While we're on the topic of musicians, I'd be remiss if I didn't
explain the immeasurable contributions of the arranger. Arranging
and orchestrating is fast becoming a lost art; very few arrangers put
pencil to paper the way arrangers did forty and fifty years ago.

At that time, an arranger would listen to a melody, come up
with inventive embellishments, and sketch out chord symbols indi-
cating what they wanted each instrument to play. Then a musical assistant (copyist) would sit and write a detailed "chart" for each
instrument. That chart would be on the music stand at the session,
ready for the musicians to play.

But the proliferation of sophisticated electronic keyboards,
MIDI systems, and home recording studios has changed the way
pop records are arranged and recorded. It's expensive to hire a
rhythm section or a forty-piece orchestra for an album and have
them sit idly while the vocalist works through their part.

Artists look for perfection in every part of their performance, and vocalists today prefer to lay down a scratch vocal and come back later to rerecord their part.

To reduce the risk of delay, I'll ask an arranger such as Patrick Williams, Jorge Calandrelli, Rob Mounsey, Rob Mathes, or Philippe Saisse to write a chart and record some basic rhythm tracks electronically in his home studio. I still record most records with a live rhythm section, for feel. After the singer lays in their part, we can embellish the recording with strings, percussion, guitar, horns, or whatever else we desire.

Do tracks that are arranged and recorded with electronic keyboards sound the same as those recorded with a real orchestra? No, but that doesn't mean that they don't work well (or, at times, better) for some projects. I've found that marrying rhythm samples and real instruments is a nice combination.

No matter who does the arrangements or how they accomplish them, I'll suggest the colors or textures that I think will work for the album. The goal is to bring a fresh perspective to the music, no matter how familiar the songs are.

For example, when George Michael made *Songs from the Last Century,* he chose to include Johnny Mercer's "I Remember You"— a song recorded by dozens of the most celebrated singers in the world. As a harp-and-vocal duet, though, George's version stands alone in its stark originality.

As the artist and I begin discussing songs, musicians, and arrangers, we often invite their manager to join us.

The manager often plays a key role in promoting the record. They can tie it into an upcoming tour, arrange for Internet and radio promotion, and book the artist on national television programs such as *The Tonight Show, The Late Show with David Letterman, Late Night with Conan O'Brien*, and *Saturday Night Live.* With MTV and VH1's shift away from straight music videos, the nightly talk and comedy shows have become an invaluable forum for exposing new music, and exposure is what helps to sell records.

While working with a manager can be a blessing, there's a flip side: some managers can be unreasonable and aggressive.

In the midst of making Ray Charles's *Genius Loves Company,* I got a scathing letter from one guest artist's manager complaining that I'd switched a line in their duet around, and that she—the manager—hadn't given her approval.

The tone of the manager's message was condescending and unprofessional, and my response to her arrogance was straightforward. "It worked for Ray and for me when we recorded it, and it's my privilege as the producer to deviate if I so desire."

Part of being a producer is that you are occasionally confronted with overinflated egos. When dealing with them, it's important to be candid—and to make decisions that preserve the integrity of the artist and their music.

Group Therapy

Peter, Paul and Mary, mid-1960s
Courtesy of Michael Ochs Archive

There's nothing like producing a rock-and-roll band.

So far, I've described the way I work with an individual artist. Producing an organized group of musicians (as opposed to a solo artist) necessitates a specialized approach.

Much as a family adapts to the preferences and behaviors of each member, musical groups that spend any appreciable amount of time together develop a policy for how the group will travel, live, write, rehearse, and record. The years I spent touring with and recording groups as diverse as Peter, Paul and Mary, Chicago, and The Band offered tremendous insight into the psychology of working with groups.

Peter, Paul and Mary personified 1960s folk music.

The trio's spirited renderings of folk songs such as "Blowin' in the Wind," "Puff (The Magic Dragon)," "I Dig Rock & Roll Music," and "Leaving on a Jet Plane" have become landmarks in the modern folk canon; "If I Had a Hammer"—a single from their first album recorded in 1962—became an unofficial anthem of the civil rights movement.

Engineering *Album 1700* and many other Peter, Paul and Mary records taught me the secrets of recording harmonies, and how to help a group maintain harmony in the recording studio.

I was charmed by the trio's sound from the moment I heard them. Their fastidious attention to detail and the way they'd harp on a phrase until it was burnished and blended to their liking blew me away. While I'd heard about how meticulous Brian Wilson was when it came to recording vocal harmonies, working with Peter, Paul and Mary gave me a sense of why Brian was so relentless when it came to his own work arranging and producing for the Beach Boys.

Each member of the trio had an ample reserve of passion, and none were shy about sharing their convictions. As individuals and as a group Peter, Paul and Mary were social activists whose spring-board for personal expression happened to be music.

Peter Yarrow emerged as the leader. He was the most forceful of the three and had an almost militaristic approach to editing.

Noel Paul Stookey was introspective—a perceptive songwriter who used humor to mediate and keep the peace.

Chicago recording session, late 1970s
Phil Ramone Collection

Mary Travers was honest, direct, and intense—a no-nonsense woman. She didn't like doing multiple takes, and would typically be the one to present a rational, persuasive argument for—or against— the specific interpretation of a vocal line. They were always healthy arguments!

For technical purposes, I recorded Peter, Paul and Mary with three separate microphones. When we recorded, the three principals would often bicker over which mike was whose. To quell the unrest, I had three small name tags made up and hung them around the mikes so we could keep track.

Peter, Paul and Mary were all about editing; most of their records were heavily edited from the best lines of all the takes.

We'd start by doing at least ten full takes of a song. Then we'd play back every take and listen. Noel (Paul), Peter, Mary, producer Milt Okun, and I each had a lyric sheet, which became our blueprint for editing. As we listened to the multiple takes, each of us would mark our comments on our lyric sheet: "Use the third line from take two, the fifth line from take seven," and so on.

If at the end of the playbacks we all agreed on which lines contained the best performance, great. If we disagreed, Milt Okun would cast the deciding vote. If Milt weighed in and we were still at an impasse, Albert Grossman—the trio's legendary manager— served as arbitrator, smoothing out any uncomfortable moments. It was during the "Which line should we use?" debates that we really heard from Mary.

With this hot-and-heavy pace, I developed a technique for creating composite takes—a practice that served me well. While I recorded all of Peter, Paul and Mary's master takes on an eight-track machine, I also ran a two-track recorder for reference.

I could make some pretty fancy edits with a razor blade, but since the group's phrasing was so tight, I'd make sample edits on the two-track before committing myself on the multitracks. As spliced up as they are, I doubt the casual listener would notice that those records aren't the product of single takes. How could I go wrong when recording at 30 inches per second?

My experience with Peter, Paul and Mary proved invaluable when I began producing Chicago, another group with complex musical and personal dynamics.

I was asked to produce Chicago's *Hot Streets* in 1978, after they ended their partnership with James "Jimmy" Guercio, who had produced their first eleven albums.

The invitation came because of my history with the group. Because I'd mixed several of their albums, I had worked at their home studio (Caribou Ranch) and I understood the inner workings of their "sound" and the politics of the band.

Hot Streets came at a bittersweet time.

Guercio, who had managed and produced Chicago since 1968, was a terrific producer who was also responsible for the sound of *Blood, Sweat & Tears*, the second, self-titled album by a band that included Randy Brecker and Canadian vocalist David Clayton-Thomas. That album's two major hits—"Spinning Wheel" and "You've Made Me So Very Happy"—won Blood, Sweat & Tears (and Guercio) a Grammy in 1969 for Album of the Year.

The magic that Guercio spun with Chicago and Blood, Sweat & Tears helped spawn a pop subgenre that artfully married traces of rock, rhythm and blues, soul, and big-band jazz. Jimmy's creative vision and business acumen were beyond compare; I had (and still have) the utmost respect for him as a friend and producer.

In addition to his creative talent, Guercio had a good business sense. He took the concept of the full-service recording studio to the limit in 1973, when he and the members of Chicago opened the Caribou Ranch Studio in Colorado. I worked there many times and it was unlike anything I'd ever dreamed of: a resort where we ate, slept, played, and recorded.

At five thousand acres, Caribou had been one of the largest private Arabian stud farms in the country, nestled nine thousand feet in the Rocky Mountains. The lodgings were plush, and the amenities par excellence.

The cabins included brass beds, leather furniture, fireplaces, hardwood floors, and high-end sound systems. Some suites had Steinway baby grand pianos, and there was a library with books, movies, and games. Then, there were horses and skimobiles. And food: A professional cooking staff was available to prepare and serve whatever snack or meal your entourage desired, twenty-four hours a day.

Caribou was the ideal place for a band to write and record, because it was all in one. You came, unpacked, and every need was tended to without leaving the property. The record companies were willing to foot the bill, and before long dozens of bands were seeking refuge at the ranch. Elton John even named one of his albums after the place.

I wasn't privy to the conflict that caused the end of the Guercio-Chicago marriage, but I knew the details of another tragedy that was affecting the band: the death of guitarist Terry Kath, who had recently died in a senseless gun accident. I had known, worked with, and loved Terry too, and was equally devastated by his loss. As we began work on *Hot Streets,* everyone involved with Chicago was grieving.

Because of Terry's death, Chicago was breaking in a new guitarist, a bright young player named Donnie Dacus. While no one could replace Terry, Donnie did a remarkable job of respecting the brotherly role that Terry had played in the band while learning to fill his musical place, too.

Upon talking about songs for *Hot Streets,* I discovered that the members of Chicago had come up with a fair plan: Each of the eight members would be given the opportunity to contribute a song for the album.

Fielding songs from eight individual members of a band—each

of whom expects to have a song on their album—wasn't easy. It wasn't just about the writing: each member also had the right to add their own twist to the mixes of the songs they'd written, *and* a share in consensus approval over the mixes for every song on the album.

With a well-known group that is as successful as Chicago, there isn't room for a B-minus song, so when I learned of the plan the question I posed was, "What are we going to do if a song that one of the members writes is not an A, A-minus, or B quality song?" We agreed that if there was any question about a song's suitability, I would be the judge.

That responsibility put me in an unenviable position. Was I thrilled about having to tell the conga player that the song he wrote wasn't good enough? Not exactly. It wasn't the percussionist's fault; he was Brazilian, and didn't have full command of our language. But it *was* my job to put the music first, so I sat down with Peter Cetera and said, "Peter, our friend needs us to help him write a better song."

The interpersonal and intersectional dynamic between the members of Chicago was fascinating. They were like a family, and

In the control room with Jim Boyer (center) during a
Chicago session, late 1970s
Phil Ramone Collection

because we spent four to six weeks (or more) together rehearsing and recording an album, I became their "uncle."

Traveling to a distant locale and settling in for a month or two to record an album helped add to the familial atmosphere. And when you traveled with Chicago, you traveled in style! Since they stopped using the Caribou Ranch studio when they split with Guercio, we were free to go wherever we wanted to record.

For the *Hot Streets* sessions we went to Miami's Criteria Recording Studios. We rented two mansions (Robert Lamm, Peter Cetera, and I stayed at the tennis club; the horn section—Jimmy Pankow, Walt Parazaider, and Lee Loughnane—stayed in what I called the Palmetto Palace because of the mammoth Florida cockroaches that seemed to be everywhere).

When we traveled, we tried to build as many comforts of home into the equation as possible. For instance, we always had a chef to prepare our meals. It wasn't about being extravagant: I knew that we would be working hard, but the temptation to play harder was sure to be there. It was better to have the places we stayed in stocked with everyone's favorite foods, snacks, and beverages so that when the band came to work there was no need to waste time sending out for food or going out to party.

As one would expect from a large family, there were often differences of opinion among the members of Chicago—and not just about songs.

I mentioned that when we were on the road, the horn section stayed in separate quarters; the brass players did, in fact, function as an individual unit. They weren't being uppity; they came to writing sessions and rehearsals, but they didn't like being around when the rhythm section was laying down the basic tracks.

When you've got so many components going into a sound and you start working through a track, getting the rhythm, guitar, and vocal parts down is intense. There were times when recording became tedious, and to thrust the horn section into long sessions and laborious debates at a time in the process when they wouldn't even be playing would have been counterproductive. It was better to have them arrive when everything was in place so that all they had to do was work their unique magic on the track.

Logistically, this didn't pose a problem. We knew that the horns would be on 90 percent of the songs (they were, after all, the major component of Chicago's sound), so we'd sketch out the rhythm parts knowing exactly what spaces we needed to leave for the brass. After the bass, guitar, drums, keyboards, and vocals were recorded they'd come to the studio and lay in the horn parts.

We made other accommodations, too.

Most of the band members didn't like to record early in the day. Robert Lamm enjoyed rising with the sun to play tennis, and I often joined him. The others were content sleeping in.

Peter Cetera and I were happy to hit the studio at ten in the morning. Like many singers, Peter didn't like anyone else around when he recorded his vocals (it can easily encourage criticism and tension), so he and I would spend hours working on his tracks before the late-afternoon sessions with the rest of the band.

It's my experience that when you work with groups—large or small—the collective personnel is "the artist." One or two members

With Chicago singer, songwriter,
and keyboardist Robert Lamm
Phil Ramone Collection

may emerge as de facto leaders (as Robert Lamm and Peter Cetera did with Chicago), but relations become thorny when a producer shows favoritism—especially if each of the artists is a successful performer in his or her own right. In those instances I'm mindful of each person's stature as an individual, yet aware that my charge is to bring them together as a group.

Paul Simon once came to me and said, "Artie, James Taylor, and I would like to do the Sam Cooke song '(What a) Wonderful World.'" The lineup was stellar, but with three distinctive artists such as Paul, Art, and James the budget could easily get out of hand, so I had to lay some ground rules.

I got them together and said, "Here's the deal: You've all got equal rights. The three of you have to sing on the initial track, and then you can each have one day to fix your guitar part or your vocal. You'll all have a say on the final mix, but when your 'fix-it' day is done, it's done. The fourth and fifth days are mine."

Cutting the record didn't take nearly as long as it otherwise might have, because I'd made my expectation of the trio *as a group* clear from the start.

I had worked individually with Paul Simon, Art Garfunkel, and James Taylor before, which gave me valuable insight into their personalities and how they worked in the studio. But we *still* met prior to rehearsals.

Every record I make presents unique obstacles. Even if an artist and I have the routine down to a science, there's still a lot of planning to do before the sessions get under way. While an established relationship makes things easier, I've got to treat everyone as a new artist, even if it's just psychologically.

A & R Recording, New York City, early 1960s
Phil Ramone Collection

The Studio

There are two places in the world where I love to be, and one of them is the recording studio.

Next to the artist and the music, the studio is the most prominent star in the recording process. It's the engineer's and producer's tool: a powerful instrument used to manipulate air, vibrations, and sound. The studio is where music and friendships are born.

My love affair with the recording arts began in the late 1950s, when I walked into J.A.C. Recording on West Fifty-eighth Street in New York to make a demonstration record.

Until that moment, I was tussling with some serious issues.

I wasn't happy studying and playing classical music, and I ached to let my violin wander into the jazz and pop worlds I was flirting with on radio, stage, and television. I wasn't even sure that I wanted to continue playing the violin at all. It was rather halfheartedly that I asked a friend (pianist, arranger, and composer Ralph Burns of the

Woody Herman band) to score two songs for my first demo: "It Had To Be You," and "Summertime."

The hour or so I spent cutting the tunes helped answer my questions and changed the course of my life. I was mesmerized by the deftness with which J.A.C. owner Charlie Leighton recorded my session, and when I expressed an interest in the process of recording, he invited me to become a trainee. Charlie's ramshackle apartment–turned–demo studio was the ideal place to start my career on the *other* side of the glass.

As an apprentice, I was expected to do everything: run tape recorders, hang microphones, balance the sound, and cut acetate discs. Leighton's philosophy was that an engineer should understand the principle behind what they were doing before they did it. "The most expensive microphone in the world isn't worth a damn if you don't know where to put it, or why it needs to go there," Charlie said. You needed to know the limitations of the final product before you put a microphone in front of an artist. How much bass could be cut into the grooves of a record? What would lend presence to a vocal?

One of the first things I learned at J.A.C. was the secret to cutting a good disc.

Condensing sound waves into the squiggly grooves of an acetate disc was an art unto itself. The width and depth of a groove was

Cutting a disc at the original A&R Studio, circa 1961
Phil Ramone Collection

determined by the dynamics of the music. You had to be careful to make the record loud enough so it wouldn't skip, but aggressive enough in terms of equalization and compression to give your demo an attention-getting sound.

The competition to make your demos stand out was unbelievable: Every songwriter and salesman wanted theirs to be louder, brighter, and hotter than the next guy's. If you became known for making the kind of demo that had an edge, word spread and you were suddenly in demand.

What was it that helped set a demo apart?

Echo.

Without echo, recordings sound tight, lifeless, and dull.

Listen to the classic sides that Elvis Presley cut at Sun and RCA Victor in the mid-1950s: The reverb is what lends a haunting, glossy overtone to records such as "That's Alright," "Heartbreak Hotel," "Blue Moon of Kentucky," "All Shook Up," and "My Baby Left Me." Drenching a vocal or guitar part with echo was a fairly new trick at the time, and the lonesomeness imparted by the reverb helped sear Elvis's ersatz R&B sound into the public consciousness.

Because few recording rooms had enough natural reverb, echo chambers made of cement or wood became acceptable substitutes.

To create the echo, speakers and microphones were placed inside the chamber. The music being performed in the studio ("dry," i.e., untreated with echo) was routed to the speaker inside the chamber, and when it bounced off of the reflective surfaces it added a "halo" or "wetness" to the music. The microphone picked up that highly reverberant sound and sent it back to the mixing board, where the engineer could add as little or as much as needed to the dry mix coming from the studio.

The fraction of a second it took for the dry, untreated sound to loop from the board, into the chamber, and back again created a slight delay. The size of the chamber and the way the walls were treated affected the quality of the echo produced.

A studio's echo became its signature, and I quickly learned that much of what you do in the studio is a mixture of echoes, reverbs, and slaps (a single, strong echo heard bouncing off a hard surface). The more imaginative you were with those effects, the more successful your studio became.

In the days before digital reverb and delay, we had to improvise for echo. Charlie Leighton didn't have the room to install a real echo chamber, and I remember Bill Schwartau slathering a small room at J.A.C. with varnish for weeks. It was improvised, but the effect gave us a nice edge around the voice and piano.

A lot of my knowledge about recording came from listening to records, and one of my favorites at the time was a Columbia album called *Delirium in Hi-Fi* by Elsa Popping and her Pixieland Band. It's still one of the greatest examples of how echo and other effects can be used creatively.

Elsa Popping wasn't a real woman, or even a bandleader. The name was a pseudonym used by French composer André Popp for his phantasmagorical technical excursions: jolly, whimsical flights of fancy in which engineer Pierre Fatosme used multiple tape machines to record each instrumental and vocal part deliberately out of synch. This created a surreal pastiche of echo, speed, and slap effects.

Popp and Fatosme's psychedelic sounds were years ahead of the LSD movement, and I spent months analyzing *Delirium in Hi-Fi* trying to figure out exactly how they did it.

Every engineer dreams of opening a studio—a place they can call their own. In late 1958, Jack Arnold (a partner in J.A.C. Recording) got tired of me saying, "I would love to have a big recording studio," and found a space for me in the Mogull Film Building at 112 West Forty-eighth Street.

I remember the elation I felt the first time I stepped into the forty-eight-by-thirty-eight-foot room that had once been a small insert stage used to shoot commercials. There was very little soundproofing, no air-conditioning, and a creaky old elevator. Despite its quirks, the place was charming and I thought Jack and I could make the place work.

We named the studio A&R Recording, for Arnold and Ramone. I asked a friend who was a calligrapher to design a logo that would be so over-the-top it would be unforgettable, and the florid script "A&R" she came up with became our visual calling card. Then we had the back wall of the studio painted with big clown-style triangular checks. If anyone spotted that wall on a jazz album cover, they would know the record had been made at A&R.

A few months after opening A&R we ran into problems.

Jack fell ill, and I was sure we were going to lose the place. There must have been something in God's master plan; Art Ward, manager of the Honeydreamers, stepped in and helped keep things afloat. Art had the entrepreneurial skills and the requisite A in his name. Although we'd started A&R with no money, microphones, or recording equipment, we were optimistic. Bill Schwartau and Don

With Jack Arnold, circa 1961
Phil Ramone Collection

Frey—two friends I'd met at J.A.C.—helped wire the studio and set everything up. If not for the generosity of all the kind souls who took an interest in its birth, this kid's dream for A&R Recording would never have become a reality.

I was lucky to have befriended Bill Schwartau and Don Frey.

Bill Schwartau was one of the unsung heroes in our industry, and every recording professional on the East Coast admired him. His ability to hear "through the microphone" was impeccable, and when Bill set up a session, what you heard in the studio matched what you heard in the control room. He used microphones and aural shading to convey subtlety and nuance in the same way a painter uses light and color.

Don Frey had worked at NBC for almost ten years, engineering the sound for live television shows such as *Your Show of Shows, The Imogene Coca Show, Omnibus,* and a series of opera programs broadcast from a large studio in Brooklyn. Don was dexterous, and when we started A&R he used his expertise to record jingle dates, commercials, and film scores.

In those days, control rooms were cramped, and the mixing console was pushed right up against the window between the con-

A&R reference disc label featuring
the studio's distinctive script logo, 1969
Phil Ramone Collection

trol room and the studio. That meant that anyone who dropped in had to watch the proceedings from behind the engineers. It was Don's idea to pull the console away from the glass and to put a couch in front of it so that visitors could sit and watch the artists while they performed out in the studio. A&R was one of the first studios in the city to do this.

Don's affiliation with A&R attracted David Sarser, a violinist with the NBC Symphony, and one of conductor Arturo Toscanini's technical advisors. David sold Ampex tape recorders and fine European microphones; we bought our tape machines from him, and he loaned us some microphones to get us started.

Our first recorders were two Ampex units: a model 300 (three-track) and 350 (two-track). We made our own mixing board out of two radio consoles and some spare parts. It had sixteen inputs, and we used a bunch of small Altec mixers to subdivide them so we had extra inputs for the strings.

David Sarser told Skitch Henderson—leader of the *Tonight Show* band—about A&R, and one day Skitch came in with Doc Severinsen and the *Tonight Show* musicians to rehearse. That session helped us test out the room for the first time. We used five microphones, and when we opened them up it sounded incredible. I knew that A&R was on the right track the moment I heard that sound. We invited them to come back on weekends to rehearse so I could experiment with setting up the room in different ways.

Then along came two more blessings: Harvey Sampson of Harvey Electronics, and the Bratmans of Carroll Musical Instrument Rentals.

In addition to having the widest variety of audio gear in the city, Harvey was a kind person who took a liking to me. "Why don't we put some of our equipment in your studio and use it as a showroom?" he suggested. Before long, microphones, preamps, and equalizers began crowding the control room.

Getting oversized instruments in and out of our tiny elevator was a nightmare. You couldn't fit a xylophone in it unless you stood it on end, and hauling timpani up the stairs took forever. To reduce the need for constant lugging, Carroll and Beverly Bratman loaned us timpani, xylophones, vibes, bells, and chimes free of charge.

The advertising agencies liked A&R, and the jingle and commercial dates we did helped pay the rent. Our reputation as a jingle house grew through word of mouth, and the big Madison Avenue ad agencies became our best daytime clients.

In time, we began doing more record dates, and when Bell Sound and the Atlantic Records studio on Fifty-sixth Street were overbooked, we received their overflow.

The first major album recorded at A&R, in 1958, was Ray Charles's *The Genius of Ray Charles*—a killer record, even to this day. Tom Dowd and Bill Schwartau were the engineers, and I was the third assistant, or gofer.

I can't overstate how much Atlantic Records engineer and producer Tom Dowd influenced my work. I met Tom through Bill Schwartau and Al Schmitt, both of whom worked with him years before at Coastal Recording.

When it came to recording, Tom was a maverick. He embraced early eight-track recording and had a knack for placing instruments on separate tracks so you could work with the individual parts later on. He was a forward thinker who tested the limits of the technology, and that impressed me.

Because of our affiliation with Atlantic, our business grew quickly. I wanted our studio to become recognized as the finest in New York City, so I experimented with mikes, equalization, and compression to find just the right sound for each artist and group.

The room at 112 West Forty-eighth Street had a nice, dry sound: the walls were wood covered in soft drapes, the ceiling was lined with acoustic tiles arranged in a zigzag pattern, and the floor was made of soft cement and vermiculite.

Whether you were recording a big band or a quartet, everyone could hear themselves and the rest of the band in the studio at 112 West Forty-eighth Street. Musicians especially loved the room because of the way the sound of their instruments reflected off the floor.

What made the floor so special?

When the Mogull Film studio originally built the room, they laid a base coat of cement but never put a finish coat over it. The unfinished concrete powdered, and when we set up folding chairs or rolled a piano across the floor it created minute fissures on the surface. The softness of the floor helped absorb certain frequencies, which altered the sound. The cracks were tiny, but with all the foot traffic, they created a chalky dust. The joke around town was that if you saw a violin player walking down Forty-eighth Street and he had dust halfway up his black pants, you knew that he'd been working at A&R!

Don Frey and I experimented with all kinds of floor treatment to duplicate the floor's special properties. Eventually we found a man who analyzed the floor's surface and formulated a topical seal. He patented the product; we later applied it to the floors in Studio A2 (at 799 Seventh Avenue), and Studios R1 and R2 (at 322 West Forty-eighth Street).

Another characteristic that set A&R apart was the echo, which was produced by portable units called EMT plates.

The EMT unit was a four-by-eight-foot soundproof box with a thin plate of sheet metal suspended in the four corners. A small transducer mounted on the plate caused it to vibrate. Two microphone-like pickups captured the sound reflecting off the edges of the vibrating plate and fed it back to the board in the control room.

When we set up our first EMT we discovered that it sounded flabby, like coiled springs or cheap guitar echo. We took the side of the box off and began experimenting with the tension on the springs. I found that if we tightened it, I could tap the plate with my fingernail and it changed the tone of the *ping*.

The secret to improving the sound of the EMT was tuning its tempered steel plate, and we worked endlessly to vary the tension on the springs that held the plate in place. Once the tension was equal (similar to the way the lug nuts on a tire are equally tightened) it sounded spectacular. The sound of the EMT-produced reverb was much better than what we got from the tiled bathroom we'd been using.

When A&R started showing a profit, we bought more EMT chambers so we could have a separate echo unit for strings, horns, vocals, and rhythm instruments.

After carefully tuning them, we suspended the EMT units from the ceilings of several rooms in the basement. The output from the basement chambers was fed to the upstairs rooms through a patch bay. I treated those EMT rooms like a bank vault; once the chambers were in place the doors were locked, and anyone who wanted to get in had to see me to get the keys.

My belief was that if you recorded with the right microphones and you had the right blend of leakage and presence, you could create wondrous echoes. Keeping the echo chambers separated gave us better control over each channel.

People began talking about the high-quality sound of the records we were making at A&R. While I was doing record dates, Don Frey and the staff engineers were recording and editing some very big commercials and jingles for the New York Yankees, Pepsi-Cola, and Marlboro cigarettes. The bulletin board in the lobby at A&R was a hub of activity; the place was like a beehive at nine o'clock in the morning.

Jingle dates were booked as all-day sessions, and they were recorded in segments. At nine o'clock the six-man rhythm section (bass, drums, piano, two guitars, and percussion) would come in. From ten to eleven we recorded the brass. Strings came in from eleven to one, and from one to three you'd have the singers. Finally, you'd mix and edit from four to five. Sessions like that were happening in each studio.

When the musicians got their hourly break they'd rush to the bulletin board, pull off their messages, and call Radio Registry—the musicians' answering service—from the direct phone lines we'd installed in the lobby.

The studio got a big boost when Burt Bacharach and Hal David booked a date to record one of their young singers—a girl named Dionne Warwick. The triumvirate usually recorded at Bell Sound. One day, Bell was busy; Burt had heard about A&R and me, and he called. Suddenly, I found myself engineering a string of Dionne Warwick's hits, songs such as "What the World Needs Now Is Love," "Look of Love," "I Say a Little Prayer," "This Girl's in Love with You," "I'll Never Fall in Love Again," "Promises, Promises," "Alfie," and "Do You Know the Way to San Jose."

As a composer and arranger, Burt Bacharach has distinguished himself as one of the true innovators in the world of pop music.

What sets Burt's music apart?

First, the idiosyncratic way that he structures a melody. Burt is audacious in pushing beyond the traditional songwriting form; his compositions are replete with unusual chord progressions, bitonal harmonies, arresting rhythmic patterns, unexpected key changes, nonsymmetrical phrasing, and offbeat time signatures—most of which are rarely found in a standard pop tune. Burt also weaves fabulous contrasts and textures into his arrangements.

Burt Bacharach and Hal David, circa 1968
Courtesy of Michael Ochs Archive

A Bacharach arrangement typically features airy, sustained strings, expansive woodwinds, felicitous brass solos (flugelhorn has been one of his favorites), throbbing timpani, and drum parts that ascend to precise, thundering crescendos.

The combination of instruments that Burt uses also adds immeasurably to the feel of his records: Rim shots, played concurrently with light brush strokes on the snare drum head, characteristically delineate the beat. Strings, voiced with the horns, thicken the sound without weighing it down.

The tonalities produced by the rhythm section are extremely important to Burt, and we always experimented to attain the exact feeling that he desired. If the snare drum sounded too bright or had too much "ring," we'd dampen the head by covering it with tape. After a time, we discovered that taping a wallet to the top head cut the sharpness and reduced the ring to just the right degree. Thereafter, a wallet was taped to the snare head before every one of Burt's sessions.

Burt's essential gift is the ability to express drama without being melodramatic, as Dionne Warwick's achingly intense recording of "This Girl's in Love with You" demonstrates. Although Don Sebesky wrote the arrangement, it has Burt's inimitable fingerprints all over it.

Throughout the song, Dionne sounds laid-back: She never loses her cool, measured approach—even when the music swells and explodes around her. Biting, edgy percussion pushes the beat along, while the strings offer a wisp of romantic warmth. The piano part could have been lifted from a country-and-western chart, and the tightly muted trumpet solo—voiced melodically—offers a sparkling contrast.

Listen, too, for the winsome flute accents that metaphorically suggest a pair of quivering hands in the line "My hands are shaking," and the urgency imparted by the percussion crescendos and timpani flourishes that punctuate the line, "I need your love . . . I want your love."

From top to bottom, Dionne Warwick's recording of "This Girl's in Love with You" is pop songwriting and arranging at its very best.

As a technician, recording Dionne Warwick was like immersing myself in a master class.

For instance, I learned that I should never shut down the string mikes—even when the strings weren't playing—because the leakage from those microphones lent an extra dimension to the sound. People thought I was crazy, but doing these things gave the A&R sound its edge.

More than this, the Bacharach-David-Warwick sessions taught me how to think like a record producer.

Burt and Hal always produced their sessions with Dionne, and they had an interesting working dynamic.

As with most teams, one person is the type A personality, the nervous one who chomps at the bit. That's Burt. He'd be out in the studio, waving his hands in the air, conducting, moving around constantly. Hal was the quiet one; he'd stay in the control room and chain-smoke, speaking softly, just taking it all in.

Once a song was recorded, Burt and Hal would listen to the playback and discuss how they felt about it. If they couldn't make a decision, I was given the chance to offer my opinion. If I felt that part of a take was special, I'd say, "I think take two had a better intro—we should keep it."

Burt and Hal had an easy give-and-take, and they were gracious in letting me join in. When we got friendly and started to understand one another, Burt stopped rushing into the control room after every take to hear the playback. I'll forever be grateful to them for being the first people to put my name on a single; seeing "Engineered by Phil Ramone" on one of Dionne Warwick's Scepter records gave me a thrill beyond compare!

Burt's parents would usually come by at the end of our sessions, and when he began dating Angie Dickinson, she'd come too.

Burt sometimes had so many visitors in the control room that I'd have to say, "Burt, can you ask them to settle down?" He would simply turn around and give them the quiet sign.

Hal David would *never* yell at anyone.

"Shhhhh," he'd say, and the room would quiet down until the second we were rolling. Florence Greenberg, the founder and president of Scepter Records, would often be in the control room and she'd cheer—*loudly*—when a song was played back.

Even my mom, Minnie—who rarely came to the studio—was drawn into the fun.

The first big hit that I engineered for Dionne Warwick was "Alfie" in 1967, and my mom attended the session. Mom was a character in the best sense of the word: a sociable lady who attracted all sorts of actors, actresses, singers, and dancers—all of whom adored her.

On the day that Dionne recorded "Alfie," Mom stopped by to say hello to composer-producer Burt Bacharach. Burt was charming, and he and my mother got along famously. After the session, Minnie knit Burt a scarf.

Meanwhile, "Alfie" roared up the charts.

At the next Dionne Warwick session we cut "I Say a Little Prayer," and Mom visited again, to give Burt the scarf. He was flattered, and they chatted up a storm.

"I Say a Little Prayer" went up the charts, too.

When it came time for Dionne to cut another record, Burt booked time at A&R. Everyone arrived, but my mom was conspicuously absent. Burt got nervous. "Where is Minnie? How come she's not here?" he asked. I couldn't resist the urge to tease him. "Look, Burt, I'm just not used to making records with my mother in the room!"

But Burt was serious; he insisted that my mother's presence had something to do with "Alfie" and "I Say a Little Prayer" becoming hits, and he wouldn't start the session without her.

I called my mother at work. "Burt would really love to see you," I explained. "He's got it in his head that you're his and Dionne's good luck charm. Can you grab a cab and come right to the studio?"

As you can imagine, my mom was bowled over by Burt's faith in her.

She didn't let him down.

The song we recorded that day—"Do You Know the Way to San Jose"—hit the Top Ten and won Dionne a Grammy Award for Best Contemporary Pop Vocal Performance, Female, of 1968.

We recorded a lot of pop dates at A&R, but the jazz guys loved the studio too. Our proximity to Jim & Andy's bar—the city's premiere hangout for all musicians—didn't hurt.

As soon as we'd call a break the musicians would stream out of the studio, down the stairs, and into the brownstone next door for a cocktail or two. More often than not, I'd have to retrieve them when the producer called for the session to resume.

On one memorable session, jazz vibraphonist Eddie Costa poked his head into the booth while we were recording a song and said, "How many bars [of music] do I have?" "Sixty-four," I replied. "Be right back!" Eddie darted out of the studio and flew down the stairs to Jim & Andy's. "Give me a shot and a beer," he asked. Eddie threw back the shot, gulped his beer, and ran right back up the steps. He looked into the control room, and I signaled "thirty-two bars left" with my fingers. He was back behind the vibes with his mallets in hand with time to spare.

Eventually I had a talkback system wired from my console directly to the bar at Jim & Andy's. All I'd have to do was push the button and say, "I need a trombone—is anyone down there?" Soon, J. J. Johnson, Urbie Green, Frank Rehak, or another trombonist of equal stature would amble in to play. Since the talkback system worked both ways, we'd sometimes flip the switch and listen to one of the guys at the bar chatting it up with some woman who may or may not have been his wife. It was madness, but we had a lot of fun.

Jim & Andy's has a special place in my heart.

Owner Jim Koulouvaris welcomed me there in the mid-1950s when I was still a kid. He'd sit me off in the corner and feed me; every once in a while he'd slip me a beer. I'd have never gotten in there normally, but Jimmy knew that I was a musician, and that I needed to meet the kind of people who were coming in and out of his place. Because of Jim's kindness I got to rub elbows with Gerry Mulligan, Eddie Safranski, Clark Terry, Patrick Williams, and many other jazz giants, never imagining that I'd be recording them in just a few years.

With Jim Koulouvaris, a friend, and Burt Bacharach
Phil Ramone Collection

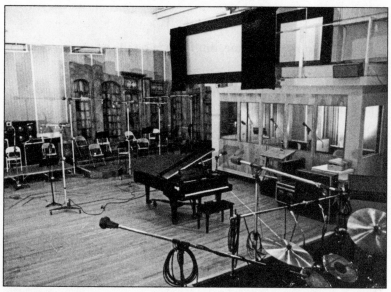

A&R Studio A1, 799 Seventh Avenue, NYC
Phil Ramone Collection

It Was a Very Good Year

Nineteen sixty-three marked a turning point for A&R Recording, and for me.

The first milestone came in March, when Creed Taylor—a producer at Norman Granz's Verve Records—came in to make *Getz/Gilberto*, an album featuring tenor saxophonist Stan Getz, guitarist João Gilberto, and pianist Antonio Carlos Jobim.

The songs were all arranged in the bossa nova style: a sexy combination of Brazilian and jazz rhythms popularized by Gilberto and Jobim in Brazil a few years earlier.

Bossa's soft, exotic beat was made for intimate dancing, and it had become extremely popular in America. *Jazz Samba,* a previous Stan Getz album, had hit number one on the jazz charts the year before, and because of it Creed decided to pair him with the two Brazilian heavyweights.

I didn't know at the time, but I was in on the beginning of a new craze.

Creed definitely knew—his previous bossa nova records had sold well and gotten plenty of airplay. There was an indescribable feeling in the room when we made *Getz/Gilberto*—a quiet energy that put everyone in a happy mood.

The biggest surprise was how the most famous version of "The Girl from Ipanema"—sung by João's wife, Astrud Gilberto—came to be performed and recorded, and how quickly it caught on. Although Astrud rarely discusses her work, she recently shared the story of "The Girl from Ipanema" as it unfolded at A&R:

"I came to the US with João, as he had a commitment to record the *Getz/Gilberto* album," she explained. "One day, a few hours prior to Stan Getz coming to our New York hotel for a scheduled rehearsal with João, he [João] told me with an air of mystery in his voice, 'Today there will be a surprise for you.' I begged him to tell me what it was, but he adamantly refused.

"Later, as they were in the midst of going over the song 'The Girl from Ipanema,' João casually asked me to join in to sing a chorus in English after he sang the first chorus in Portuguese. So, I did just that. When we were finished performing the song, João turned to Stan, and said (in 'Tarzan' English), 'Tomorrow Astrud sing on record—what do you think?'

"Stan was very receptive—in fact very enthusiastic. He said it was a great idea. The rest, of course, as one would say, is history. I was a bit nervous; [it was my] first time in a recording studio. But I felt reassured by the presence of my husband, João, and of Jobim, who at the time was a supportive friend. I'll never forget that while we were listening to the song in the studio's control room, Stan said to me—with a very dramatic expression—'This song is going to make you a star,'" Astrud concluded.

As I recall, Norman Gimbel walked into the studio at about

ten o'clock that night with the lyrics. Creed looked them over and said, "Jeez, it would be nice to get this song to Sarah Vaughan."

João intimated that Astrud might sing the song, which we could record as a demo for Sarah. I didn't even know that Astrud could sing; all she did was quietly sit in the corner of the studio while her husband and his cohorts recorded their album.

Astrud was sweet, and her version of "The Girl from Ipanema" turned out to be the most charming demo I'd ever heard. Others were captivated by Astrud's understated interpretation too. Why wouldn't they be? It was beguiling: sexy and coy, yet innocent at the same time.

I cut a disc and sent Astrud's "The Girl from Ipanema" to Quincy Jones, and was later surprised to learn that Sarah Vaughan had declined to record the song. But I was delighted to learn that Verve had decided to put Astrud's version on the back of a Stan Getz single—"Blowin' in the Wind"—which he had recorded with a large orchestra.

In those days, 45 singles had designated A and B sides.

The A side was reserved for the song the label believed would be the hit, while the B side contained a filler tune.

Astrud's recording may have remained an obscurity if not for a disc jockey at a small radio station in Columbus, Ohio, who turned the single over and began playing the B side on the air.

Within weeks, stations across the country were playing it too, and "The Girl from Ipanema" reached number 5. It also became the defining moment for Brazilian music—in its native country, and in America. The *Getz/Gilberto* album—which had been relegated to the vault after the onslaught of the Beatles—reached number 2 and stayed on the charts for two years.

I've been given a lot of credit for my work on *Getz/Gilberto,* but the truth is that it was pure magic because of the players and how they sounded in the room at 112 West Forty-eighth Street. I'm apprecia- tive that Creed trusted me to record it, and especially proud that the album went gold and earned me my first Grammy Award for Best Engineered Recording, Non-Classical, in 1964.

The more I engineered and watched producers I'd come to respect, the more I yearned to move into the producer's chair. The producer had more control over the aesthetics of a recording, and I felt I could use my skills as both a musician and engineer to make better records.

Creed Taylor deserves my special thanks, for he was one of the first people to suggest I step out of my role as engineer and move into the studio.

Creed is a quiet soul, and I think he was uncomfortable telling someone, "I don't like what's being played." When we worked together I became his interpreter, and he gave me tremendous leeway to evaluate and constructively criticize a performance from take to take, and to interact creatively with players like Jimmy Smith, Kai Winding, J. J. Johnson, and Wes Montgomery. That was a big responsibility for me and a risk for Creed, and I benefited immeasurably from it.

For example, one of our clients at A&R was Solid State Records, and they had a nifty marketing gimmick: Their albums were made using 100 percent transistorized equipment, and they were all recorded in our studio. As Solid State's audio director, I had the plum assignment of recording and producing jazz artists like Thad Jones, Mel Lewis, Manny Albam, and Jimmy McGriff in the 1960s.

Another momentous occasion of 1963 was one Sunday morning in April when Quincy Jones showed up at A&R with Lesley Gore, a sweet sixteen-year-old from Tenafly, New Jersey.

Lesley had been studying with a vocal coach, and when some voice-and-piano demos she made came to the attention of Mercury Records president Irving Green, he was impressed enough to send them to Quincy. There was a swell of female pop singers and girl groups in the early sixties, and Lesley had the voice and moxie to rank with the best of them.

Although I didn't record the original session, our association began with one of her first songs—"It's My Party." As Lesley recalls, she and Quincy cunningly trumped another producer named Phil to snag the hit:

"We recorded 'It's My Party' on a Saturday at Bell Sound. That night, Quincy hosted a Mercury Records event at Carnegie Hall. He was standing outside of Carnegie when Phil Spector came up to him, bragging about a new record he was making with the Crystals. 'Quincy, it's the greatest song I've ever recorded in my life.'

"With a poker face, Quincy said 'Oh, really? What's the name of the song?' Spector said, ' "It's My Party." ' Quincy, being a smart guy, realized that the music publisher who owned the song had double-dealt him. One of the partners had given Quincy and me an exclusive for the song, while the other partner gave Spector the same deal," Lesley explains.

Late that night, Quincy called me at home. "Can you meet me at your studio first thing in the morning, Phil?" he asked. "I'll be there at eight," I promised.

While I readied the room, Quincy went to Bell Sound to retrieve the unmixed tape. When he came to A&R we mixed it, and then cut a hundred acetates. On Monday morning the acetates went out via airmail to the biggest radio stations across the country; we ended up scooping Phil Spector's record, which wasn't even finished yet!

I'm still bowled over by "It's My Party."

As soon as I heard the punchy arrangement and Lesley's assertive take on the vocal, I knew that she and Q had hit on something extremely rare. She wasn't even seventeen when she made that record! "It's My Party"—a very adult song sung by an innocent child—shot to the top. Lesley Gore became a hot commodity, and she began recording all of her records at our studio. Everyone loved the cavernous echo and gorgeous string sound we got on her next hit, "You Don't Own Me," and that helped A&R become a hip place to record.

Producers would hear a record or commercial on the radio and say, "I want whoever made that record." They wanted to duplicate the success of the records we were making and demanded to use the identical studio, musicians, equipment, and engineer.

A&R grew quickly—much faster than anyone expected. Soon, we had two studios at 112 West Forty-eighth Street (A and B), and a mix room. But we needed more. We became so busy that I told the business staff, "We've got to open this place twenty-four hours a day."

We spent nearly all of our waking hours at the studio, which became our nesting place. If passion overtook us, the vocal booth sometimes served as the center of activity.

Sometimes the overnight stay was really necessary: On one of the rare occasions when I did go home to rest I overslept and missed a morning session. The extra sleep cost me $3,000 that I couldn't afford.

One of the most important things I did when we opened A&R was to implement a strict training program for prospective recording engineers. I wanted to have reliable people who could step in and take over if necessary. Everyone who wanted to work in any serious capacity followed the same routine.

An intern's first stop was the tape library, where he or she would work for two or three months. Recording tape was our most valuable asset, and it was imperative that everyone who worked with it knew how to flat-wind, label, and store it. While in the tape library, an assistant would also learn the ins and outs of documentation.

A&R's track sheets were something I prided myself on.

We never attached labels to or wrote track information on the back of tape boxes: All of the data pertaining to the music recorded on a reel of tape (artist, date, master numbers, titles, and technical data) was scrupulously noted on our track sheets. The track sheets were prepared in triplicate, and when we sent a tape out, whoever received it would have a clear, accurate log with all of the recording's pertinent information right inside the tape box.

Interns in the tape library were forever being peppered with questions.

"Where are the tapes for this project?"

"Are the track sheets in the box?"

"Can you read your notes?"

"Are the reels filed correctly so we can find them easily?"

Next came the production room, where you would learn to dub (copy) tapes and magnetic film.

Then came the mastering room, where an assistant learned how to cut the discs that went to production. Cutting masters gave some guys conniptions! I loved watching interns try to cut a disc for the first time; they'd usually bury the diamond needle in the acetate. With practice, an apprentice would learn what a burnish on the stylus was and how to make it work to their advantage, how to adjust the angle at which they were cutting, and how deeply to cut the groove.

If an intern continued to show aptitude, they would be moved up to second or third assistant engineer. Being a second or third assistant was the proving ground: It gave one the opportunity to demonstrate their skills—and their potential—to senior engineers like Don Frey, Bill Schwartau, and me.

Eventually the day would come when another engineer or I would see that someone was ready to become a first assistant, and

Original A&R track sheet & master
tape reel for *The Stranger,* 1977
Phil Ramone Collection

they'd get to work their first real date: a jingle, commercial, or week-end rock session, perhaps.

In a typical week, a first assistant could expect to work sixty or seventy hours. To most, the exhausting hours were mitigated by the thrill of being involved in the creation of many historic records—and the experience gained by working alongside the main engineer. Whether operating the tape machines, adjusting the cue mixes sent to the artist's headphones, or mixing a record, every task performed by the first assistant offered a valuable lesson.

By the time an assistant came to work for a senior engineer at A&R, they knew their job thoroughly. Amongst the three or four big studios in New York in the 1960s, '70s, and '80s, A&R had the finest help—people who you could trust to invest the same time and care in a session as the primary engineer would.

Things kept rolling along at A&R until one day in 1968 when we received some disturbing news: Mr. Mogull was selling the building at 112 West Forty-eighth Street. As a stopgap measure, we found space in the Leeds Building at 322 West Forty-eighth Street. But we *still* needed more room.

There are times in your life when fate turns your way. Through a series of fortunate events, we learned that Columbia Records was closing their flagship studio at 799 Seventh Avenue, a place with an enviable pedigree.

The building at Fifty-second Street and Seventh Avenue was the site of CBS Radio's first New York broadcast studio (opened in the 1930s), and when CBS formed the American Columbia Records in 1939, they began recording there.

Acoustically, nothing beats an A-frame, the architectural model that has graced churches for hundreds of years. To my delight, studio A1 at 799 Seventh Avenue was an A-frame.

The room's dimensions were sixty-five feet by fifty-five feet with a forty-foot domed ceiling. The exterior of the dome was metal, which cut out almost all of the interference from radio signals. I liked the design of the ceiling, but it was too reflective for my taste. Inside the room, the ceilings were plaster, and we placed high-diffusion tiles—in a V pattern—on the ceiling to help cut down on the amount of reflection and natural reverb in the room. This gave the sound a warm ambience and the sweet, crystalline top end I was looking for.

A well-designed room produces a balanced blend of high (treble), middle (midrange), and low (bass) frequencies. Too much of any one frequency range can mar an otherwise terrific record. Treble and midrange tend to reflect off hard surfaces, while bass is absorbed by soft surfaces. If your room is overly bright, music recorded there will sound shrill. Too much midrange lends stridency (a nasal sound, like a voice coming through the telephone) to the recording. Excess bass booms, making the lower frequencies sound muddy and undefined.

To control the midrange and high frequencies and create spacious sound, Don Frey and I covered the walls with soft fiberglass and fabric. These "drapes" had two layers, but there was some space between them so the fabric side didn't touch the fiberglass side. Because of this, the midrange would pass through the fabric and be absorbed by the fiberglass, while the high frequencies would bounce off and back into the room.

We also redesigned the bass response in the room by creating "bass traps" (fiberglass-covered battens that protruded eighteen inches from the wall) that would prevent unwanted bass frequencies from running along the wooden floor. Doing this reduced low-frequency muddiness, and gave our bottom end a clean, well-defined edge.

One of the first things we did to the smaller studios at 799 Seventh Avenue (and each of the studios at 322 West Forty-eighth Street) was put in a floor that was similar to the one in the studio at 112 West Forty-eighth Street. It was spring-loaded (it floated inside the shell), and was a mixture of vermiculite and cement.

But the existing floor in Studio A1 at 799 Seventh Avenue was oak—the first wood floor I ever worked with. The room had large acoustic panels that could be raised or lowered by chains, which helped diffuse the little bit of sound that was reflected off the floor.

I built a special platform for the drums (I isolated them, but kept it so that the drummer was visible to the other musicians), and came up with a technique that gave us a very pretty string sound.

We also built a large, suspended booth with sliding doors directly across from the control room window. The booth's frame was anchored to the steel I beams of the building; it was so strong it could bear the weight of a full rock group without collapsing.

The booth could be split in two by a divider, so we could put a soloist on one side and a vocal group on the other, or open the divider to accommodate a large group. The front doors were removable, and when a vocalist who preferred to hear more of the orchestra came in, we would take the doors off so he or she could be isolated yet still hear the musicians playing outside in the studio.

Having an area with separation was helpful on dates at which we recorded a solo singer and a vocal group together. Dionne Warwick's sessions with Burt Bacharach and Hal David are an excellent example.

Dionne's sister (Dee Dee) and their aunt (Cissy Houston) often provided backup vocals on her records, and to prepare for an evening session, Dee Dee and Cissy would rehearse with Dionne in the afternoon, with Burt and Hal.

Recording began at seven. Everything was recorded live with the orchestra in the room. I'd put Dionne on one side of the vocal booth, and Dee Dee and Cissy on the other, and it worked beautifully.

Since the studio was on the top floor of the building, we had seven floors of hard steel in the back stairwell. When Columbia Records owned the building they used the stairwell for echo. Microphones and speakers were placed on different landings; the sound that bounced off the hard surfaces was folded back into the mix.

While that worked well for some recordings, I found that the stairwell yielded a far different sound than my EMT plates, and rarely used it.

The late David Smith and I were friends from the day he came to work in the maintenance department of A&R in 1973. David was a respected engineer and world-class microphone collector. Later, he worked as vice president of engineering at Sony Music Studios in New York.

David spent years working in Studio A1, and valued its acoustics more than anyone I know. Shortly before his untimely death, David described what he believed made the studio special:

"The most remarkable characteristic of A1 was the leakage. No matter what you recorded there—mass ensembles, big bands, little bands, or a soloist—it sounded good. There was a formula: You knew that the ambience, leakage, and echo sounded a certain way and if you put the instruments where they needed to go, you got an unbelievably smooth, transparent sound.

"There were places in the room where certain instruments sounded their best. When I heard the elongated string sound on the *Midnight Cowboy* theme, I was blown away—and that was before I worked there! I later learned that the strings were purposely recorded in the back left corner, which had a high-frequency air to it.

"A1 was a large room—the footprint was nearly 2,000 square feet—and once the sound left an instrument it was reflected off the floor because the walls were so far away. If you stomped on the floor, it went *Boom!* It sounded like you'd struck the head of a drum, because of the way it was floated. There are only three other places in the world where I know this happens: Skywalker Ranch, Symphony Hall in Boston, and Carnegie Hall in New York," David concluded.

Hearing is believing, and if you'd like to hear why everyone loved the sound of 799 Seventh Avenue, you might sample some of the important singles that were recorded there: B.J. Thomas's "Raindrops Keep Falling on My Head"; the *Midnight Cowboy* version of Harry Nilsson's "Everybody's Talkin'"; Dionne Warwick's "I'll Never Fall in Love Again," "Do You Know the Way to San Jose," and "This Girl's in Love with You"; and Simon and Garfunkel's "My Little Town."

Then, there are the famous albums: Van Morrison's *Moondance;* Elton John's first American concert broadcast, *11-17-70;* Paul Simon's *Still Crazy After All These Years;* Phoebe Snow's *Phoebe* and *Second Childhood;* Kenny Loggins's *Celebrate Me Home;* Billy Joel's *The Stranger, 52nd Street, Glass Houses,* and *The Nylon Curtain;* and the very last recording I made before the building was razed in 1984, Frank Sinatra's *L.A. Is My Lady.*

When I think about A&R and the other defunct East Coast studios of that era, I remind myself that while the structures may be gone, the records that were made there will outlive us all.

Listening to the Orchestra "in the room," 2003
Phil Ramone Collection

The Session

Few music lovers get to hear music as it sounds when it's being created in the studio.

Once you start locking doors, turning off the phones, and hanging up signs that say CLOSED SESSION, people get curious.

Who can blame them? The allure of the studio is what brought me into the business, and knowing a bit about what happens during a recording session will help bring you closer to the music.

I'll start by explaining how I operate on a typical day when I'm recording.

On the first day of a project I need to be as focused as possible. I get up early, have a cup of tea, and leave for the studio. The time I spend alone in the car gives me a chance to think about the work we're about to do. During my hour-long drive I concentrate on the music, listening to the artist's rehearsal tapes and demos.

If I call anyone from the car, it's my production assistant or the engineer. I'll ask if everything is on schedule, and whether they have looked at the drawing that shows how I want the musicians seated and where the microphones should be placed. While the assistant engineers will get them in position, I still like to tweak the placement of microphones myself.

I expect everything to be set when I arrive at the studio.

Production is a team effort, and when I go into the studio to begin a new project I feel confident that the key players on my team are watching my back.

A dedicated office staff is essential to keeping my professional life on track, and through the years I've been blessed with some of the best executive assistants in the business. Today, Nancy Munoz and Lisa Perez keep my schedule on an even keel.

One of the people I rely on most to keep things running smoothly in the studio is my production coordinator, Jill Dell'Abate. Jill sets up recording budgets, hires the musicians, and books studio time. She knows the very best musicians in each city we work in, whether it's New York, Nashville, Los Angeles, Paris, or London.

A savvy production coordinator can make or break a project. So can a competent recording engineer and technical crew.

I've noticed that many of my technical associates share a work ethic that's similar to a professional athlete's.

In baseball, players are rated according to five tools: speed, power, instinct, defensive skills (fielding), and offensive skills (hitting). A five-tool athlete is considered an elite player who's in a league of his own.

The same rubric can be applied to recording engineers and record producers—and how they approach their responsibilities during a session. Here are the five tools that will help insure success in the studio:

1. Treat your artist well
2. Know the most direct way to record
3. Know which microphones to use

4. Know where to place the microphones

5. Trust what you hear

There are hundreds of electronic connections in the recording chain, and the time to find out that there's a hum in the line or that a recorder isn't working is not when we hit "Record." Unnecessary delays cost time and money, and cause tension.

Before a session, I question the crew:

"Did you test the microphone by having someone sing into it?"

"Has someone sat and played the drums to get a rough balance?"

"Have you checked the headphones and cue mixes?"

"Did you make a test recording to be sure that all of the cables and recorders are working as you expect? Just because the meters work doesn't mean that the sound is good . . ."

The cue mixes—what the musicians and vocalists hear in their headphones—are vital to me, and I encourage my engineers to keep a pair of headphones handy so they can listen closely if the singer goes out of tune, which is the first sign of a problem with their cue mix.

Have they got enough pitch? Are their phones too loud, or too soft? Is there enough rhythm? Can they hear themselves, or are they hearing too much of their own voice? A glitch in any of those areas can send a vocalist off key in a second.

I expect my engineers to be in tune with the room, the artist, and me at all times. If a guitarist is playing a guitar solo and I say, "Punch in the middle four bars," I count on the engineer who is running the recorder to listen closely. If the solo is over but the player is still blazing away, I don't want to have to say, "Don't punch out—keep recording it."

When the artist arrives at the studio, I greet them myself.

If the artist isn't familiar with the arranger or musicians on the date, I'll make the necessary introductions. I'll offer them tea, coffee—whatever they need to help keep them fresh. Vocalists especially need hot beverages available to hydrate the vocal cords and keep congestion at bay.

I'll go out into the studio to be sure that the music stand and lighting are adjusted to their liking, that their headphones are comfortable, and that the cue mix we're giving them is what they need.

Listening "in the room" also gives me a snapshot of what we should be striving to capture on tape. The most important thing I can do for the artist before we begin recording is to make sure that they're singing or playing into the right microphone.

I lavish generous attention on the selection and placement of microphones, and the types of microphones and techniques engineers and producers use to capture the sounds of the orchestra could fill a book.

Because I often work with singers, getting a clean vocal is my number one concern. The voice is a superb instrument with infinite color, and there are many variables that go into choosing the right microphone for a vocalist.

Some singers (such as Elton John and Billy Joel) have a lot of dynamic range; they can go from a whisper to a shout in an instant. Others (such as Paul Simon and Dionne Warwick) have good tonal range, but they don't sing loudly.

When I begin working with a singer, we'll put up a selection of two or three mikes and record them singing into each one. When we play back the sample recordings I might say, "My personal favorite for you is number two—I think it expresses your warmth," or, "This microphone will allow us to hear all of the color in your voice, but you're going to have to 'play' the mike."

The mike I choose also depends on the physicality of a vocalist's performance style. Some artists can stand still in front of a directional microphone and stay within the scope of its sensitivity. Others move around when they sing, which requires either a different microphone or another sensitivity pattern setting.

Generally, condenser and ribbon microphones work best for vocals.

When Judy Collins came to A&R to record *Judith* (which included "Send in the Clowns"), I wasn't pleased with the sound that my standard vocal mikes were giving me. Judy's voice is delicate, and I found that a Sony C37—a microphone I wouldn't normally use on a vocalist—gave her vocal timbre extra body and warmth.

The C37 also helped me bring the warm expressiveness of Peter, Paul and Mary to their records that I recorded, including two of their biggest singles: "Leaving on a Jet Plane" and "I Dig Rock and Roll Music."

As I mentioned earlier, when I first began recording them, Peter, Paul and Mary all sang into one microphone. I'd set them up around a single omnidirectional mike, and away they'd go. After a while we switched to using three microphones because they felt it gave them better control over their sound.

I favored placing Mary's microphone in the center, with Peter to her right and Noel to her left, in a semicircle. Giving them each their own mike definitely helped me: I fed each vocal mike to a separate track on the tape, and it was much easier to make edits with three separated vocal tracks. I wanted a close, intimate sound on the guitars, and miked them with a pair of Neumann KM54s.

Billy Joel's vocal mike was a Beyer M160 dynamic ribbon, and it worked well because of the rejection—its ability to nullify all but the sound that came directly into the top. Since we recorded Billy live with the band, the Beyer helped keep most of the piano and drums out of his vocal track. That microphone also gave Billy a big, smooth sound without a trace of distortion.

Because he overdubbed his vocals, I didn't need to worry much about leakage of other instruments into Paul Simon's mike. The

Neumann U87 or a Sennheiser shotgun condenser microphone re-
produced his voice beautifully.

I kept special microphones—such as those used by Judy
Collins, Paul Simon, and Billy Joel—wrapped in velvet bags, and
locked them in engineer Jim Boyer's microphone case, or my office.
Our vocal mikes never left their cases unless the artist was in the studio. Vocal microphones were rarely used on other instruments—
and *never* on an instrument that produced high sound-pressure
levels, such as a drum, trumpet, or electric guitar amp.

Conversely, I took the precaution of keeping the microphones
that I liked to use on bass and drums out of circulation.

Assigning microphones to specific instruments or artists, then
keeping them out of circulation is critical.

When a vocalist sings into a microphone, the fine misting from
their saliva coats the inside of the capsule, making it in essence their
own personal instrument. If you send that microphone out to be
cleaned, it will never sound exactly the same again.

To maintain consistency, I ask every engineer I work with to keep
a record of the make, model, and serial number of the microphones
we use on a session. I also ask that the studio keep the most critical
microphones used on a project (vocal or instrumental soloists mikes)
out of circulation until the record has been mixed and mastered.

What happens after we've set up the microphones and the musicians are in place? I begin setting the levels by calling for each instrument to play:

"Strings, letter C, first four bars please. Thank you."

"Muted trumpets, letter B. Okay, can I hear them open?
Thanks."

"Percussion, can you give me a timpani roll, please? All
right . . ."

I move through each section, and they respond as quickly as I
speak. This exercise assures me that everything is working properly.

Are the faders set at the appropriate volume? Is there any distortion? Does the sound I'm hearing through the board match what I heard while I was standing out in the studio?

Once I'm satisfied, I'll ask the conductor to run through a song so I can get a balance.

The best way to get a starting mix in the control room is to open up microphones quickly and get the padding (how loud or soft each mike should be) established right away. Then, you can begin finessing the color, and adjusting how loud one instrument is compared to another. *That* becomes a mix. What doesn't become a mix is when you're fussing around with things to satisfy your ego.

The time you have to get a rough mix is limited, and in the early days I could be impatient about it.

When I was coming up the ranks no one ever said, "You've got fifty minutes to get the balance—take your time and give us your best sound." What they said was, "Give us your best sound in rehearsal—we're going to roll the tape *now*." I can't tell you how many times I wasn't ready. You adjust on the fly, and on the playback if you can. In those days we weren't recording on multitracks, and once you set your balances, you were stuck with it.

Once I'm satisfied with the setup and balances, we're ready to record.

Before I bring you backstage to visit Bob Dylan, Paul Simon, and Billy Joel in the recording studio, I've got to mention my philosophy on two things that often cause distractions during a session: telephones and visitors.

There are two places where phone calls are unwelcome: the bedroom and the studio.

Years ago, when we called a break the musicians would rush out to the lobby and call their answering services to find out where their next gig was. Nowadays, a sea of cell phones comes out and everyone makes calls from the studio. I have no qualms about telling an artist that unless it's a dire emergency, the studio telephones must be turned off until the break.

The topic of visitors is a bit thornier.

I prefer to maintain a closed-door policy when we're recording, but it's not uncommon for an artist or band member to ask if they can bring a cousin, friend, music student, or their mom to a session. When the visitor arrives I politely say, "Please sit next to me and wait for the break to ask questions."

Why is having a visitor in the studio such a big deal? Visitors can cause distractions.

You've also got to trust those who visit the studio, and be certain that they understand that what they're seeing and hearing is in its most basic form. Eavesdropping on a recording session is like watching the rough cut of a film: There are notes to be fine-tuned, volumes to be adjusted, and instruments to be balanced so they sound proportional. Those things won't happen until we edit, mix, and master the record.

If I know that we're expecting a visit from someone special— the artist's mom or dad, let's say—I'll be sure to stay late to prepare a couple of mixes for them to enjoy. Why not? They're the ones who made sacrifices—got the kid lessons and maybe moved from place to place with them for the sake of their talent when the artist was young. I think about things like that because I remember the sacrifices my family made for me.

Although it may be rough, what we play for any visitor has to sound good. I don't want Mom, Dad, the artist's manager, or a record company representative to say, "I can't hear my son/daughter/client's voice."

Like many stars, Billy Joel traveled with a small entourage, and we devised an equitable way of handling all the family, friends, and record executives who wanted to visit his sessions.

When we were recording, Billy's retinue wouldn't come to the studio until the end of the week. It took the heat off of Billy. "Tell them it's *my* house rule that visitors can only come in on Friday night," I said. Billy (or any other artist) could overrule me—and they sometimes did—but Friday seemed like an appropriate time to relax and enjoy the work we'd slaved over all week.

If it had been a productive week, we might have one or two finished songs to play for everyone. I'd get a couple bottles of wine, the band and their friends would sit around, and we'd enjoy the fruits of our labor.

Those Friday-night soirees were great fun.

Elizabeth Joel (Billy's first wife and manager), Brian Ruggles (his concert soundman), and Steve Cohen (his lighting director) would usually show up. We knew when they liked what they were hearing 'cause they'd holler and cheer like mad!

After listening, we'd either open more wine and replay the songs, or go out for dinner. There were many Friday afternoons, though, when we found ourselves in the midst of a bang-up session and said, "Let's not have any interruption tonight."

I must say that I loved when my wife and sons dropped by the studio. My older boys, Simon and Matt, enjoyed seeing "Uncle

En route to the Grammys with Simon, Matt, and Karen, late 1970s
Phil Ramone Collection

Paul" (Simon's namesake), or "Uncle Billy." When my youngest son BJ was born, we named him after Billy Joel.

Record company people *always* wanted to visit, and they had the right to come in at any time to hear what we were doing. In addition to hanging with the stars, they liked to keep an eye on their investment.

I never wanted to play an executive or A&R rep something that was too far removed from the final product, so I'd say, "Why don't you come in after the second week, and I'll play you three tracks?"

In the days before they arrived, I would obsess over every detail. Which tracks should we play? How should I mix them? What order should we play them in? How loud should we play them?

Record executives loved getting the royal treatment, and Billy Joel has a way of schmoozing 'em like no one else I know. When we held playback sessions for the label people, Billy would mingle and share some of the stories behind the songs. His presence—and his irrepressible passion for the records he was making—went a long way toward keeping the label people happy.

Although it can be intrusive, one can't discount the value of having an objective set of ears preview works in progress.

I knew presidents of record labels who would play new records for anyone—the bellman who delivered his bags, or a room service waiter—and ask, "What do you think of this song?"

Brian Wilson was famous for doing that sort of thing. He'd invite all kinds of delivery and service people into his home to hear whatever he was working on at the moment. The opinion of the average listener is important.

Perhaps the guy in question loved what he heard—or maybe he didn't pay much attention and said, "It's okay." Either of those opinions could easily change the direction a record was taking—and it often did.

Dennis Arfa (Billy Joel's booking agent) used to come to Billy's playback sessions, and I was amazed at his prescience. His feet would tap to the wrong rhythm, and his head would nod out of time, but he could pick singles like no one else could. Dennis would listen to a song and say, "That's the hit single." I'd cock my head and look at him quizzically. "Really?" He'd almost always be right.

Bob Dylan
Blood on the Tracks

Bob Dylan, circa 1974
Courtesy of Paul Natkin/WireImage

I was delighted to receive "the call" from John Hammond in September 1974 asking me to engineer some sessions with Bob Dylan.

"Phil? John Hammond. Listen, Dylan's in town and he's ready to record for us again. He wants to come back to 799 Seventh Avenue, and we need to capture the magic."

Although he'd made his name at Columbia Records, Bob had briefly left the label to record two albums for Elektra. Hammond, who'd recognized Bob's talent and signed him to Columbia twelve years earlier, wanted to bring him back to the CBS "family."

I'd toured with and recorded Bob Dylan and the Band in 1974, but *Blood on the Tracks* was the first and only Dylan studio album I ever recorded. Like many fans, I was in awe of Bob's talent and respected his polite, distant attitude. I'm private too, and I'm tenacious about protecting the privacy of artists. Traveling with Dylan gave me a glimpse of his idiosyncrasies, and I'd developed a real affection for him and his music.

Since many of Dylan's early recordings had been made in studio

A1 at 799 Seventh Avenue when it belonged to Columbia, his return to A&R brought everything full circle.

It was clear that this album was going to be personal. Bob was going through a separation; he was emotionally fragile and at a creative crossroads. I was elated that he'd chosen A&R, and felt privileged to be the engineer who'd preserve this watershed moment.

Things didn't seem to be planned, and that didn't unnerve me. If you understand who Dylan is and what his music is about, you know that he comes to the studio with what I call "prepared spontaneity." You're never quite sure what Bob is going to play, or what key he's going to play it in. He doesn't like to overdub, so you learn to build around him.

I didn't see Bob until he came to the first session on September 16. Earlier that day, Hammond called and asked if I could line up a few musicians. I didn't think the request was odd; I expected that Bob would just come in and lay down some voice and guitar tracks. But at the last minute, Bob decided that he wanted a few extra players.

The New York studio scene was flush with work, and I was expecting to find that most of the A-list session players had already been booked. Luckily, Eric Weissberg—a versatile guitarist who was riding high on his hit song "Dueling Banjos" (the theme from *Deliverance*)—was recording at A&R that day. I bumped into him in the hallway, and told him of my dilemma.

Eric quickly pulled together a small band consisting of Charlie Brown and Barry Kornfeld (guitar and banjo), Richard Crooks (drums), Tony Brown (bass), and Tom McFaul (keyboards). All of them admired Dylan and were excited about working with him.

A few hours later Dylan arrived.

Other than the musicians, the only people in the studio were Columbia's Don DeVito, John Hammond, and me. Now, you've got to understand that Bob Dylan is a bit eccentric: He'll come into the studio and just start playing. And when he does, he concentrates solely on the music. When Bob came in, we got a quick level on him, and he launched into the first of more than a dozen songs.

To some, it probably seemed like Dylan was in his own world.

There was no structure to the session, no feeling that he was being guided or limited by anyone or anything. I didn't yell out, "Ready to roll? This will be Take Two." I'd stopped making those mistakes long before. Attaching numbers to a performance increases the artist's anxiety, however subtly.

I could tell that the free-form way that Bob stopped and started a song without paying attention to when a verse or chorus came around rattled those musicians who had come expecting a more focused collaboration. But that's how Dylan creates—it's stream of consciousness.

On these dates, the songs poured out of him as if they were a medley. Bob would start with one song, go into a second song without warning, switch to a third midstream, and then jump back to the first.

Bob hardly ever played anything the same way twice, which was disconcerting if you weren't accustomed to it. On the first go-round he'd play an eight-bar phrase; the second time, that phrase would be shortened to six.

The sessions were unscripted and unpretentious. I saw them as a spiritual release—a letting out of the man's insides. When he stepped up to the mike and began singing, I saw a sensational album start to unfold. For four days, Dylan stood at the mike and bared his soul on record. The intensity of songs like "Tangled Up in Blue," "Idiot Wind," "If You See Her, Say Hello," and "You're A Big Girl Now"—which he arranged as he went along—proved that this was a cathartic exercise. Dylan was purging in the only way he knew how, and I respected that.

There were no charts and no rehearsals. The musicians had to watch Bob's hands to figure out what key he was playing in. Don

DeVito also gave them a suggestion: "To stay in the groove, you've got to watch his feet," Don explained. "It's something I learned from [producer] Bob Johnson, and that I witnessed on earlier sessions with Dylan." Between takes (of which there weren't more than a few), Bob would come into the booth for the playback. His comments were brief and decisive. "I don't like that. Let's do another one."

Bob's a nice guy, but he's not a conversationalist. You don't need that when you're making records: You have camaraderie with someone, and you enjoy them for who they are. Bob's self-imposed isolation wasn't some antisocial posturing; it was clear from his mood and body language that he was vulnerable. My way of working is that you don't break the code of privacy that the artist sets up, whatever that may be. Dylan shares what he needs to, and nothing more. At one point, we found ourselves in the men's room. I said, "How are you feeling?" He said, "I'm okay." That's Dylan.

I'm amused that I was later criticized for not paying enough attention to the musicians' pleas to get Bob to communicate more, and that I wasn't attentive enough to their needs. I understand the criticism and accept it. My view from the booth, as someone who understood the artist in front of me, was that I needed to stay out of the way as the music came down. When Dylan walked into the room with guitar in hand, I knew that it wasn't about balancing the guitar against the vocal, getting a better sound on the guitar, or moving the bass player around. I instinctively did what I knew was right.

Because of the subdued tone, I even let some small imperfections slip by, like the clicking sound of Bob's pick brushing against the microphone. I didn't interrupt the performance to correct it; I went into the studio while Bob was playing and carefully pulled the microphone back a couple of inches. What was I going to do, tell him he had to do another take because I screwed up, or because his pick was clicking in the microphone?

I knew that what I didn't do for Bob Dylan was as crucial as what I did, and that in this case I needed to step back and allow the poet before me to shape the music as he saw fit.

Except for a minor fix here or there—and a part or two that Bob decided to add at the last minute—we didn't overdub. The only corrections we made on the Dylan tapes were a few spots where John Hammond said, "We're missing a couple of words here," or, "The guitar gets strident during this phrase."

After that first prolific night (which yielded about thirty takes in all), Dylan came back to A&R on three successive nights to finish *Blood on the Tracks*.

The second date—on the next night—was far more intimate than the first, as other than Bob only bassist Tony Brown and organist Paul Griffin were present. Dylan was more introverted than I'd ever seen him.

For the final session, Bob asked steel guitarist Buddy Cage to listen to the tracks and overdub some parts. Columbia's Don De-Vito made the call.

"I knew Buddy from the New Riders of the Purple Sage, and when Bob said he wanted a steel guitar player, I got word to Buddy," DeVito recalls. "Buddy called me and said, 'A Dylan session? It's a joke, right?' 'No, Buddy—it's not a joke. It is really a Bob Dylan session.'"

Although Cage brought a special feel to "Meet Me in the Morning," it took some prodding by Bob to extract the brash nuance he was looking for. It was, as Cage recalls, a session he'd never forget:

"I'd brought along my entourage—I had a limo driver, bodyguard, secretary, and two crew guys. When we arrived at the studio, Dylan motioned toward the group and said, 'What's all this?' 'Ah well, you know,' I explained.

"Bob laughed. 'Well, can any of them go out and get us some wine?'

"Phil Ramone was on the board and Mick Jagger was there too, observing. I looked at them and thought, 'Holy Christ—what I do had better be good.' I went out into the studio, where I found myself alone. It was a cavernous room and I had a sinking 'Oh, God' sort of feeling.

"Dylan said, 'Phil, play him the tunes.'

"They played back a mess of tracks—maybe eighteen in all—and what I heard were some of the most incredible masterpieces that anyone could ever hope to hear. Remember: Bob Dylan had made two, maybe three albums that everyone hated. I didn't hate them, but everyone else panned them. And here I was, sitting in an empty studio listening to a record that everybody in the fucking world was dying to hear.

"The songs were so good the way they were that I wondered why they'd asked me to add anything to them. I looked at Dylan, then at Ramone. 'What the fuck am I supposed to do?' I asked. 'They're masterpieces, they're already finished!'

"My praise took Bob by surprise. 'Oh, thanks—but I'd like you to put some steel guitar stuff over what's there,' he explained. 'Well, I honestly don't know where to begin,' I responded.

"Bob turned to Phil. 'Play them again,' he directed.

"I listened to all of the songs again and bookmarked 'Meet Me in the Morning' and one or two others. But I was afraid to start playing, because I feared that once I got going I'd record over everything till I burned out spiritually. It's the way I like to record; once I'm finished, I don't care what happens—you can do whatever you want in the final mix. Dylan hated working that way. He preferred to keep trying until he got exactly what he wanted.

"Phil cued up the tape and I did one take on 'Meet Me in the Morning.' Then, I did a second and a third. After each one, there was nothing but silence from the booth. The red light went off at the end of the third try, and I sat there all by myself. I was scared shitless, but I found the courage to do a fourth take. Again, silence.

"I could barely see into the control room, but if I squinted I could make out Phil Ramone, sitting behind the glass with his head in his hands. After what seemed like a long time, the door opened and someone came in. It was Dylan. He was wearing a motorcycle jacket, blue jeans, and a pair of black cowboy boots. He walked up, stuck the tip of his boot under my pedal board, looked me dead in the eye and said:

"'THE FIRST SIX VERSES ARE SINGING—YOU DON'T PLAY. THE LAST VERSE IS PLAYING—YOU PLAY!'

"He turned on his heels and walked out. And in that split second, I felt pure contempt for Bob Dylan, and the old punk ass in me came out. Fuck you, Jack, I thought. I deserve to be here. You're not getting away with talking to me that way, you twisted little bastard.

"Phil came on the talk-back mike and said, 'Buddy, do you want to practice one?' I gritted my teeth. 'No—hit the tape.'

"When the red recording light came on, I was still thinking about what a motherfucker Dylan was, and I tore right through my part—I took his direction and played it just the way he wanted. I did one take on that last verse, and had the picks off and the bar down before they were done rolling the tape.

" 'There, you son of a bitch,' I thought, as I stomped out of the room. I shoved the door to the control room open and saw Dylan sitting back in his chair. He and Ramone were giggling like two kids.

"Bob looked at me and grinned. 'That was great! Play it for him, Phil.'

"At that moment I realized that I'd been had. Bob's bullshit was all a ploy to goad me into turning out a combustible performance. After the playback I turned to Bob and said, 'That was the toughest three and a half minutes of my life. I don't mean the playing—I mean sitting here listening to it with you.'

" 'Can you go and out and do some more?' Bob asked. 'Yeah, I'll go out and do some more,' I said."

I thought that what Bob had created during the four A&R sessions for *Blood on the Tracks* was momentous: moving, yet redolent with the understated sarcasm that had marked the best of Bob's early Columbia albums. It defined the dichotomy of Dylan.

Whenever an artist lets a recording lie around for any length of time, the temptation to redo—or add to what he or she has done—grows exponentially, and the impulse affected *Blood on the Tracks*. As Dylan aficionados know, Bob is a restless wanderer, and half of the songs we did in New York were rerecorded a few months later in Minnesota, with other musicians.

For those collectors who'd like to hear the acoustic sessions recorded in New York, they're out there: A test pressing was prepared, and Columbia sent a few promotional LPs to select radio stations before Bob decided to reimagine the album.

Although it's thirty-four years old, *Blood on the Tracks*—a Bob Dylan classic—has retained its relevance.

So has the man, whose influence has nothing to do with age or the era in which one discovered him.

In recent years I've had teenagers and young adults come up to me and ask about *Blood on the Tracks*. Heartened by their interest, I smile. "How old are you? You couldn't have been *born* when that record was made!"

With Paul Simon, A&R Recording, New York City, circa 1975
Phil Ramone Collection

TRACK 14

Rhythms of a Saint
(Recording Paul Simon)

I'll never forget the day I met Paul Simon.

Our first collaboration was in 1972, on Paul's hit "Me and Julio Down by the Schoolyard." Paul was cutting his first solo album (*Paul Simon*), and I was asked to engineer the session because Roy Halee—Paul's longtime engineer and producer—wasn't available.

One afternoon the phone in my studio rang.

"This is Paul Simon," the voice on the other end said.

"Sure it is," I replied, thinking that one of the other engineers was pulling my leg.

"No—it's really Paul Simon," the person said. "I heard you're a good engineer. I'm doing a solo project, and I'd love to work on a song with you."

At the time, Roy Halee was one of Columbia Records' most progressive producers, and I admired him.

Simon and Garfunkel's *Bookends* and *Bridge over Troubled Water* were albums that reflected a high musical and technical watermark; both records opened my eyes to the possibilities of production.

I distinctly recall hearing *Bookends* for the first time in 1968.

I was at a party, and the host had an elaborate stereo system with speakers in every room. The bathroom was probably the quietest place in the house, and when I chanced to use the facility, the sound of Simon and Garfunkel songs such as "Bookends Theme," "America," and "Old Friends," offered a welcome respite from the cacophony outside the door.

"America" was a whimsical precursor to Simon and Garfunkel epics such as "Bridge over Troubled Water" and "The Boxer"— both of which established new rules for the standard three-minute pop single. The album's contrasts—the understated gentility of the "Bookends Theme" juxtaposed with the dissonance of the violins in "Old Friends"—were especially haunting. I bought a copy of *Bookends* the very next day, and listened to it three times in a row.

There are few albums recorded during the last forty years in which almost every song on the album has become embedded in the musical lexicon. *Bridge over Troubled Water*, released in February 1970, is one such record.

The production and the sound of Paul Simon and Art Garfunkel's harmonies on this album are astounding. Then, the spacious sonority of songs such as "The Boxer," "El Condor Pasa," "The Only Living Boy in New York," and "Bridge over Troubled Water" are unparalleled examples of Roy Halee's expert touch.

When I prepared to make "Me and Julio Down by the Schoolyard" with Paul, I considered the high standard that he and Roy had set with these groundbreaking records. How can I give "Me and Julio" an innovative bite? I wondered.

The answer came as the session began.

As guitarist Dave Spinozza rehearsed on his unamplified, solid-body electric guitar, I noticed that his pick made a percussive *chukka-chukka* sound when it hit the strings. There was no tonality and it was subtle, but I liked it. Instead of amplifying it, I placed a microphone directly in front of Dave's guitar.

Paul began running down "Me and Julio" for the band, and I rolled tape. The combination of Paul's acoustic guitar and the odd-sounding rhythm made by Dave's guitar created a new percussive sound, and when we played it back Paul said, "I really like that." I was thrilled to have pleased Paul, and thankful that I'd stumbled upon something that brought a fresh sound to one of his records.

I didn't know if I'd ever see Paul in my studio again.

While he expressed delight in how "Me and Julio Down by the Schoolyard" turned out, Paul didn't say, "We should work together again." But about a year later I got another call—again, from Paul himself—and shortly thereafter we began work on *There Goes Rhymin' Simon*.

Our personal and professional relationship grew slowly, as Paul began to call more often. I was proud to have received the "Paul Simon Seal of Approval."

What I've always loved about Paul is his inquisitiveness, and his voracious thirst for regional and world music. While he has become renowned for integrating the native music of Africa, Peru, Brazil, and other nations into American pop, Paul was among the first superstars to recognize the wealth of regional talent here in America.

Earlier, I mentioned the Muscle Shoals Sound Studio and the Muscle Shoals musicians. It was Paul who introduced me to the wonders of Muscle Shoals, Alabama, in 1973, during the sessions for *There Goes Rhymin' Simon*.

The Muscle Shoals Sound Studio—immortalized in Lynyrd Skynyrd's "Sweet Home Alabama"—was the legendary home to a four-man rhythm section of unrivaled brilliance. Many artists (including the Rolling Stones, who cut "Brown Sugar," "Wild Horses," and two other tracks for *Sticky Fingers* there) flocked to the studio for the fresh approach of the band, and the unique sound of the room.

The Muscle Shoals Rhythm Section (Jimmy Johnson, guitar; Roger Hawkins, drums; David Hood, bass; and Barry Beckett, keyboards) first began playing together in 1967, as part of the acclaimed Fame Recording Studio rhythm section.

Within a short time, the band became one of the most sought-after group of studio players in the country. The quartet opened their own studio in Muscle Shoals in 1969.

The rhythm section's endemic style and solid backbeat helped propel such explosive records as Aretha Franklin's "Respect," Wilson Pickett's "Mustang Sally," Paul Simon's "Kodachrome," Bob Seger's "Old Time Rock & Roll," and Rod Stewart's "Tonight's the Night." During their years together, the group earned more than seventy-five gold and platinum albums.

When you worked at Muscle Shoals you made records *organically.*

No written arrangements were necessary. The Muscle Shoals Rhythm Section used a musical shorthand that enabled them to create and play a chart quickly without having to spell out every note and chord change. Instead of writing chord symbols, the Muscle Shoals guys wrote down numbers. It was a technique based on solfeggio, and it was the common musical language of the South.

I can close my eyes all these years later and see keyboardist Barry Beckett playing the piano while calling out chord changes: *"Bridge, bridge, two bars—1, 2, 3—turnaround—4,"* he'd bark. Then, *"Go to cymbals!"*

Paul admired Aretha Franklin's Atlantic records—many of which were made in Muscle Shoals—and when he was thinking of ways to bring a twist to *There Goes Rhymin' Simon* he said, "I love that sound—why don't we just record where Aretha did?"

We both marveled at the way Muscle Shoals was set up.

"When you came into the studio you turned on a switch, and the sound was there," Paul explained. "The drums were never moved, the bass was never moved. It wasn't like it was in New York or

Los Angeles, where you had the studio for a block of time, and when you were finished you had to break down so another act could come in later that night. Because the instruments, musicians, and studio were always ready in Muscle Shoals, you never had to struggle to find the sound."

The interplay between the Muscle Shoals musicians was unlike anything I'd seen anywhere except Nashville. The group played with a classic R&B style that, despite the studio's location, wasn't influenced by country or regional music.

Muscle Shoals cofounder Barry Beckett played piano on *There Goes Rhymin' Simon*, and has vivid memories of recording with Paul in Alabama:

"The excitement of Paul coming in enabled us to psych ourselves up for at least two weeks before he arrived," Barry explained. "We got some inkling of what to expect when we found out that he had booked four days to do one song! That surprised us, because [we normally finished] one song in an hour, or an hour and a half.

"The [first song we recorded] with Paul was 'Take Me to the Mardi Gras,' which had a reggae feel. I remember Paul walking over to me at the piano, and making a suggestion. 'Barry, by every indication, the gentleman in the song is going to get to go to the Mardi Gras,' Paul said. 'He wants to go, so he's going to go. Nowhere in the song does it say he *might not* get to go. Is it possible to get that feel?' 'Sure,' I said.

"We cut 'Take Me to the Mardi Gras' within thirty minutes. Paul was flabbergasted that it took us so little time to get the groove and the attitude of the song. Attitude is something that Paul really concentrates on. He goes for attitude, then groove, and then color, and we caught all those ingredients very fast—and all at once," Beckett concluded.

But recording in Muscle Shoals wasn't just about the music or musicians. The entire Muscle Shoals experience was a slice of

Americana: the people were sweet, the food was delicious, and the businesspeople went out of their way to make you feel at home.

Some examples:

When Paul and I arrived at our hotel, a huge sign greeted us: WELCOME PAUL SIMON AND PHIL RAMONE. Seeing it made me feel very special. I'd never seen my name on a marquee before, much less on a Holiday Inn.

That night we had a sumptuous southern dinner—catfish, biscuits, and vegetables like you've never eaten—for a quarter of what it would have cost us to eat in New York. I left a tip on the table, and as we were leaving, the waitress came over and said, "You forgot your money."

On a subsequent trip to Muscle Shoals I woke up with a horrific toothache. It was a Sunday, but Jerry Masters—the studio's chief engineer—called a local dentist. "We don't want you suffering," the doctor said. "I'll come and pick you up, and take you to the drugstore. Bill [the pharmacist] will meet us there, and make up a prescription for you." Can you imagine such a thing happening in New York, much less on a Sunday?

The Muscle Shoals experience offered Paul the chance to infuse his music with loads of color, and I loved taking part in his impulsive flights of fancy.

One never knew what direction—literally and musically—Paul's whims would take us in, as I discovered during the *There Goes Rhymin' Simon* sessions.

After cutting the basic track for "Take Me to the Mardi Gras" at Muscle Shoals, Paul decided that he wanted to take the sixteen-track master tape to New Orleans to overdub the Onward Brass Band. It was a masterstroke—one of those spontaneous decisions that lend Paul's music just the right degree of verisimilitude.

I began making some calls, and was shocked to learn that none of the studios in New Orleans had sixteen-track recorders. The idea, though, was just too good to abandon, so I persisted until I found a studio—Maleco Sound in Jackson, Mississippi—that could handle sixteen-track masters.

Jackson was halfway between Muscle Shoals and New Orleans, and the Onward Brass Band agreed to meet us halfway. Paul and I piled into a car and headed for Maleco Sound. We got lost, of course, and during one desperate moment we pulled into a gas station to ask for directions. I still laugh when I think of the puzzled look the attendant gave Paul and me; we were tired, unkempt, and at least one of us was famous—even in Jackson, Mississippi!

I didn't know what we were stepping into when we'd agreed to go to Maleco, but I quickly learned that working with the Onward Brass Band was much like working with the Muscle Shoals musicians; it gave me a new perspective on professionalism.

For the Maleco session, the Onward Brass Band members came to the studio wearing their uniforms. It might not sound like such a big deal, but that gesture really impressed me, and I know it impressed the hell out of Paul. Image and propriety were clearly important to them, and it was reflected in their look, style, and performance.

There Goes Rhymin' Simon represents Paul's coming-of-age as a solo artist, and yielded a number of Paul Simon classics including "Kodachrome," "Something So Right," "Take Me to the Mardi Gras," "St. Judy's Comet," "One Man's Ceiling Is Another Man's Floor," and "Loves Me Like a Rock."

Muscle Shoals (and Maleco Sound) influenced the tone of *There Goes Rhymin' Simon*—and the direction of Paul's work for years to come.

Another wondrous moment that Paul and I spent together was in Brazil, when he was making *The Rhythm of the Saints* in 1989.

By then, *Graceland*—Paul's groundbreaking world music album—had been hailed a masterpiece. With *Graceland*, and songs such as "Diamonds on the Soles of Her Shoes," "Gumboots," and "You Can Call Me Al," Paul skillfully blended his American pop music sensibilities with the seductive, unrelenting rhythms of traditional South African music.

With *The Rhythm of the Saints,* Paul extended the concept, this time emphasizing the underexplored polyrhythms indigenous to West African music.

Roy Halee supervised production on *Rhythm of the Saints,* but Paul also asked a friend—Brazilian producer Mazzola—to assist. Although portions were recorded in New York and Paris, much of the album was recorded in Brazil.

For the Brazilian sessions Paul booked time at Transamerica, Impressao Digital, and Multi Studios in Rio de Janeiro. Because I had been on tour with Paul (and since Roy Halee opted to stay stateside and mix the tracks later, at the Hit Factory in New York), I accompanied Paul to Brazil.

Recording in Brazil was complicated.

Foreign engineers and producers weren't permitted to bring recording tape into the country without prior authorization (the government wanted to know who you were recording, and where you were recording them). If permission *was* granted, the amount of tape you could get through customs was limited. Traveling to the country with recording gear of any kind—microphones, mixers, or tape recorders—was out of the question. The sessions at Transamerica were allowed because of Paul's connection with Mazzola, and because only Brazilian studio space, engineers, and materials were being used.

Working around the restrictions was worth the result; the locale brought a spirit to the music that could never be duplicated in the United States. Everyone involved with the project knew that like *Graceland* before it, *Rhythm of the Saints* would signify an epochal moment in Paul's world-music canon.

Paul's international recording adventures on *Rhythm of the Saints* weren't confined to Rio—or the studio.

One evening, Paul, Mazzola, and I left Transamerica after a

session and drove to the countryside for dinner. While driving back to our hotel, we passed through Salvador, Bahia.

It was a hot, muggy night, nearly eleven o'clock, and the car's windows were open. We'd had a long, fruitful day in the studio, and a satisfying (albeit late) meal. Both enhanced our weariness, and as Mazzola whisked us home, our conversation ebbed. When it became quiet, we heard the sound of drums in the distance.

I instinctively perked up, knowing that Paul would want to investigate.

"Drive in the direction they're coming from," we begged.

Mazzola wound his way through the narrow streets of cobblestone, and we soon found ourselves in front of a cluster of buildings.

"Let me get out first," the producer implored. "I don't know if this is a safe area, and I don't want either of you getting hurt." Ignoring Mazzola's warning, Paul and I sprang from the car, intent on finding the musicians.

When we did, we were speechless.

There, playing in the street, was what appeared to be a marching band. The heart-thumping resonance of the sound their drums produced was mesmerizing.

Paul and I looked at each other knowingly.

The visceral punch of the sound reverberating off the buildings was unlike anything we had ever heard in a recording studio, and would fit perfectly on *Rhythm of the Saints*.

Mazzola spoke to the group, and discovered their name was Olodum.

Using Mazzola as an interpreter, Paul hastily explained what he was doing in Brazil, and that he wanted to record their music for *Rhythm of the Saints*. They expressed interest, and he made arrangements to return and discuss the details the following day.

During their meeting, Paul learned that a recording agreement would come with stipulations.

First, Olodum was eager to publicize their social and political agenda, and they wanted a worldwide forum. Then, any recording sessions would have to take place outdoors, in Pelourinho Square.

Paul was sympathetic—and persuasive. Concessions were made, and the session planned. I was excited by the prospect of recording the ensemble, but concerned with the lack of suitable facilities.

"What the hell are we going to record this on?" I asked Paul.

We were lucky to have gotten permission to bring a few rolls of multitrack tape into the country for the studio sessions; we didn't have extra recording tape, nor did we have any portable recording equipment. But Mazzola—God love him—scrounged up a battered eight-track recorder, ten or eleven dynamic microphones, a few mike stands, and two reels of tape.

Paul's manager alerted the media.

When we returned to Pelourinho Square at the appointed time, we found Olodum's members dressed in snappy uniforms: white shirts with red sashes. The walls of the courtyard had been painted a brilliant white, which accentuated the starkness of their dress.

The scenario was very theatrical; everything that Olodum did was deliberate—and aimed at maximizing their exposure. I was surprised at the number of people who gathered in the square and impressed with the considerable press coverage that Paul's publicist had arranged.

The working conditions were, as expected, primitive.

I'll never forget what happened when I asked for some electrical power. The man who was helping me set up calmly reached into the street, lifted a manhole cover, and pulled two bare wires from the opening. "Here," he said, shoving them in my direction. As I backed away, he touched them together. They began to spark. "These will do," he said, calmly taping them up.

We had enough tape for an hour's worth of recording, and I didn't have complete faith in our power source. I put a few microphones on stands and slung the rest over the branches of nearby trees. Motion played a major role in Olodum's sound, and I wanted to impart the spatial depth of the performance as Olodum briskly moved through their routine.

After a quick run-through for levels I started the tape machine, and the band's director—Antonio Luis Alves de Souza—gave the drummers their cue. The music wrought from the session added a marvelous texture to "The Obvious Child," which became the opening song on *Rhythm of the Saints*.

The impromptu location session in Brazil was the kind of zany situation that I came to expect with Paul, and is indicative of the unexpected directions that my recording life sometimes takes me in.

Paul's *Graceland* and *Rhythm of the Saints* are momentous musical records, but they made their mark technically and socially too. It's important for a songwriter or musician to blend the music of many worlds, but downright heroic to go as far as Paul does to preserve its authenticity.

Liberty Devitto, Doug Stegmeyer, Billy Joel, & Richie Cannata
Phil Ramone Collection

He's Got a Way About Him
(Recording Billy Joel)

When Billy Joel makes a record, spontaneity trumps all.

There was seldom any fixing or polishing on Billy's records; if there were minor flaws in the performance, they stayed in.

As I touched on earlier, Billy's method of writing songs during his recording sessions was unlike anyone else's.

With Billy, the melody came first.

He would sit at the piano and start with a riff that caught his ear, and build the melody around that. As he played the basic chords, the band would fall in, improvising a head arrangement; one that came together as they played. After a time we'd play back these attempts, then continue to experiment with the instrumentation.

During the playbacks, Billy and I would talk about instrumental nuances that we each thought would improve the song.

When I listen to a song and imagine how it might be arranged, I listen for melodic lines in the background—a haunting phrase that's not fully developed—or another piece of the melody that could benefit from emphasis.

With Billy, when such a phrase popped out we might double its line by having him play it on piano with his left hand (lower notes). Or, we might notice a phrase that Billy was playing with his right hand (higher notes) that clearly said, "This theme should be repeated elsewhere in the song."

If Billy became impatient or discouraged, I would urge him to keep at it. I never wanted him to settle.

Once the framework was established, the band would start playing the song to get its general feel. When I sensed that Billy and the band were headed for a peak moment, I'd signal for Jim Boyer or Bradshaw Leigh to start rolling the twenty-four-track machines. Most of Billy's songs were recorded in three or four takes.

If for some reason a tune *didn't* feel great, we'd put it aside, then try it again a few days later, or after Billy played it at a few concerts. The rationale was that a song sounded better after they'd played it on the road and worked out the kinks.

The process of writing and recording continued every day and by the third or fourth week of work, we'd have hit our stride. Billy would cheer when he passed what he thought was the halfway mark and say, "Phil, I think we've broken the back of the album!"

Bradshaw Leigh became my engineer in 1979, while Billy was making *Glass Houses*. Here, he recalls what impressed him most about Billy's sessions:

"The thrill of working with Billy was watching him sit down, jam on the piano, and come up with an idea," Brad explains. "Witnessing him write and polish a song was invaluable. It was like watching your favorite band in concert for the first time, every time.

"For me, the most incredible part of the process was what would happen *after* Billy and the band had recorded a particular song.

"Let's say that Billy and the band had worked through the initial phases of laying down a tune: Billy had delineated an idea, he and Phil had worked out a skeletal arrangement, and the band had gotten comfortable with it. They would run through it a few times, and then record it. What was in the can at this point was, for all intents and purposes, the final master—a perfectly acceptable performance.

"We would move on to other songs. Two or three days, maybe even a week might go by, and the band would be running down yet another tune that was 'in-progress.' Suddenly—just for fun—Billy would count off the song they'd completed a few days before, and the band would launch right into it.

"Nine times out of ten the band would hit it dead on, and that impromptu take would supplant the earlier one, because it had so damned much energy! It usually sounded better because in the band's minds, the pressure was off—the master take from the previous session was already in the can.

"I was twenty-one years old, and I was amazed by what I was seeing and hearing. I have never seen anything like it in all the years I spent engineering, and I'll probably never see it again," Leigh believes.

When Billy discovered what he wanted to say musically, the palette was wide open. I always felt that we could be irreverent; I wouldn't dare stifle Billy by restricting tempo, style, or feel.

Because of our mutual flexibility, "Just the Way You Are" moved from a somewhat stiff nightclub ballad into an endearing love song; "Allentown" became a ballsy anthem; "Only the Good Die Young" went from reggae to rock; "The Stranger" evolved into an evocative mood piece; "Stiletto" developed a discernible edge; and "Zanzibar" dripped with the ambiance of a sultry, after-hours jazz club.

Billy's willingness to experiment with offbeat instrumentation also gave us wide latitude.

One example of a seemingly outlandish idea that worked is the effect we achieved on the tag line of "Pressure" (*The Nylon Curtain*) in which the piquant sound of the balalaika—a three-string Russian guitar with a triangular body and elongated neck—imparts a decidedly peculiar sound.

Balalaika players weren't exactly clamoring for work in New York City at the time, but I happened upon a balalaika band from Brooklyn one day and asked them to come to the studio. The musicians were accustomed to performing at Russian Orthodox weddings— they had no idea who Billy Joel was. But they graciously appeared, and their contribution helped make "Pressure" one of the more unusual pop records of its day.

Another area where I enjoyed freedom was with vocal effects.

Billy liked to hear vocal effects when he was singing, and to help him find the right voice when he was recording I made him a control box with Echoplexes, MXR phasers, and flangers. We labeled the buttons "Elvis," "Doo-wop," "R&B," etc., and put it right on the piano so he could switch the effects around until he hit on one that he liked.

He loved Jimi Hendrix's *Electric Ladyland*, and when Billy made *The Nylon Curtain* we experimented extensively with panning, phasing, and compression. Almost every song on *The Nylon Curtain* has a different vocal effect.

On "Goodnight Saigon," for example, we used an echo chamber with a noise gate to cancel out the normal ringing effect. The combination gave his voice the sweet, high "youthful innocence" that he wanted, but at the same time it made him sound breathless, frightened, and agitated.

After my first few sessions with Billy, I made an interesting observation: He never warmed up by singing his own songs—not even the ones we were currently working on.

Instead, he would start a session by doing impersonations.

"Remember when Otis Redding sang this?" he'd ask, and start singing like Otis Redding. Then he would slide into a Ray Charles song, or start wailing Percy Sledge's "When a Man Loves a Woman." He did the same thing when he overdubbed background vocals.

It was odd: Here I was trying to get Billy Joel to sound like Billy Joel, while he was trying to sound like anyone but. I was curious, and it took two albums before I had the nerve to ask, "When are you going to just come in and sing like Billy Joel?"

What I learned was that singing in different styles not only helped Billy warm up before a concert or session; it helped him break through his shyness and fear, too.

Billy once explained his love-hate relationship with singing:

"The human voice has lots of nuance, and I like to use humor to drive my point home. I don't think of myself as a singer; I'm a piano player and songwriter. I don't have a lot of confidence in my singing voice, so I'm constantly fooling around with it. When I have to listen to my voice cold in the studio, I cringe. I try to give it a 'live-in-the-arena' setting on record because I think it's pretty boring.

"I like to compose and play in such a way that I don't have to sing all that many round notes, keeping the emphasis on syllabic bursts filled in with drum beats and guitar licks. I sound better when I'm socking out a tune to one degree or another than when I'm crooning."

A vocalist is far more exposed when singing a ballad than when they're singing an up-tempo tune, because it's easier to hide a crack in the voice behind the brashness of a busier arrangement. Belting 'em out definitely brought fullness and vigor to Billy's vocals.

So did singing at the piano.

When Billy sang and played simultaneously, he put his entire body into the performance. The crook in his neck and the way he faced the mike are what gave him his sound.

Billy plays an extremely full piano, and to help isolate it from his vocal mike I built a "doghouse" shell for the piano and draped it with thick blankets. The studio was arranged so that the piano was in a direct line with Liberty, who was six or eight feet away on a small platform.

I was big on putting the drums right near Billy and having Liberty DeVitto play as loud as he wanted. The pressure from the two instruments sounded like a hundred tons spilling into each other, and the leakage is why Billy's records have such incredible energy. It also didn't hurt that Doug Stegmeyer could play the electric bass as ferociously as Billy played piano.

"Doug Stegmeyer, God rest his soul, was like Billy's left hand," explains Richie Cannata. "When musicians talk about Billy playing a 'full' piano, it meant that he played the way a singer playing in a piano bar would—using the keyboard broadly. Doug embellished the bass notes [that Billy was playing with his left hand] by following it exactly."

The guys in Billy's band weren't shy when it came to sharing ideas.

Billy Joel recording at the piano,
New York City, circa 1986
Courtesy of Sony/BMG Music Entertainment

They had plenty of opinions, and the discussions that followed a take would usually end with good-natured attacks on each other. Things could get wild during the sessions. Billy had what we called the "Billy Joel Guilt Complex" because of his relationship with the guys in his band—Liberty in particular.

As a drummer, Liberty had control and power, and he asserted it in a positive way. He didn't like to play to a track without lyrics— he needed to hear words. Billy knew that, but he'd sometimes come in after the weekend, and we'd discover that he hadn't made much progress insofar as lyrics were concerned. Billy would feel bad if he had only the words for one song, and *really* awful if he didn't have any at all.

If Billy hadn't come up with any lyrics by the time we were ready to record a song, he would hum the main melody, or make up nonsensical words. There were lots of dummy lyrics (usually devised by Liberty) that filled in for as-yet-unwritten words. Some of them were quite funny: An early incarnation of "She's Always A Woman to Me" was "She's Only A Widow to Me," and in lieu of a firm song title, the word *sodomy* was substituted for "Honesty" when we were making *52nd Street.*

Like most drummers, Liberty was the band's engine: he drove everyone, and he made Billy toe the line. Liberty thought nothing of chiding Billy for not completing his work; he'd throw his drumsticks across the room and say, *"I'm not playing this shit—go finish it!"* And Billy would do it.

Liberty also wasn't averse to telling Billy when something was awful. In fact, I think he sadistically delighted in doing so, and I laughed like hell one time when Billy jibed him back. Liberty had written a song, and he played it for Billy in the car. Billy listened and said, "Hmm, that's not bad." Then, he caught himself. He sneered at Liberty and said, "I'm gonna do what you do to me. That *sucks!*"

In those days there was an untenable bond between the guys in Billy's band, and sessions were as wild as a garage band's rehearsal.

As Billy explained:

"If someone ever saw footage of our recording sessions and it looks like we're fooling around too much, it's because we were. It's a recording technique we came up with. If the musicians are having fun—if they're having a good time—it shows in the music. You have to do things to relax because recording is tense. You're creating something out of nothing; you're conjuring something out of thin air. It's a source of amazement to the musicians, too, that we're doing this. There's a joyful feeling you get when something works. It's like, 'Wow, we did it!' It's exhilarating."

"We were a bunch of twenty-year-old guys, and it was effortless," says Richie Cannata. "But it's important to mention that Phil was the fifth member of the band—the glue. He had the facility to give us leeway, but he knew how—and when—to bring it all together."

Food was a source of fun for the band, and I kept the studio stocked with snacks, in case someone came down with an acute case of the munchies.

There was always a big bowl of candy on the table: Three Musketeers, Baby Ruth, and Snickers bars. I'd also put out a few jars of peanut butter and jelly, a loaf of white bread, and some fruit. On breaks the band would have peanut butter and jelly tasting contests. They'd give an assistant a few bucks and say, "Get a jar of Jif, and a jar of Skippy—both crunchy and smooth." Then they'd make sandwiches, and debate over which peanut butter tasted best.

Leaving the studio for meal breaks interrupts the flow of a session. It changes everyone's attitude, and more often than not, neither the food nor the break ends up being fulfilling. After four or five hours of intense work, it's better to bring in some food, turn on a ballgame, and hang out in the lounge.

A funny phenomenon happens when you take a break and somebody hears what I call a "through-the-door mix." Music sounds different when the speakers aren't in your face and you're not concentrating so hard. I can't count the number of times an artist came walking down the hall, happened to overhear something that the engineer and I were doing in the other room, and said, "Jeez, what was I thinking? Let's fix that," or "That could be great if we changed one little thing." Hearing the music casually gives you another perspective—one that you wouldn't necessarily notice or enjoy if you were outside of the studio, eating in a restaurant.

I discovered early on that food was a valuable incentive for the guys in Billy's band, and when necessary, I'd hold it over their heads.

The hands-down favorite among band members was Chinese food, and our debates over which take sounded best—the pre- or post–Chinese food take—are legendary.

Here's how it worked:

When everyone started getting hungry, the band's energy level would drop and the session would come to a halt. They'd pile into the control room, and we'd order in Chinese. Then, I'd send them back out into the studio to continue doing takes until the food arrived.

After a half hour or so, the deliveryman would come in and put the bags of food down on the counter in the control room. When they saw the deliveryman through the window, the guys would start salivating. I'd open the door between the control room and the studio to allow the aroma of the Chinese food to waft into the other room. When they had finished the take, everybody would come in to eat. They would scarf their food, and before they got too comfortable, I'd shoo them back out into the studio. "Okay—go back out there and do it again."

Everyone would grumble, but they'd go out and pick up where they'd left off. Many songs—"Honesty," for instance—sounded better *after* everyone had eaten. The food slowed their metabolism and curbed their aggression, which is exactly what the tempo of certain songs needed.

As Richie Cannata remembers:

"We especially loved ribs, and wonton soup. There would always be some sort of fried rice, too—probably a 'Phil Ramone Special' that the local Chinese takeout place had on the menu, because he ordered it so frequently. The whole Chinese food thing sounds casual, but after a while I realized that everything Phil did was calculated. He had a plan, and he held us to it."

As Cannata also recalls, there was one memorable time when we *did* go out to eat, and someone at Columbia Records decided to hold an impromptu shoot for the back cover photo of *The Stranger:*

"We were planning to have dinner at the Supreme Macaroni Company on Ninth Avenue and someone said, 'Let's take some pictures for the cover of the album.' It was spontaneous: no makeup, hairstylists, or fashion consultants. All of us wore exactly what we'd worn to the studio that day. After they took the pictures, we sat down and ate. It was all great fun; for a long time, the restaurant kept copies of the photos on the wall of the back room."

In addition to food, humor helped elicit cooperation.

Getting the band to show up on time was a real pain in the ass. I walked a fine line on this one: I couldn't allow them to take advantage of Billy and me, nor could I let them waste precious studio time. But I couldn't piss them off, either.

To keep a check on their tardiness, we agreed on a penalty system in which I would arbitrarily levy fines based on the severity of the tardiness and the originality of their excuse. It was all in good fun.

Here are a couple of their cockamamie stories:

LIBERTY DeVITTO: You won't believe this, but I was sitting in front of my TV set with my daughter when the TV set exploded. The explosion broke my glasses, and I had to go to the optician to get a new pair. It took a lot of time, but I have a note signed by the doctor.

Everyone knew that Liberty had forged the note; I imposed a five-dollar penalty for creativity alone.

RUSSELL JAVORS: I was on my way to the studio in a cab when a guy with a gun showed up at the window and robbed all of my money. He took my wallet, and I couldn't pay for a cab, so I had to walk all the way from 34th Street.

Russell's was one of the most ridiculous stories I'd ever heard. "What? You couldn't call me collect?" I asked. "That'll be ten bucks!"

During production of an album, I made a large grid on poster board listing each of the songs we were recording and what the progress on each was. I hung the chart on the wall of the studio, and as we progressed, I'd check the appropriate box. Often I'd come in to find that Billy or one of the other guys had taped a couple of *Playboy* centerfolds (or worse) over the top of my list.

I'll admit that I was as much of a prankster as any of them. Our practical jokes weren't always confined to the studio, either.

Because I spend a lot of time traveling to and from work, the quality of the sound system in my car is extremely important. One day, we were sitting around after a session, and I made the mistake of mentioning that I was looking for a new car stereo.

A short time later, the guys called and said they were stopping by the house to bring me a present. I got all excited. When they drove up to my house, it was in an old jalopy that they'd bought for three hundred bucks. It had a top-flight stereo in it, but nothing else worked. They left it right on my front lawn, and I couldn't move it because it wouldn't start. It sunk into the mud, and I eventually had to pay to have it towed away.

On another occasion, Billy gave me a beautiful turntable. The only problem was, he had rigged it so that when you put a record on, the tonearm skated straight across the record, irreparably scratching it.

But I got Billy back.

I presented him with a gift: a nice clock that I had a friend encase in plastic. The clock told you the time on the minute: "It's one-oh-one, it's one-oh-two, it's one-oh-three . . ." The clock nearly drove Billy insane! He would kick it, throw it across the room—he'd just abuse the hell out of it. But no matter what he did to it, the clock wouldn't stop telling the time.

The closeness we enjoyed, however, occasionally put me on the spot.

At times I had to be assertive, and when I really put my foot down the guys didn't always know how to take it. "Is he serious, or is he joking?" they would wonder. Sometimes they'd laugh nervously and say, "Uh-oh, the teacher's getting mad."

Meanwhile I'd be wondering too. Should I step in? Do we need to take a break, or send everyone home, or move on to a different song?

Like a parent who uses tough love on a child, I'd have to rein them in. One such occasion was when guitarists Russell Javors and David Brown's foolery irritated Billy. We were recording *An Innocent Man* at a studio on Forty-second Street in 1983 when things boiled over.

Russell and David were horsing around while Billy and I were trying to talk. They were trading some great guitar riffs, but the fooling around was distracting, and it drove Billy crazy. It got to the point where I asked Russell and David to leave so we could sketch things out and cut the track without any intrusion.

After the session, Billy cornered me and asked, "What are we going to do about Russell and David?"

I had an idea that I thought might put a stop to the chaos.

I called Eric Gale, who was playing in Paul Simon's band, and asked him to sit in on Billy's next session.

As a sideman, you've got to know your place in the hierarchy, and Eric understood his role. He also knew how to play *inside* of a band—how to listen to a song and add to it without stepping on everyone else. More important, he was a superb lead guitarist: a respected player who was imposing enough to help me make a point with Russell and David.

I warned Eric of my ploy in advance.

"I'll have a chair in between Russell and David," I explained. "Your Roland amp will be set up and ready to go. Just come in, sit down, plug in, and start to play. Be yourself and set the groove."

On the night of the session, Eric came in without saying a word. He sat down between David and Russell, and started playing during the first rehearsal. Russell and David didn't play a note—they just looked at him.

We went to the next take, and Eric immediately fell in. I didn't speak to either Russell or David during the entire session; all of my comments were directed to Billy, Liberty, Eric, and Doug Stegmeyer. I could tell that my sternness—coupled with Eric's formidable presence—was rattling Russell and David.

After that session, Russell and David snapped back into line. "Things are much cooler when you guys cooperate," I said casually on the subsequent date. "What we're doing isn't about you or me— it's about the guy at the piano."

It's every producer's hope that their love for music and their respect for the artist and musicians rings true—both in their attitude toward their work and in the final product. What was most satisfying about the years I spent producing Billy Joel and his band was our camaraderie and the positive effect it had on our records.

Here is Liberty DeVitto's description of the unique understanding we shared, and his perspective on my role as the producer:

"Phil knew how we could enhance Billy's music, and he was able to get us under control. Someone told me that on *The Stranger* it sounded like someone had tied my balls to the drum seat to hold me back. That was true; it sounded that way because Phil taught me how to play in the studio. Drummers are mostly concerned about fills: 'What am I going to do to impress the audience that hears this record?' With Phil it was a solid 'two-and-four' beat all the way. 'Got to have the two-and-four, Lib,' he'd say.

"The two-and-four beat aside, Phil allowed me to do some crazy shit. I could play backwards, invert a rhythm—everything was cool, as long as it felt right. He never smothered our creativity. Everyone thinks that I sat down and wrote all those drum parts, but it wasn't that way at all. I didn't think about starting 'Allentown' or 'Uptown Girl' with the beats they begin with—it just happened. All of us were making it up as we went along. We played what felt natural.

"Phil would let us do whatever we wanted in the studio—for forty minutes or an hour. He'd be in the control room talking to Jim Boyer or Bradshaw Leigh, and we'd be all over the place, thrashing through a song.

"Then, Phil would come on the talkback mike and say, 'Okay, guys—you've been noodling around long enough. Do you want me to tell you how it should *really* go?' We thought that he was absorbed in his conversation, and that he wasn't tuned in to what we were playing. But it turns out that he'd been listening all the time! Sometimes he would say, 'What you've been playing is really cool—why don't you come in and listen to it? We've got it on tape.'

"One of the few arguments I ever had with Phil occurred when we were recording 'My Life,' but it was funny, not tense. He wanted me to play a very straight beat, and I bucked him. 'I ain't playin' that disco bullshit!' I said. Phil got up, slammed something on the console, and scolded me like he was my father. 'You've been in this business for what, twelve minutes? And you're gonna tell *me* how you're gonna play? Just get the hell out there and play it the way I told you to play!'

"I grumbled about it then, but every time I see the gold record I received for 'My Life' on the wall, I mutter, 'Fucking guy was right.'

"With Phil, there was never the separation you typically see between a band and their producer. We were a team, and he was our coach. I can still see Phil walking around the studio with headphones on: He wanted to hear how the sound was shaping up, but he wanted to be right next to us at the same time. Phil was like a member of the band.

"The studio was Phil's home, and we were invited in. It was like a bunch of city kids going to their uncle's house in the country, and having him say, 'Hey, kids—wanna go in the pool? Want some ice cream? Don't worry that it's almost dinnertime. Go wild—have fun.'

"We had some great times, and made some incredible records. The best thing about it was that in spite of the madness, Phil never lost track of who Billy Joel was."

TRACK 16

It's All in the Mix

Great records aren't recorded. They're mixed.

Creating a mix is like preparing a fine meal: if the ingredients are of top quality and the chef knows the secret to combining them, the results can be sumptuous.

As in a gourmet dish, a well-crafted mix allows individual instruments and soloists to shine while complementing and strengthening the whole.

The mixing engineer is the star of the record-making process— an artist in every sense of the word. There's a place for everything in a mix, and it's the mixer's job to put everything in its place.

Where will the organ or twelve-string guitar live? What about the horns? Does the piano sound better up front, or placed further in the background? How much air should be around it?

All of these questions will be raised—and answered—during the mix session.

A person's response to a record has a lot to do with how their body moves when they are hearing it. How many times have you been in the car and found that you're tapping your feet to a song on the radio, or pounding out the rhythm on the steering wheel? Have you ever played air drums or guitar, or been moved to tears by a song? Evoking that kind of response is a compliment to the artist, producer, and mixing engineer.

There are infinite ways to mix a record; the best mixes are designed to sound good anywhere—at home, on a boom box, in the car, or on an iPod. But the most important place a mix has to sound good is on the radio.

Radio was our target in the 1960s, '70s, and '80s, in the pre-Walkman days. I kept a small, white kitchen radio in the control room at A&R, and we'd play our mono mixes through it to preview how they'd sound on AM radio.

I also had a car speaker setup so we could hear how it would sound coming through the single-cone, full-range speakers found in automobiles. When FM stereo came into play, we had to adjust the mix to compensate for the heavy compression of the FM signal.

Clarity, space, and movement are all essential to achieving a harmonious sound. So are subtlety, balance, and decisiveness.

An instrument doesn't have to jump out and clobber you over the head to make its point. Part of the charm of accent instruments like the Hammond B3 organ or a winsome flute, oboe, or French horn comes from how subtly they're layered into the mix.

The most effective mixes take full advantage of psychoacoustics, which is why I mix in two dimensions: in stereo and in depth.

Creating a good layer from front to back and left to right offers depth and allows the instruments to breathe, which amplifies their tonal qualities. It also brings clarity to the mix.

Although ultrasophisticated computer-based systems such as Pro Tools have revolutionized the way we mix, my philosophy is the same as when we mixed in analog: start from the ground up by setting a strong foundation, and build on it.

A solid mix begins with a clean, tight rhythm track: bass, drums, piano, and guitar. Heart-stopping bass is one of the toughest things to get; a bristling top end comes easy, but it's hard to keep things clean and funky on the bottom.

I've found that one of the best ways to really hear what's going on in a mix is to listen at a low volume.

Unless the artist wants to hear something played loudly, I set everything to a predetermined volume and never change it. Low-level monitoring helps reduce ear fatigue and gives you a better sense of how the mix is shaping up. If you're worried about *not* hearing something at low volume, relax—your ears will adjust.

If you ask any mixing engineer what the bane of their existence is, they'll probably tell you it's the artist who continually says, "I want to hear more *me.*" Vocalists especially feel they have a proprietary right to have their part stand out front and center, and they're not entirely wrong.

Whenever I mix something for an artist, I make three samples: one with the vocals out front, one with the vocals where I think they should be, and one with the vocals mixed back. After a week or so they should be able to select a clear winner (hopefully, it will be the one right in the middle).

There is a physiological reason for the "three mix" technique: the limitations of human hearing. As the volume on a radio or stereo is turned down, hearing the lowest and highest frequencies on a recording becomes difficult. Comparing the three mixes allows us to adjust the mix so it sounds good at all listening levels.

Another thing I like to do is run the choice vocal against the rhythm mix to see how it sounds *before* I add any sweetening (other instruments, percussion, etc.). If the vocal doesn't blend well with the rhythm track, it won't improve when the rest of the instruments are added later.

Transparency is a virtue, and if the mixing engineer and I have done our jobs, none of the characteristics I've described should step out and say, "Here I am."

Jim Boyer and I spent hundreds of hours together recording and mixing Billy Joel's records, and his recollection of our techniques is vivid:

"In crafting a mix, Phil painted a sonic picture. The rule was that when it came to mixing, there were no rules. He would EQ something in a squirrelly way and I'd look at him funny, but when you heard it in the mix it made sense. He'd narrowband something and make it sound very thin, but in the context of the mix it sounded just right. He taught me the trick to using the old Fairchild limiters, and how to use saturation to your benefit.

"Phil had me start mixing without looking at the meters, because he wanted me to understand the relationship between level hearing and where '0 VU' was on the meters. I'd never given it a thought, but it was a fundamental relationship, and a lot of engineers didn't

Jim "Flying Faders" Boyer mugs for the
camera during a mixing session, early 1980s
Courtesy of Larry Franke

understand it. They don't understand how what they're seeing on the meters relates to the decibels being heard, so they're either pinning and distorting, or recording under level."

Spending a few minutes listening closely to a representative mix—one that reflects the qualities and subtlety of technique that I've described—will give you a sense of what a top-notch mix brings to a record.

As an example, I'll use Billy Joel's "Scenes from an Italian Restaurant," as the mix has excellent dynamic range and a myriad of color. I would say that it's one of the mixes I'm most proud of. Most people are familiar with it, too. To appreciate my descriptions, it would be advantageous to listen to the recording through a set of headphones—even the comparatively lo-fi ones that come with most iPods.

Generally we used as little EQ as possible when mixing "Scenes from an Italian Restaurant." Consequently the bass and drums are focused and tight, and the cymbals ring without being harsh. Each instrument occupies a meaningful spot in the mix; more importantly, the mix possesses the requisite clarity, spaciousness, and movement.

Here are some specific sections, and the characteristics you should listen for in each:

1. MAIN THEME: "A BOTTLE OF WHITE, A BOTTLE OF RED . . ." (at 0:14):

The opening section features piano, accordion, vocal, and guitar. There's a slight reverb on the vocal, with a boost in the upper vocal range to emphasize the *T* and *S* sounds. This section offers an example of *complementary equalization.*

With complementary equalization, instruments that have frequencies in common are equalized to remove or enhance some of the shared frequencies. This helps each instrument stand out, and allows it to retain its own designated space in the mix.

In the introduction, the acoustic guitar (which comes in on the second verse) was equalized with a fair amount of treble. If it hadn't been, the sound of the guitar would compete with that of the accordion. Heard on its own, the equalized guitar would sound thin and weak; blended into the mix, it sounds terrific. Every note being played retains its sharpness and clarity. Notice how the guitar (and, at the end of this section, the drums) are heard in both the right and left channels; this effect offers great dimension.

2. INSTRUMENTAL INTERLUDE (saxophone solo) (at 1:07):
There is little (if any) compression on the saxophone; the sound of the instrument is natural, and reflects the dynamic range of the original performance. This is an important characteristic.

Compression squeezes a signal's dynamic range. Mixing engineers use compression to even out a record's levels by raising the softer notes and lowering the louder ones. Excess compression can easily reduce a mix's dynamic nuances, and with them, a bit of emotionality.

In this instance, each note that Richie Cannata plays is discernible.

At the end of the saxophone solo, you can hear how we rode the gain (turned the volume control on the console up when the playing was soft, and down when it was loud).

3. INSTRUMENTAL INTERLUDE (Dixieland band) (at 2:23):
The exuberant melody in this section offered an opportunity to add lots of color to the mix, and in addition to the bright instrumentation, we used *panning* (moving the instruments across the soundstage) to impart depth and dimensionality.

In many cases, the mixing engineer would have mixed the trombone, clarinet, and tuba to the left, center, and right respectively. But in this case, the trombone is placed slightly left of center in the stereo image, leaving space for the other instruments to breathe.

4. THE BALLAD OF BRENDA AND EDDIE (at 3:00):
Listen for the piano boost (with accents) after the first *"Brenda and Eddie . . ."* vocal line in this section.

Overall, there's a midrange bite, which allows every note that bassist Doug Stegmeyer plays to cut through without sounding offensive.

Then, the lowest frequencies in the bass guitar have been rolled off to help accentuate the kick drum. This is another example of complementary equalization: Here, the tone of the kick drum and electric bass are adjusted so that they're each defined in their own space. I didn't want to lose any of the fabulous interplay between piano, bass, and drums at the end of this section.

I could list hundreds of similar examples, using dozens of songs and techniques. But you get the idea.

Billy liked listening to the mixes and had the ultimate approval, although he wouldn't necessarily come to the mix sessions. Even when he was physically in the building, he wouldn't sit with Jim and me while we were mixing. He'd come in and listen when we were done, or we'd send him the mixes and he'd get together with the band and then give us feedback. Either way, we'd take his suggestions and remix the song until he was satisfied.

In addition to blending the music elements, the mixing session is when sound effects (if being used) are added.

Many producers use canned effects from stock libraries, but I enjoyed recording my own sound effects whenever possible. There's nothing like the challenge of devising and reproducing an effect you're looking for. Sometimes the chase is more exciting than the catch.

I recorded more offbeat sound effects for Billy Joel's records than anyone else's.

The screeching tires and roaring engines on "Movin' Out (Anthony's Song)" from *The Stranger* were the first ones we did, and they were fairly easy to re-create.

Bassist Doug Stegmeyer had a couple of Corvettes and a motorcycle, and we sent an engineer out to Long Island to record Doug's car peeling out. The engineer strapped a crappy dynamic microphone to the tailpipe, and after several unsuccessful tries, got the right sound.

Although it's not an effect per se, I'm frequently asked about the whistling on "The Stranger." Yes—that's Billy Joel whistling, and it was an idea he unwittingly came up with early on.

"The Stranger" has mysterious underpinnings, and Billy wanted to heighten its drama. He wrote a short prelude to preface the main song. He whistled it to demonstrate it for me, and asked what instrument I thought we should use.

The melody—and the way he whistled it—sounded great.

"That's it—you've just done it," I said.

We recorded him whistling, and added a bit of echo. The whistling prelude extended the understated atmosphere of "The Stranger," giving the song's shadowy protagonist an appropriately ambiguous identity.

To end the album we reprised the whistling theme—this time adding strings—thus bringing the idea full circle.

Occasionally something funny would happen and we'd laugh about it for days. For "Stiletto" (*52nd Street*) we needed the crisp

DAVID S. RAPKIN RECORDING ENGINEER JU 6-3700	EDITED DATE:		TIME	
			PART OF	
TITLE Motorcycle start & depart			SPEED ☐ 3¾ ☐ 7½ ☒ 15	
SELF CONTAINED	PROGRAM NUMBER	IN A SERIES OF	☒ MONO ☐ STEREO	
PROGRAM DESCRIPTION			☐ DATED MATERIAL	
SOUND EFFECT			HOLD FOR	
			RETURN TO	
			ORIGINATOR	
			TAPE THICKNESS ☐ STANDARD ☐ THIN TAPE TYPE ☐ STANDARD ☐ L.N. ☐ DO NOT RECYCLE	
REMARKS ¼ track			DUBBED FOR	
MASTER BY	DUBBED BY			
DATE 8/18/77	DATE			
LOCATION			INDEX UNDER	

Original tape box for the motorcycle sound effects
on "Movin' Out (Anthony's Song)"
Phil Ramone Collection

snap of a switchblade knife clicking open. It had rained that day, so we got an umbrella and Liberty practiced opening it so the timing would be right. We begin recording . . . here comes the take . . . and *SNAP!* The umbrella flew right off the top of the handle. The timing—and the sound—couldn't have been better.

Other attempts to replicate a specific effect weren't as simple.

The sound of breaking glass that opens "You May Be Right" at the beginning of *Glass Houses* was a difficult effect to achieve.

We didn't want a typical glass-break effect; we wanted the kind of sound that comes when a large plate glass window breaks, and there's a split-second delay between the *crack* and the entire sheet crumbling to the ground.

I can't tell you how many pieces of glass we broke—and how many ways we fractured it—before we found the piercing sound that's heard on the record.

First we took two pieces of cinder block, covered them with wood, placed the glass on top, and hit it with a sledgehammer.

It didn't sound right. We tried seven or eight different kinds of hammers and we still couldn't replicate the frightful shatter that our hearts were set on.

Then I remembered a trick that one of our engineers had used when *he* needed a glass-break effect for a record: He tossed a few five-gallon drinking-water jugs down the back stairwell of the studio at 799 Seventh Avenue. We didn't have drinking water in the studio the next day, and the stairwell was a mess, but hey—he was making a record.

I was preparing to toss a few jugs myself when another engineer walked into the studio and learned of our dilemma.

"You're breaking the wrong glass—it's too thin," he said. "If you really want a bloodcurdling shatter you've got to use sheets of glass that are more than a quarter-inch thick, and you've got to suspend them."

The following day I ordered the right glass. When it was delivered, I placed a piece over two wooden horses and smashed it from above. I miked the hell out of it; there were microphones all over the studio—above, below, to the right and left sides, far and near. It took nearly thirty sheets of glass, and the best-sounding take came on the last piece, with one crack of the hammer.

The time and expense was worth it: The harrowing glass-break we captured gave *Glass Houses* the pluperfect kickoff it deserves.

Larry Franke, an A&R engineer who worked on *The Nylon Curtain* and *Songs in the Attic*, witnessed the creation of another sound effect we devised for *Glass Houses:*

"Billy and Phil wanted to create a Spanish flavor for the breaks on 'Don't Ask Me Why,' and were looking for percussive things to achieve the effect. Billy noticed that our receptionist, Laura Doty, was wearing shoes with heels. 'Can I borrow your shoes?' he asked. 'Sure!'

"We set up to record on a little white table in the lobby at 322 West Forty-eighth Street, between studios R1 and R2. Billy grabbed the shoes, we rolled the tape, and he used Laura's heels to tap out a flamenco-style rhythm."

I had a Pentax 35mm camera with me, and I jumped up on the chair and snapped a few pictures. In those photos, you can see the Shure SM57 microphone we used to record it. Ultimately,

Billy Joel overdubs handclaps and heels for the
flamenco-inspired bridge of "Don't Ask Me Why," 1980
Courtesy of Larry Franke

the flamenco break featured handclaps and castanets. "But somewhere in the mix are Laura Doty's heels, too," Franke concludes.

The Nylon Curtain also offered several opportunities for us to creatively use sound effects.

Engineer Jim Boyer and I searched like hell for the steam whistle and industrial sounds that open "Allentown." We listened to stock sound effects, and scoured small factories and industrial sites. We finally found a steam shovel working on a skyscraper near the studio; the natural echoes of the buildings surrounding the construction zone are what gave us the huge sound you hear on the record.

Liberty DeVitto remembers an unconventional trick we used for another effect on "Allentown":

"Billy and Phil were looking for industrial sound effects for 'Allentown,' and they located a pile driver sound effect in the tape library. But the canned effect was too thin—it needed bulking up.

"Near my drums was a box of small percussion instruments that came from Studio Instrument Rental: cowbells, maracas, triangles, and such. The box was always in the way, and I had noticed that whenever I picked it up, the instruments tipped to one side. All of them banging together made an elongated *'Shhhheeeooow'* sound—it was very sibilant. When Phil was talking about the pile driver effect, I ran over to the box and tipped it on its side. 'How's this?' I asked.

"Phil liked it, and when you hear the pile driver effect on 'Allentown,' the weird sloping sound is me, jumping up and down so that all of the percussion instruments in the box would crash together on the beat. When we later opened the box, we found that all of the stuff inside had been smashed to bits."

The sounds we incorporated into songs like "Movin' Out," "Stiletto," "You May Be Right," "Don't Ask Me Why," and "Allentown" were fun. But when we recorded "Goodnight Saigon" for *The Nylon Curtain,* we reverentially strove for authenticity.

We auditioned many sound effects for *The Nylon Curtain*: airport, factory, battle, gunshot, helicopter, and rain forest sounds. We also pulled up stock recordings of troops in the jungle, night sounds, and chirping crickets; a priest talking, and an announcement; and ambient sounds reminiscent of Mexico, Vietnam, Brazil, and France.

The whirring of the helicopter blades in "Goodnight Saigon" is a mixture of the Roland JH 720 synthesizer and Liberty's tom-toms, which he loosened so that when he hit the batter side it gave us a flaccid *thwack*. The effect was such an integral part of the song that I had to program it on Billy's synthesizer so he could reproduce it in concert.

The cricket, military, and helicopter sounds on "Goodnight Saigon" were so effective that we began receiving letters from Vietnam vets, telling us how real it all sounded.

The transfer of a realistic-sounding mix to the final master tape occurs during *mastering*: the last and most influential step in the recording process.

During mastering, the album is sequenced, and the recording levels and equalization of each song are adjusted to make for smooth song-to-song transitions on the final album. At the end-stage, the production master—used for manufacturing—is created.

The hallmark of an expert mastering job is latency. If an album unfolds smoothly and you don't notice any jarring changes between songs, the mastering engineer deserves the credit.

"The first rule of mastering is, 'Do no harm,'" explains Bob Ludwig of Gateway Mastering. "The secret to being a good mastering engineer is being able to listen to a mix, imagine how it could sound, and then push the right buttons to achieve the sound you have in your head. For most of the recordings I work on, great mix engineers and producers have spent lots of time trying to get it right in the first place, and I honor what they send me."

As Greg Calbi of Sterling Sound in New York points out, "Mastering is the last stage of mixing, where the mix is finished in terms of its sonic quality and balance. The perspective of the mastering engineer is, 'Can this mix be improved in terms of excitement, clarity, unity, or emotion?' A good recording engineer can make a clean digital transfer, but they still look to the mastering engineer for a fresh perspective or opinion. Recording engineers have such a complex job, and are usually deeply focused on the project they are recording. The mastering engineer has an enormous range of listening experience, a consistent, high-resolution monitoring environment, and the luxury of working without the distractions of a recording session. His or her ear training is very different from that of the recording engineer."

When we cut records thirty years ago, they sounded good in the control room, but it was hard to channel that sound onto an LP. Session tapes underwent a lot of tweaking during their transposition to vinyl, and the compromising to compensate for vinyl's deficiencies began in the mixing phase and ended in mastering.

In mastering a tape for LP, you had to cut back the bass, crank up the mid-range and high end, and use compression to make it sound pleasing on an average record player. There was a complex physiology behind groove width and depth, and the width of the grooves changed as you got toward the end of the record. The last track on an album was the most problematic; if you didn't master the tape and cut the disc properly it would sound distorted. You could have the most dynamic mix in the world, but it would sound awful if you couldn't squeeze it into a record's grooves.

In the LP era, we had a daily flow of discs between the mastering studio (often Sterling Sound) and A&R. The mastering house would master the disc, send us an acetate of the song or album, and we would preview it. How did it sound on a hi-fi system, and on a rinky-dink record changer? Invariably, we'd make corrections and when we did, another set of acetates was cut for our approval.

With the CD, groove physiology is no longer a factor. But since digital recording's high resolution can magnify a mix's flaws, mastering becomes even more critical in the digital domain.

"Vocals are particularly important," says Bob Ludwig. "People want to hear the words to a song, and the first thing I listen for in a mix is the vocal. Is it prominent enough in the mix? Is the equalization correct? Too much vocal in a mix makes the music uninteresting; too little is annoying to the listener. I work hard to find the equalization and compression that will keep the vocal in place. At one magical point, something happens that makes the vocal blend perfectly."

The qualities that make for a great mix can be enhanced under the careful hand of an expert mastering engineer. Thanks to the finely-tuned ears of such distinguished mastering professionals as Greg Calbi, Ted Jensen, Bob Ludwig, George Marino, Darcy Proper, Doug Sax, and Mark Wilder (to name a few), the recordings supervised by this producer shine.

Original 10" acetate test disc label
Phil Ramone Collection

Live from the President's House

Watching Marilyn Monroe rehearse at
Madison Square Garden, May 1962
Phil Ramone Collection

When it comes to energy, excitement, and musical vibrancy, nothing beats a live performance.

Back when I started engineering, it was a challenge to provide decent sound in the concert hall itself, much less reproduce it on an LP. But because I started out as a performer, I was always attuned to the acoustics in the venues I played and recorded in.

As A&R Recording's reputation grew, people began asking Don Frey and me for advice on how to make their studios and performance spaces sound better. We got so many requests to work on television productions and concerts that in 1963 we decided to start an offshoot business as audio consultants.

By that time, Don and I had been working for our most prestigious client for almost two years: President John F. Kennedy. Why start at the bottom when you can start at the top? Our White House affiliation helped solidify our credibility and marketability as sound-reinforcement experts.

How did a New York engineer like me land a dream job in the White House?

One day, songwriter Richard Adler was producing a commercial at A&R, and out of the blue asked, "Can you come to an evening in tribute to the arts, at which President Kennedy is the keynote speaker?" It was a live remote broadcast from the Washington Armory, with orchestral pieces being performed in Washington and New York—a real black-tie, Washington society party. I thought it would be fun, so I tagged along.

The sound in the Armory was atrocious. There were no absorptive surfaces; the acoustics were so bad that everything sounded like a blur. When the National Symphony Orchestra began to play, all we could hear was feedback. Predictably it was President Kennedy who got blasted for it in the press.

Shortly after that debacle, Richard received a call from the head of the Democratic Party asking him to remedy the situation before a fundraiser marking the anniversary of Kennedy's inauguration. Richard called again, this time asking Don and me to help improve the Armory's acoustics.

Neither Don nor I had formally studied architecture or acoustics, so we invited Tom Dowd along. All we had were our ears; Tom had the benefit of golden ears *and* a Columbia University degree in physics. After surveying the cavernous Armory and conferring with Tom, I drew up a plan that I thought might work. It was easy to do, since cost wasn't a concern.

First, we built a set of risers, stuffed fiberglass insulation into every crevice to prevent rattling, and carpeted them.

Then, I asked Altec to design a speaker system that could be hung in tiers going straight up toward the audience. I wanted one pair of speakers for every twenty people in the room. It was overkill, but I was determined to get the best effect.

Finally, I treated the ceiling to help reduce the reflections in the room.

I knew that NASA was using an experimental weather balloon, and it seemed like just the right thing. We called for and received a bunch of NASA's weather balloons, stuffed them with Styrofoam, placed them against the ceiling, and swathed them in netting to hold them in place. The party planners hung ten thousand red, white, and blue balloons from the netting, creating a panorama of all-American color. The brick walls on either end of the Armory were decorated with drapes; the set design made the interior look like a classic theater. The program was a resounding success.

At seven o'clock the next morning, the phone in my hotel room rang. I answered groggily. A voice on the other end said, "Phil? This is Jack Kennedy." Thinking it was one of the guys playing a practical joke, I said, "Yeah, right. Lemme sleep!" I slammed the receiver down and drifted back to sleep. Within minutes, the phone rang again.

This time, I recognized the inimitable Boston accent. "Mr. Ramone? This is President Kennedy." I was never so embarrassed or apologetic in my life. "I'm sorry, Mr. President. I can't believe I hung up! I feel terrible." Despite my faux pas the president laughed and complimented me on our work. He then extended an invitation for me to meet him in the White House.

It was an inspiring and fruitful visit. He expressed a desire to improve the sound in the East Room, where the Kennedys were making history with a series of historic music and theater programs. I was elated to hear that the president was concerned about the quality of the sound in the mansion. He was especially eager to please Mrs. Kennedy, who had redecorated the public rooms in the White House and didn't want unsightly cables marring their beauty.

Richard Adler summoned the great theatrical designer Joel

Mielziner and lighting designer Jules Fisher, and they explained that we could install architectural elements to hide the equipment. Sound, lighting, and design were incorporated into the East Room without compromising the decor.

I suggested to the president that he consider recording all of the events in the East Room—and the speeches he made wherever he spoke—and install a recording system inside the Oval Office with microphones that could be switched on and off. Until then, the only extant recordings were those done for radio, television, and newsreels. I felt that having a high-quality archive of the president's conversations would be invaluable.

Then I asked if I could make another suggestion. Could we get rid of all the unsightly news microphones that were on his podium and replace them with a simple, two-microphone system that would feed both the public-address system and the press?

THE WHITE HOUSE
WASHINGTON

Dear Mr. Ramone:

I wish to thank you for your participation in the Second Inaugural Anniversary Salute.

I particularly appreciate your efforts in making the sound at the Armory truly superb. Your contribution in making the evening a resounding success should certainly be commended.

Both Mrs. Kennedy and I are most grateful to you.

Sincerely yours,

Mr. Phil Ramone
112 West 48th Street
New York City, New York

Phil Ramone Collection

Visiting and working at the White House wasn't just fun—it was intriguing, too. President Kennedy was so poised that it was easy to forget that we were in the midst of a cold war, and that there were some terrifying threats facing the nation.

All of us had thorough background checks and security clearances before we were allowed to enter the White House.

When you entered the compound, both you and your vehicle were searched. If you left the mansion and returned, you were searched again. If you walked from the East Room to the president's office, you were searched yet another time.

If the buzzer that signaled the president was coming through the hallway sounded, everyone cleared the area. Even butlers who were carrying trays of food would instinctively duck into the nearest doorway!

When you arrived to work each day, you were given a color-coded button. The color was changed every few hours, and if for some reason your button hadn't been replaced and a Secret Service agent saw you, you'd be led out.

It's funny now, but the first event we did for the Kennedys inside the White House was a disaster.

The president loved show music, and to please him and Mrs. Kennedy, Richard Adler produced an evening of Broadway favorites featuring music and dance.

Agnes de Mille choreographed a special ballet to the music from *Oklahoma!* As the stage in the East Room was too small to hold all of the musicians, I suggested that we prerecord the music at the United States Marine Corps studio, using their orchestra.

The show began, and the first three numbers were well received. During the de Mille piece, however, the room was suddenly plunged into darkness.

The tape machine stopped, and the dancers froze in position. The Secret Service swept into action.

Before long, the White House electrician discovered that the fuses in the White House were only fifteen amps, which wasn't adequate for the demands of our equipment.

The poor electrician got the fuse replaced, and the tape picked up where it left off. The dancers unfroze and finished the number to a rousing ovation.

I felt like my White House career was over before it got started. I felt as though I had embarrassed both the president and myself. It was one of the few times in my life when I felt mortified.

Mingling in the reception hall afterwards, I felt a hand on my shoulder and heard the reassuring voice of the president. He'd seen how distraught I was. "This is not something you could have controlled. It was still a sensational evening."

I was stunned.

I was a visitor in the president's home, and here he was trying to console me. "Think about how many people will talk about this, and never forget being in the White House when the lights went out," Kennedy said. "It's still a damned shame," I replied. "We have to do something about the electrical system in the East Room."

A week later I received a lovely thank-you letter from President Kennedy. Soon after, the White House social secretary called and asked if I'd be available to do the next state dinner.

Because of my Kennedy affiliation, I got another unexpected assignment in May 1962: doing the sound for the president's birthday bash at the old Madison Square Garden.

It was the first time I'd done sound at the Garden, and because of the unions, I was limited in what I could do. I did, however, install special microphones, speakers, and equalizers. Madison Square Garden was, at the time, a fight arena, and the sound wasn't easy to control. The star of the event, however, wasn't the sound.

As a special gift, the president's friends had arranged for Marilyn Monroe to cap the evening by serenading him with "Happy Birthday."

Marilyn came to rehearsal at seven thirty a.m. wearing sunglasses, white pants and blouse, and a simple kerchief. Even casually dressed, she was stunning.

Her first move was to greet the members of the orchestra, some of whom had played on her album. She was charming, and as she spoke with the musicians I understood why she had such an entrancing effect on people.

Then she walked over to me.

"Hi, I'm Marilyn," she said.

I introduced myself, and Richard Adler told her that I'd done his Hertz commercials and White House events. She put her arm in mine as we walked back toward the piano. "Where are those damned White House photographers when you need them?" I muttered to myself.

Marilyn needed to do a sound check, and I don't think I ever spent so much time preparing a microphone. We discussed how to approach her performance, and Marilyn rehearsed with jazz pianist Hank Jones. It was pretty imposing to be on stage with Marilyn Monroe, Hank Jones, and a nine-foot grand piano!

Since Marilyn was notorious for being late, they used that as the setup for her introduction: Peter Lawford, Jack Benny, or George Burns would announce her, the spotlight would pan across the arena and shine on where she was supposed to make her entrance, and— no Marilyn.

After doing this several times, Peter Lawford stepped up to the microphone and simply announced, "Mr. President, Marilyn Monroe."

Marilyn came out swaddled in that flesh-toned, skintight Jean Louis gown, cooed "Happy Birthday, Mr. President," and floored the audience.

Marilyn was very sweet to me, and we spent a few minutes talking at the cocktail party afterward. There were, however, several other influential men vying for her attention.

One of the last events I worked on in the Kennedy White House was held on October 1, 1963—a performance by the Joffrey Ballet. Not long after, a White House secretary who helped coordinate musical events asked my opinion on something. "We've been reading about this new group from England that American teens are going crazy over. If it can be arranged, would you be interested in helping to produce a White House concert by the Beatles?" Imagine the possibilities . . .

THE ROBERT JOFFREY BALLET
PRESENTED BY
THE REBEKAH HARKNESS FOUNDATION

TUESDAY, OCTOBER 1, 1963
THE WHITE HOUSE

Original tape box for the recording of the last event I recorded at the Kennedy White House
Phil Ramone Collection

Barbra Streisand, Central Park, June 1967
Courtesy of Sony/BMG Photo Archive

Greetings from Central Park

Of all the venues in the world, my favorite place to hear and record live music is New York's Central Park.

The social aspects of attending a concert in the park are beyond compare; acoustically, it's among the most neutral settings I've ever heard. The lack of reflective surfaces (except buildings) and the natural absorptive properties of the grass (and the audience, when the park is full) allow for better acoustics.

For me, the adventure of working in Central Park began in June 1967, when I first met Barbra Streisand.

Marty Ehrlichman (her manager) called and asked, "Could you design the sound system for a concert in Sheep Meadow? We're expecting about ten thousand people. Columbia Records will be recording it for an album, and CBS-TV will be videotaping it for later broadcast."

No one had ever wired the Meadow for sound.

Barbra was already a star, and I figured that the concert would draw many more people than Marty anticipated. How could we set up the sound system so the people farthest from the stage— thousands of feet away—would hear the music at the same time as those who were right up front?

The vastness of the outdoor setting required a high-powered system with many speakers, so I suggested that we create a series of speaker towers, and called JBL—one of the biggest and most innovative loudspeaker companies. "I know you're experimenting with long-throw horns. I'm doing sound reinforcement for a concert in Central Park. Could I borrow some?" They sent them over immediately.

The power amplifiers needed to drive the humongous speaker system necessitated cooling, so I rented an air-conditioned trailer. I also hired a recording truck and assistant engineer for the night.

It rained like crazy the night before and the day of the concert, so we couldn't rehearse in the park. The organizers were so concerned about the possibility of rain spoiling the event that they took out rain insurance from Lloyds' of London (who refused to include "mud insurance" because no one could agree on a definition of mud).

I hadn't met the man who'd be working alongside of me before, and I hoped that he'd make my job easier. It was wishful thinking. The fool brought along his dog, a Weimaraner that barked incessantly, and a bottle of bourbon, which he began drinking in the afternoon. By dusk, he was well into his cups—and of no use to me.

Wiring the speakers took hours, and about an hour before showtime I heard a loud *crack*. A lighting truck had backed up and dropped its tailgate on the thick bundle of microphone cables running from the stage to the sound truck.

The entire cluster of wires was severed, cutting the connection between the stage and the Meadow. Thankfully my friends from Columbia Records understood what a disaster this was, and six engineers—plus a Good Samaritan—sat there for forty-five minutes splicing the wires back together.

We inched toward showtime. Our final sound check—at the begrudging courtesy of conductor Mort Lindsay—was the "Overture."

In the park, the audience awaited Barbra's entrance.

As the orchestra segued into the first number, Barbra began singing offstage. Then she appeared, wearing a stylish, billowing gown (a perfect choice for a balmy summer's eve). The audience roared in approval. In return she delighted them for two and a half hours, singing thirty-three songs, kibitzing all the way.

Earlier in the week I had suggested that we put out a few more sets of speakers, "Just in case there are more people than expected." Well, just in case . . .

More than 125,000 people came to enjoy the hot June night when Barbra Streisand turned Sheep Meadow into a giant living room.

The recording truck engineer that I'd hired wasn't one of them. He had long since passed out, missing the entire show.

He awoke at the very end, when the audience—surging to rush the stage as Barbra took her bows—nearly toppled over the sound truck. Worse yet, his dog—upset with a policeman—was about to take a chunk out of the cop's leg. "The dog's just protecting his owner," I explained, hoping the officer wouldn't take more aggressive action.

Here's how Barbra remembers our first meeting, and that auspicious night:

"I met Phil after a two a.m. lighting rehearsal in Central Park. I had shot a scene for *Funny Girl* in Los Angeles that Friday morning, then got on a plane and flew to New York. I arrived at JFK Airport around midnight and went directly to the park for the lighting rehearsal. My business associate Marty Ehrlichman had warned me that twenty-five thousand people might show up for the rehearsal so I was prepared for a big crowd. To my disappointment, nobody was there, and I thought, 'Oh my God, what if nobody shows up to hear me sing for the concert the next night?'

"When the rehearsal was over I was introduced to Phil, and was told he was responsible for making sure that all ninety-nine acres of Sheep Meadow would have the proper sound. It was clear to the audience that most people wouldn't be able see me, but if they couldn't hear that would be terrible—there would be a riot.

"Phil told me that his plan was to erect [twelve] sound towers throughout Sheep Meadow, and that they would be on tape delay so the people farthest away could hear as well as the people in the front row. Of course, what he didn't tell me was that no one had ever done this before. Had I known that, I never would have slept as well as I did!

"The next day when I went back to the park for a sound check, I was relieved to find sixty thousand people there. What we discovered was that the park closed at midnight, and that's why there wasn't anybody at the rehearsal the night before.

"By the time the concert started, all ninety-nine acres were filled with people: in front of me, behind me—a few were even hanging out of their windows on Central Park West, which made me feel right at home because it reminded me of Brooklyn. We escaped the rain by about forty-five minutes, and it turned out we didn't need any cops at all because of all the people who made the happening happen. There were no disturbances, no arrests, no problems—just five tons of debris.

"Everything went off beautifully that night, and for the first time the Ramone sound was heard by an audience of a hundred and twenty-five thousand people."

It wasn't the last time, either.

In 1981, fourteen years after Barbra's incredible outdoor show, Paul Simon mentioned that he was thinking of doing a concert in Central Park.

By then, Paul had enjoyed success as a solo recording and

concert artist, made numerous television appearances, and had starred in his first feature film, *One-Trick Pony*. A high-profile concert in Central Park would expose him to an extremely large audience and underscore Paul's social awareness—and his generosity.

Saturday Night Live producer Lorne Michaels offered to produce the event and edit the show for television; producer Roy Halee and I would supervise the sound and coproduce the album.

Not long after Paul told me about the idea, I received word that Art Garfunkel would be joining him, and that the concert would be promoted as a Simon and Garfunkel show. The idea was attractive: Besides playing for a staggering number of people in the park, the show would be televised to millions.

Apart from an occasional appearance on each other's solo records or at a show, Paul Simon and Art Garfunkel hadn't done a full concert together in years, and a reunion was bound to be fraught with peril.

To the world, Paul and Artie's relationship was famously bad. To those who knew them personally, it was a conundrum. Although they'd been friends since childhood, they were complete opposites—even in terms of musical taste. They argued as fiercely as any two brothers I've ever known. Yet when they harmonized, it was pure magic.

Paul Simon & Art Garfunkel, 1981
Courtesy of WireImage

We began by rehearsing at the Hudson Theater and the Palladium. From the first day, I thought there'd be bloodshed. The bickering started over the most fundamental decision: a concept for the show.

Because the program had been conceived as a solo concert, Paul felt that he and Artie should use Paul's band. Paul already had horn and rhythm arrangements for all the songs, and they were well suited to the songs he and Artie made popular as Simon and Garfunkel.

But Artie wasn't comfortable with using Paul's band; when the set list was drawn up, he groused because Paul would be singing several of his familiar solo hits, while Artie had only one. He also expressed particular concern about whether Richard Tee could play the piano solo on "Bridge over Troubled Water" the way Larry Knechtel had on the original record. "I think we'd be better off if it was just us—a guitar and two vocals," he said.

I disagreed. "Progress is progress," I said. "You'll have the chance to do four or five songs from the past with just voice and guitar, but the two of you should be doing 'Bridge over Troubled Water' with a full-blown arrangement."

Eventually a compromise was reached: they'd use the band, but they'd also do some songs in the classic Simon and Garfunkel style. But the squabbles continued through the end of rehearsals, mostly over things so petty that I've long since forgotten how they began. There were many times during the week when everyone thought the concert would be cancelled.

Paul and Artie weren't the only problem.

A couple of days before the show, the television remote truck nearly got stuck under one of the bridges inside Central Park. The only way to pass through without shearing off the top of the truck was to deflate the tires. When the truck finally reached the concert staging area and the driver pulled onto the grass, the truck sank four feet into the mud. The vehicle had to be winched out, the tires filled, and a suitable parking area found so the crew could set up for taping.

The day of the dress rehearsal finally came. The rain that had soaked the field for two days subsided, and the weather looked promising for the next night's show. Our rehearsal and sound check began at six as planned.

When Artie arrived, he looked around and said, "You didn't tell me that there were going to be cameras." I was shocked. "You know the show is going to be televised, and a dress rehearsal sound check for a television show usually includes cameras," I reminded him.

"My hair isn't right, and I'm not dressed for the cameras!" Artie said. The jeans and shirt he was wearing seemed fine for a rehearsal, but Artie apparently felt that he needed something dressier.

He disappeared.

We only had until nine p.m. to perform the sound check, and New York City Parks Commissioner Gordon Davis was adamant about the cutoff time. The sound check began without Artie, and when he returned—this time sporting a nicer outfit and neater hair—it was almost over.

At nine, Commissioner Davis said, "You've got to turn off the outside PA." We turned off all of the amplification except for the stage monitors.

"I can't hear," Artie complained.

"You're going to have live with what you hear on stage," I said. "You won't be able to hear the audience towers tomorrow anyway—it's not like you're in a theater."

As we finished the rehearsal, a policeman approached me. "We measured the decibel level with a sound pressure meter, and it's much too high," he said. "If it goes over 85 dB during the performance tomorrow, we'll shut you down."

I'd designed the amplification system with towers and delays, and the sound was good—and loud. Jeez, I thought. With peaks, we're sure to go over a hundred.

I'm normally cool, but I went at it hammer and tongs with the commissioner. "This is not the New York Philharmonic," I conceded.

"But it's not Led Zeppelin, either. Simon and Garfunkel have soft, sweet voices. We've got to be able to push the volume up a bit."

The commissioner wouldn't budge.

Fans had begun camping out in the park two days before the show. They'd endured the rain, and were exhausted. I had visions of Streisand, circa '67.

"Some of these people have been here for days," I said. "I can assure you that if the audience can't hear the concert tomorrow, there might be a riot."

"What do *you* know about riots?" he asked.

"Well, I know that a lot of people are going to fill the Great Lawn tomorrow night, and if they can't hear the show they'll be extremely upset!"

By the next afternoon, Central Park was teeming with people. As we inched toward showtime, I noticed a cop walking the area with a meter. Amused, I went backstage and warned Paul about the commissioner's edict, and the meter-toting cop.

Paul didn't say much, but I could tell he was thinking.

Starting on time was a priority, because television director Michael Lindsay-Hogg wanted to capture the sky's transition from dusk to dark. We stalled the audience for almost an hour, and when Mayor Ed Koch appeared and announced, *"Ladies and Gentlemen, Simon and Garfunkel,"* they went wild.

Artie and Paul strode out and sang their first two songs.

At the end of "Homeward Bound," they surveyed the audience. "Well, it's great to do a neighborhood concert," Paul said, as though he was playing a coffeehouse. *"Can you hear me?"*

"No," they screamed.

"Turn it up, Phil!" Paul shouted.

I beamed, and the parks commissioner seethed. With the mayor and audience on our side, there was no way he could ask me to lower the volume!

Near the catering tables, I noticed that the fencing they'd set up to separate us from the crowd was rather flimsy. "How will that stop anyone? What if they start coming over for food?" I asked a nearby police lieutenant. "Don't worry. If the crowd is well behaved, they won't bother you."

It wasn't the answer I wanted to hear.

"But what if the crowd doesn't behave?" I asked.

The lieutenant gave me a quizzical look. "Do you see that pond over there, behind the Delacorte Theater?" he asked. "It's filled with weird fish and crap. If the crowd storms the area, just follow me. We'll both go in the water—fast!"

My fear was unfounded—the audience's behavior was beyond reproach.

As I prepared to leave, the police lieutenant came up and said, "Knock on wood—we didn't have any problems during the show. No muggings, no fights, no emergencies to speak of."

The post-concert atmosphere blew me away.

I tried to get backstage, but all the paths were jammed. As I walked out of the park with the rest of the crowd, I witnessed something I'd never seen before: people carrying lit candles and boom boxes, playing back the cassette tapes they'd recorded during the concert. All I could hear was Simon and Garfunkel music blaring from every direction.

At the small after-party held downtown, I gazed at Paul and Artie.

That night they'd pulled off what everyone who writes, plays, and produces music aspires to do—they'd killed the audience. The pair had battled each other all week, come together for one brief moment, and were now separately greeting guests on opposite sides of the room. "Paul Simon and Art Garfunkel may be separate," I thought. "But they'll always be bound by their harmony and its incredible blend."

Another Side of Live

Aretha Franklin
Courtesy of Kevin Mazur/WireImage

There's nothing more satisfying than using music to raise money for worthwhile causes, and over the past ten years I've had the opportunity to produce some musically rich benefit shows, including the annual Songwriters Hall of Fame tributes and the National Academy of Recording Arts and Sciences' MusiCares concerts.

MusiCares is a foundation that raises money to aid musicians in need. The Songwriters Hall of Fame is a branch of the National Academy of Popular Music; their mission is to preserve the history of the American popular song, and award scholarships to promising songwriters.

Creatively, SHOF and MusiCares concerts give me wide latitude to experiment and pair artists with songs they're not normally associated with. I've found that artists—regardless of the area they work in—have genuine respect for one another, and that you can't stereotype a singer or musician according to their chosen genre.

When we were putting together the MusiCares tribute to Billy Joel, Garth Brooks asked to perform "Shameless," and I wasn't thrilled with his choice. Everyone around him said, "Forget about changing it. Don't even mention it to Garth—he's made up his mind."

I've often found that "handlers"—the cadre of press, publicity, and peripheral management people who accompany a celebrity—don't always know the artist's opinion on certain issues. The handlers are there to minimize bumps in the road, keep the artist on schedule, and make that schedule flow as smoothly as possible. Each group tries to protect the artist, and in doing so they sometimes act overzealously.

During rehearsal I had the chance to chat privately with Garth, and I decided to ask him how he felt about Billy's music.

ME: What's your favorite Billy Joel song?

GB: Oh, jeez—"Goodnight Saigon."

ME: Do you know it?

GB: Yeah!

ME: Would you sing it in the show?

GB: You must be crazy.

ME: No—no one is likely to ever cover that song, and I think it would be a terrific song for you to sing tonight.

I've got to admit that I was taken aback by Garth's choice—"Goodnight Saigon" is a heavy song for anyone to select as a favorite. But its symbolism resonates with many people—especially musicians—and I said to myself "Why wouldn't I want to present that song in a completely different context?" It was something that few in the audience would ever imagine a country singer like Garth Brooks doing.

The MusiCares house band was very good, but they didn't know "Goodnight Saigon." I grabbed an intern, gave him twenty bucks, and asked him to find the nearest record store and buy a copy of *The Nylon Curtain*.

Meanwhile I could see that the public relations folks were getting nervous because Garth was spending so much time with me. They tried to pry him away. "Yeah, just a minute," he said, stalling them. Before anyone realized what was happening, the intern returned and a CD player was blaring "Goodnight Saigon."

"Can anyone copy the arrangement for us?" I asked the band.

Four guys stepped forward and offered to transpose the chart. We didn't have any horns in the band, so they created parts for the guitars, drums, and synthesizers. Everyone—including stagehands—pitched in to sing the background parts. By the time that Garth finished his second run-through, those present at the rehearsal—including Garth's publicist and manager—were crying.

"I'm thrilled that you think that I can do this," Garth said after coming off the stage. "It's going to be amazing—you've got to close the show," I said.

Garth looked puzzled.

"Who's on before me?" he asked.

I went through the lineup, mentioning Tony Bennett last. "I'm going *after* Tony Bennett?" Garth asked incredulously.

"Yeah—I'd like you to close the show."

"Absolutely not," Garth said. "Tony closes. I am *not* going to follow Tony Bennett!"

At the end of the show Garth received a stomping ovation, and as I watched from my seat I felt confident that my earlier hunch was right: No one could possibly follow Garth's performance of "Goodnight Saigon."

Then, the announcement came: *"Please welcome Mr. Tony Bennett!"*

Tony—in his inimitably cool way—glided effortlessly on stage, snapping his fingers to a Gershwin tune. *"I got rhythm, I got music . . ."*

After a few bars Tony stopped, and began singing Billy's "New York State of Mind." The place was ours; Tony and the audience became one, basking in the mutual warmth flowing freely throughout the room.

"Okay," I admitted to myself. "Garth was right: No one can top Tony Bennett."

I rarely sit in the audience during these events, but on this night I'd decided to sit with the honoree. As Tony hit his final notes, I turned to Billy Joel and ribbed him. "Okay, Billy—try to follow *that!*"

There's something to be said for flexibility.

When MusiCares honored Bono in 2003, I juggled the entire running order of the show to accommodate the opening act: President Bill Clinton.

Mr. Clinton—a big U2 fan—was delighted, and just before the show began I decided to deviate from the program. "It'll be impossible to have you sit in the audience for two hours—you'll be mobbed, and no one will watch the show," I explained to the president. "Would you mind opening the show?"

We rearranged the order so that President Clinton could present Bono with the award up front and then speak for ten minutes. From there, everything would proceed as scheduled. Well, the president and the Irish rebel played off each other so naturally that what had been planned as a fifteen-minute prelude turned into one of the best half hours of entertainment I've ever seen.

Who follows the president? It wasn't easy, but B.B. King, Sheryl Crow, and Mary J. Blige did a fantastic job of entertaining the crowd.

Traditionally the president of the Recording Academy wraps the MusiCares show with a short speech about the artist. Before the Bono show I took NARAS President Neil Portenow aside and said, "I wouldn't wish that spot on a leopard!" Neil laughed, but we both knew that the *real* president had gotten him off the hook.

Instead of giving a speech, Bono sang Frank Sinatra's "That's Life."

I didn't tell Bono what I had planned for this number. All I said was, "I have a surprise for you." When he came on to do the finale, the curtain parted and a brass and saxophone ensemble began playing a sophisticated, punchy chart written by Rob Mathes. Hearing a band like that playing right behind you is inspiring, and as a closer, "That's Life" was as rousing as the show's opening.

I believe in good karma. There have been many times when I've looked at how certain situations have unfolded, and walked away reassured that most things happen for a reason.

The first MusiCares concert I produced was a tribute to Luciano Pavarotti at Radio City in 1998, and in planning the event producers Tim Swift, Dana Tomarken, and I were discussing which artists we might possibly ask to perform. I knew that Aretha Franklin loved Pavarotti's music, and having Aretha on any show never failed to lend it an extra-special dimension.

I called Aretha, and when I told her that the program's honoree was Pavarotti she agreed to perform—with one condition. "I've got to sing Puccini's 'Nessun Dorma,'" she said. The aria was her favorite Pavarotti recording, and she was dying to sing it. I scrambled

With Luciano Pavarotti and my son, BJ Ramone
Phil Ramone Collection

to find a suitable arrangement; Rob Mounsey came up with a classic chart for her.

Aretha's rendition was electrifying and moved Pavarotti to tears.

Two nights later, Pavarotti himself was scheduled to sing "Nessun Dorma" at Radio City, where he was receiving a Grammy Award for lifetime achievement. Twenty-five minutes before his cue, the maestro summoned me. He pointed to his throat. "I can't go on," he rasped.

At that moment we were live on the air, and "twenty-five minutes out"—twenty-five minutes away from Pavarotti's spot in the show. The news spread quickly, and Grammy president Mike Greene and television producer Ken Ehrlich immediately responded and asked if I could convince Aretha Franklin to take Pavarotti's place.

It was our only option, and if Aretha agreed to fill in, we'd have to work quickly. Engineer Hank Neuberger located Pavarotti's performance from that afternoon's dress rehearsal, and dubbed it to a cassette. As soon as Hank was finished, I grabbed the tape and took the stairs to Aretha's dressing room two at a time, with Pavarotti's conductor in tow.

Although she was familiar with the music, agreeing to fill in at the last minute would take enormous courage on Aretha's part.

Pavarotti's arrangement had an introduction that she was unaccustomed to, and it featured a choir. "The choir will sing the intro, and the orchestra will be behind you," I explained. "The key is a little lower than you're accustomed to, but there's not enough time to make changes. You'll have to sing it in Luciano's key," I explained.

Aretha listened to the cassette three times. Time was running short, and we anxiously awaited her verdict. "Yes," she said. "I'll do it on one condition: You must turn off all of the air-conditioning in the theater before I go on."

It was a small but considerable request.

Aretha detests air-conditioning; it has a deleterious effect on her throat and voice. Although the theater was packed with six thousand people and a truckload of television lights and cameras, the cooling system was shut down.

I informed Ken Ehrlich of Aretha's approval, and he rewrote Sting's spoken introduction. Despite the slapdash changes, Aretha took the stage and performed as though everything had been planned. When she left to a standing ovation I hugged her. Aretha gave a little sniffle, and offered an admonishment. "Phil, it was still too cold out there!"

On the set with Paul McCartney and engineer Clarke Rigsby, 1986
Courtesy of Alan Dahl

Hooray for Hollywood!

When I was a child, I dreamed of being a movie director.

Every Saturday, my sister and I would go to the movies. I sat for hours, studying those wonderful M-G-M and Warner Brothers musicals of the 1940s and '50s. All I could think about was playing, singing, and acting in them—and maybe even directing them.

Although that dream hasn't yet been fulfilled, I've never lost my love for film. I'm just as enamored of the art and science behind filmmaking as I am recording, and was privileged to have played a small role in the creation of numerous films and music videos (not from behind the camera—from behind the mixing desk).

My first involvement in a feature film project came courtesy of Quincy Jones, who asked me to record the score he'd written for *The Pawnbroker* in 1964.

Quincy and I had made many records together, and I was excited by the prospect of breaking into the film world. But it would be a big step, given my relative inexperience with the art of film recording.

"I would love to record it, but I know nothing about movie scoring," I explained to Quincy. "Neither do I," he replied. "But I've spoken to Henry Mancini in London, and Armando Travioli in Rome. They've helped me understand how synchronization works. They also taught me a few tricks about how to arrange and record so that the film mixer can bring out the best in the music."

I'm a problem solver, and this puzzle was one that I wanted to piece together. The score for *The Pawnbroker,* a Sidney Lumet film, took Quincy two months to write, and two days for us to record.

Quincy hired the best jazz musicians on the east coast, including Freddie Hubbard, Elvin Jones, Anthony Ortega, Dizzy Gillespie, Oliver Nelson, and Bobby Scott, and asked Billy Byers to help write the orchestrations. The sessions were frantic: At one point, Quincy and Billy kept a full orchestra waiting while they arranged the last cue that Quincy had written.

The Pawnbroker was a revolutionary film.

The film challenged the Motion Picture Code, and brought the issue of frontal nudity and censorship to the fore. As a result, *The Pawnbroker* helped establish a precedent, and an acknowledgement that in certain situations, nudity had an undeniable moral purpose in films. But behind the scenes, *The Pawnbroker* also confronted another looming issue: the acceptance of black composers in Hollywood.

Until 1954, very few blacks were welcomed into the ranks of Hollywood's film studio orchestras. It took influential actors such as Marlon Brando—a real jazz fan—and the efforts of black musicians such as Buddy Colette and Nat Cole to integrate the inimitable talents of African American musicians into the studios.

The musicians may have staked their claim to a small piece of the Hollywood studio scene, but black film composers were practically unheard of.

So solid was the white line—and Hollywood's misperception of black composers—that Henry Mancini received a call from a *Pawnbroker* producer before Quincy was hired. "We know he's gifted," the producer told Mancini. "But he's also black. Will he be reliable?"

They needn't have worried. Quincy's jazz-inflected score—dynamic, yet appropriately brooding and dark—underscored the picture's dramatic theme, and garnered both Quincy and the producers of *The Pawnbroker* considerable praise.

After *The Pawnbroker,* my recording for film was limited to the commercials that A&R was cutting for the top Madison Avenue advertising agencies.

Then, in 1967, Burt Bacharach asked me to supervise the recording of the soundtrack for *Casino Royale,* which was recorded in London.

The plum to emerge from *Casino Royale* was Dusty Springfield's rendition of "The Look of Love," a performance that brought sensuality in film music to a hitherto rarefied level. Burt had written all of the music in the States, but when he and Hal arrived in London for the sessions, they were told that the script had changed. Consequently some of the melodies that Burt had written didn't fit the new story.

Fortunately Burt was in the throes of fleshing out a melody that he'd devised for another spot in the picture; a pretty, Brazilian-influenced melody that he believed could be expanded into a song. Using Ursula Andress's beauty for inspiration, Burt completed the melody, and Hal wrote the lyrics on the spot. Bacharach may have been thinking of Ursula Andress, but "The Look of Love" fit Dusty Springfield's voice (and persona) beautifully.

Years later I was back in London to produce another James Bond film soundtrack: John Barry's *On Her Majesty's Secret Service.*

I owe a great deal to composer John Barry, for teaching me about how film music is written and recorded.

John Barry's scores were always rhythmic, and he often went against the grain. For example, a John Barry cue written to accompany a high-speed car chase was unlike anything you'd expect. Instead of a pulsating theme to underscore the scene, John would go in the opposite direction. Brilliant!

London had become a popular place to record film scores, and I enjoyed my work there. While British union rules prevented me from touching the board, the English technicians—Jack Clegg on *Casino Royale,* Gordon McCallum, John Mitchell, and John Richards on *On Her Majesty's Secret Service* were sheer professionals, and eager to fulfill my wishes as the soundtracks' producer.

I had gotten a taste of the film world from my small part in bringing the music for *The Pawnbroker* and *Casino Royale* to life. Why can't New York become a hub for film soundtrack recording, too? I wondered.

We could easily fit sixty or seventy men on the scoring stage in Studio A1 at 799 Seventh Avenue, and I set out to make our studio one of the premier film-recording facilities in the East. I started by purchasing the best 35mm magnetic film recording system I could afford.

Traditionally film music and dialogue are recorded on 35mm magnetic film, the advantage of which is quietness and fidelity. The space between the heads on a magnetic film recorder is wider than on an eight- or sixteen-track magnetic tape machine, and the hiss level is much lower. The amount of headroom is double or triple that of a conventional tape recorder, offering increased dynamic range and lower distortion.

Before digital recording, the fidelity of 35mm film was so highly regarded that engineers in standard recording studios began using it to record certain sessions, and many labels used it as a marketing tool. On the East Coast, Bob Fine was the master of magnetic film recording; I had taken note of what he was doing even before I became an engineer.

In the early 1950s, Bob and his wife, producer Wilma Cozart Fine, made some startling symphonic recordings for Mercury's classical Living Presence series. The earliest of those classical sessions were monophonic; Bob suspended a single U47 microphone over the conductor's head and recorded direct to 35mm film. When stereo came into vogue, Bob designed a three-track magnetic film recording head, devised a multiple microphone system, and made some of the finest stereo orchestral recordings of all time.

Bob was also among the first engineers to design and use a mobile sound truck, and in the mid-1950s he opened his own studio, Fine Sound, where he recorded dozens of high-fidelity jazz albums for Mercury and Verve Records, including Count Basie's sonic and musical tour de force, *April in Paris*.

Many of Bob Fine's orchestral recordings were made in the ballroom of the Great Northern Hotel, and when the hotel closed down, some of his engineers came to work at A&R. They were valuable assets; because of their expertise with 35mm magnetic film recording, A&R became one of the best film-recording facilities in New York.

One of the most important film-music recordings made in our studio was *Midnight Cowboy* in 1969, and participating in the production was a milestone for me.

Midnight Cowboy was a controversial film.

Expletives, the suggestion of homosexuality, or anything resembling prostitution practically guaranteed an X rating in 1969, and an X rating branded a film taboo. *Midnight Cowboy* touched on those themes, and the X rating it received caused quite a stir.

I clearly recall going to a screening of the film at Movie Lab with an invited audience of seventy or eighty people. John Schlessinger became upset because the audience hadn't laughed in the spots where he thought they should have. To Schlessinger, that meant the film was doomed.

"How can you judge what's going to happen?" I asked.

I was with both Johns—Schlessinger and Barry—when I saw the film for the first time in a theater with a regular audience, and they screamed, hollered, and did all of the things an audience does when they like something.

The comparison taught me a lot about what and what not to expect from a film. It also made me aware of how narrowly the person responsible for each portion of a film's production views the final product. During both screenings I was hypersensitive; I wanted to be sure that the music mixes came across the way I'd intended them to.

Following what is still film-studio tradition, we scored *Midnight Cowboy* "to picture," meaning the musicians sat in the studio and played each cue as the film was projected on a screen.

As we spent time together, I discovered that John Barry preferred to record long sections of scoring in one piece. For this reason, we decided that in addition to the short cues that were cut to the picture, we'd also record extended versions of the Theme, Main Title, and several other important cues, which could later be used on the soundtrack album or released as singles.

In those days, we didn't waste much time recording a film.

The bulk of the music for *Midnight Cowboy* was probably finished in three or four days, in large part because John Barry's scoring and orchestrations were so precise.

Midnight Cowboy is a good example of how scoring and mixing a film in New York differs from scoring and mixing it in Hollywood, where they have individual mixers to record dialogue, music, and effects. The recording setup was fairly simple: We recorded the sessions on eight-tracks of magnetic tape (which were later transferred to 35mm film), and I premixed the score and songs to three separate stems (tracks). Later, film sound mixer Dick Vorisek added dialogue and effects on his board for the final mix. He was happy just to move the music up and down, with a pencil taped to three faders!

The most memorable song to emerge from *Midnight Cowboy*

was Harry Nilsson's new interpretation of Fred Neil's "Everybody's Talkin'."

Harry had originally recorded "Everybody's Talkin'" in 1968, for his second RCA album, *Aerial Ballet*. For *Midnight Cowboy,* we rearranged the song, and had Harry rerecord two versions: one for the opening credits, and a reprise for the end. The most noticeable difference between Harry's RCA recording and the *Midnight Cowboy* versions is that the film renditions include harmonica, played by Toots Thielemans.

The inclusion of "Everybody's Talkin'"—already familiar to many because of Harry's first recording—helped make the United Artists soundtrack album for *Midnight Cowboy* a best-seller. "Everybody's Talkin'" was not, however, a song that the producers had planned to include in the film.

When a film nears the end of production, the director assembles a rough cut: a draft version of the film that approximates their vision for the final cut.

Rough cuts are truly rough. Scenes that have not yet been filmed are missing, edits are choppy, and the film's color hasn't been corrected. Since music cues often are incomplete, the rough cut's soundtrack often contains only bits of the actual score, and temporary music in between.

At first, John Schlessinger put "Everybody's Talkin'" into the rough cut of *Midnight Cowboy* as a placeholder, since Harry Nilsson and John Barry were still working on an original song, "The Lord Must Be in New York City." But as often happens when everyone lives with the temp track in a rough cut, John and producers came to love "Everybody's Talkin'," and the way it blended with the visuals. Nilsson had the voice of an angel, and his folksy rendition of "Everybody's Talkin'" was exactly the kind of theme song the picture needed.

The scoring for many motion pictures (in whole or in part) took place at A&R, including *The French Connection* (1971), *Cops and Robbers* (1973), and *Fame* (1980).

I went to Hollywood to work on films, too.

Earlier I described how I came to supervise the recording of *A Star is Born* in 1975. It was one of the proudest moments in my life.

It's rare for someone like me to join a film production team as the script is being completed, and rarer still to be accepted as one of the crew. I was relieved when everyone who was working on *A Star Is Born* welcomed my participation. When I took the assignment, I promised Barbra (and myself) that I'd do whatever was necessary to make the soundtrack reflect what she had in mind.

Regardless of the sensationalized stories you may have heard, Barbra is a kind, sensitive person who demands from her colleagues only what she expects of herself, and *A Star Is Born* is a film of consequence. With it, Barbra opened the door for things that people in the film industry had long wished for. From true live action to technological freedom, working on *A Star Is Born* expanded all of our horizons.

Were there tensions on the set? Of course there were. With all of the aggregate talent working on the picture, there were bound to be squabbles.

With my wife, Karen Ramone, and
Barbra Streisand, 1983
Courtesy of David McGough

By the time I got to Hollywood, there had been numerous script changes, and there was a pressing deadline to start production. The issue of song selection also hung in the air.

When I arrived, Barbra was sifting through dozens of songs submitted by Paul Williams, Kenny Ascher, Rupert Holmes, Leon Russell, Kenny Loggins, and others. "Let me help you preview them," I requested. "That's part of the music supervisor's responsibility, and as the film's producer, you've got enough to worry about."

One of the memories I savor is hearing "Evergreen" for the first time.

Barbra was learning to play guitar so her movement would look real in the film, and she'd improvised a pretty melody while practicing one night. The next day she came in and played it for us and it was superb—almost classical in its simplicity. She also played the song for Leon Russell, who also affirmed its beauty.

Barbra was very proud of "Evergreen." She was reticent about contributing to the film something she'd written, but it was by far the finest song in the picture. Paul Williams took Barbra's melody, added lyrics, and "Evergreen" became the movie's theme. It went on to win both an Oscar and a Golden Globe for best song, and is still one of Barbra's most-requested tunes.

Original tape box for mix of "Evergreen"
Phil Ramone Collection

To that point, *A Star Is Born* was the most ambitious project I'd ever done. We were recording live on the sets, then editing and mixing the sound in several places: in the sound truck on location, at the Burbank Studios, and at Todd-AO. To help us work efficiently I had forty Class-A phone lines installed between the Burbank Studios and Todd-AO, and we began feeding the mixes from Burbank to Hollywood, where Barbra was supervising the assembly of the D/M/E (dialogue, music, and sound effects) track.

When I called to request the forty phone lines, the head of Pacific Bell's technical department asked if we'd like to use an experimental satellite to bounce music off Mount Wilson. It had never been done before, and when they said they'd give us sixty lines, I jumped at their offer.

The soundmen in Burbank thought I was crazy. There were trucks with receiving dishes scattered all around, and maintenance men constantly calling, "Where's Phil? Where's Phil?" We compared the sound of the satellite transmissions to that of the Class-A phone lines and found that the satellite worked very well.

I would prepare one or two mixes at whichever studio we were in and send it via satellite for Barbra to hear. Barbra would listen to the mix, fix the vocal line from where she was, and bounce it back to us wherever we were. I spent more than enough time driving back and forth between Burbank and Hollywood! The payoff came when everything Barbra had imagined came together and the studio, critics, and audiences reacted favorably.

One of the things I'm most proud of is that *A Star Is Born* was the first magnetic Dolby surround sound film, and that it premiered in true surround sound in fifteen theaters. The late dialogue mixer Buzz Knudson and I personally tested the print and equalized the first five theaters so they would sound like the mixing theater at Todd-AO. Then the Dolby technicians tuned each theater to what we called the "Todd-AO curve."

While the pace of working on *A Star Is Born* was frantic, I had my share of fun, too.

Because Barbra and producer Jon Peters had disagreed with director Frank Pierson over the first cut of the film, Barbra decided to recut it herself. To accomplish this, she installed a full editing suite in a cottage on her Malibu ranch.

I spent a lot of time there with Barbra and Jon, and was treated to all of the estate's amenities, including the gym and pool.

One night, I decided to take a swim in the buff.

It was late—maybe two o'clock in the morning—and no one else seemed to be alive. I dove into the cool water, and when I surfaced found the barrel of a gun pointed at my head.

The assailant was one of Barbra's round-the-clock security guards—a serious bunch who patrolled the borders of the property. As I treaded water, I frantically tried to explain that I was not an intruder but an invited guest who was staying in the guest house. The guard eyed me dubiously.

I was splashing around, trying to stay above water, when I heard a familiar voice from the apartment above the cottage.

"Who's that in the pool? Is everything okay down there?"

It was one of Barbra's assistants, a lady who was staying in the apartment above me.

"Tell him who I am!" I screamed.

"Well, who *are* you?" she yelled back, having a good laugh at my expense.

She knew I was swimming in the buff, and all she wanted to see was my embarrassment when I was forced to come out of the pool naked. The story was the hot topic at breakfast the next day.

Flashdance (1983) was a terrific film and a great challenge.

The team of Jon Peters, Peter Gruber, Jerry Bruckheimer, Don Simpson, and Dawn Steele were out to produce an original musical, and they asked if I was interested in producing the soundtrack. To help them capture a modern spirit, they signed Adrian Lyne to direct.

Although Lyne had only directed commercials, I admired his work and hoped I'd get the chance to work with him on his first feature film.

Because of the producers' efforts, *Flashdance* has the two most important elements that make for an entertaining picture: a good story and exciting music. After reading a script that offered an elaborate view of the characters and plot, I signed on as coproducer of the music for the film.

For a musical to be successful there has to be a reason for each song, and the songs have to interlock with the story. Few people could write to the style of the period as well as Giorgio Moroder, who was at his peak.

Giorgio's "What a Feeling" (sung by Irene Cara) was upbeat, and Michael Sembello's "Maniac" provided the relentless, driving beat punctuating Jennifer Beals's frenetic dance sequence. "Manhunt" has since become a camp classic, and the movie's big ballad—"I'll Be Here Where the Heart Is," written by Kim Carnes, Duane Hitchings, and Craig Krampf—signaled a pivotal moment in the film, and in Kim's career.

The dance form was far different in the early 1980s than it was during the days of Fred Astaire, Ginger Rogers, and Gene Kelly. Marrying music and dance can still be a Herculean task.

Dance is like an Olympic sport; it's physically demanding, and professional dancers are as strong and agile as any athlete. Choreographing a tight dance routine for a film requires concentration and repetition. Allowing ample time for rehearsal is essential.

When we first ran through *Flashdance*'s dance sequences, we rehearsed in one half of a trailer on the studio lot. I quickly realized that doing so successfully would be damn near impossible.

I had Jennifer Beals and the other dancers streaming in and out to hear what we were doing with the music, and when they started dancing, the trailer shook like mad. When that happened, the writers on the other end of the trailer would yell, *"Shut up! Turn off the music—we're trying to write a script in here."* The only place with enough room for our dance rehearsals was the commissary, which was available only between two and four in the afternoon.

To keep the peace, Jon Peters consented to renting us a house off the studio lot where the choreographer, songwriters, a few keyboardists and I could work without distraction. Being secluded from the rest of the production staff for those twelve to fourteen hours a day calmed our nerves and let us do much more than we would have otherwise.

One night when I was back in New York, I called Don Simpson and said, "You won't believe this, but there are a group of kids on the corner of Fifty-ninth Street, playing music and spinning themselves around on a piece of cardboard! You've gotta see this—it's incredible. It would be just right for the Pittsburgh scenes."

Simpson sent a friend down to shoot some videotape of the break-dancers. He loved what he saw, and worked them into the movie.

"Should we write original music for the scene?" he asked.

"Giorgio Moroder and I agree that we don't have to write anything new," I explained. "Let's lease the music track that the kids on the street were using."

The kids had thrown their mix together from a bunch of dance records, and God only knew whose records they'd sampled. Today it would be unaffordable to license every sample they had used; when we made *Flashdance* it was easier—and far more cost-effective.

There's a lot to be said for this kind of spontaneity, and that's what made working on *Flashdance* so interesting.

I also have a special fondness for *Flashdance* because it let me work with the young woman who had recently become my wife—singer-dancer Karen Kamon, whom I'd met at a Peter, Paul and Mary concert in 1979. Karen was their production assistant, and I thought she was cute.

Karen's coming to *Flashdance* happened in a funny way. I wouldn't have suggested that she audition; I didn't think that mixing business and family would be a smart move. But Ken Topolsky—my production assistant at the time—saw Karen's potential and snuck her into the studio to do the demo of "Manhunt."

For Karen, the song was a natural.

At the time she cut the demo, Karen was pregnant with our son BJ. There was a greater chance that the song would be cut from the movie; Karen never thought she'd be coming back in her eighth month to record her final vocals!

Karen was quite uncomfortable, and she called Donna Summer for advice. "How the hell did you record 'Last Dance' when you were pregnant?" Donna laughed. "Sing it in phrases," she suggested. "Take a deep breath, hold on to your belly, and sing your ass off!" Donna and Karen were ahead of their time, singing to their babies in utero before it became fashionable.

Flashdance also affirmed Ken Topolsky's eye for talent. After leaving the A&R nest he moved to Hollywood and became a producer of the hit television series *The Wonder Years.*

As actors Bob Hoskins and John Goodman have said, "No good film enjoys a trouble-free ride." *Flashdance* was no exception.

The studio lost faith in the director and only halfheartedly supported the production, and no one expected the film to do well. But after the first preview, I got a call at home from Dawn Steele. She was so excited I could barely understand what she was saying. "They're dancing in the aisles!" she exclaimed. "Come on—that's what publicists write," I retorted. "No, Phil—I'm not joking. *They are dancing in the aisles!*"

At the next screening there was more dancing, cheering, and jumping up and down, and *Flashdance* became one of the biggest films of the eighties.

On Broadway

With composer-lyricist Stephen Sondheim
Phil Ramone Collection

Musical theater has always been a part of my life.

When I was a teenager, I could rarely afford tickets to a show, so a friend and I would go down to Broadway and search for discarded *Playbills* outside the theaters. The next night we'd go back to the theater, tuck the programs under our arms, and scavenge the ground for ticket stubs. During intermission we'd give the usher a story like, "We're sitting upstairs—would you mind if we stand in the back of the theater for the second act?" Most of the time she'd let us in; many of the ushers were would-be actors who knew what it was like to crave something you couldn't afford.

I've recorded a number of stage shows—both on Broadway and in London—and they're among the sessions I get the most pleasure from.

The assignment of recording or producing such cast albums as *Promises, Promises; Pippin; The Wiz; Chicago; Little Shop of Horrors; Starlight Express; Passion; Company; A Funny Thing Happened on the Way to the Forum; Big (The Musical); The Wild Party; Seussical (The Musical); The Boy from Oz;* and *Billy Elliot (The Musical)* has brought me backstage, and into the minds of the composers, producers, and performers who put every ounce of their body and soul into giving us a rich, satisfying theater experience.

The best stage musicals dazzle the audience with color, movement, and lighting cues that stimulate the senses, but the record producer doesn't have the benefit of those elements when he or she is bringing the show from stage to record. This prompts the question, "Is it possible to transpose all that the audience sees and hears in the theater into a credible cast recording?"

It all depends on what your idea of a Broadway cast album is.

To me, a cast recording is more than a souvenir—it's history. Because of Actors' Equity union rules and music licensing issues, producers aren't prone to film or tape a Broadway show for commercial purposes, so once a production closes it's lost to the ages. A cast album lets you hear it over and over again.

A good cast album preserves the spirit of what the story is about, and what the audience saw in the theater. Since each person leaves the theater with a unique impression, structuring a cast album can be complicated.

As Hugh Jackman recently said:

"It's deceptively hard to do a live version of a show album because the temptation is to make it like a studio recording. What often happens is that the cast recording doesn't resemble the show. People who buy the CD want to remind themselves of what it felt like to be at the show."

The producer's mind-set has a lot to do with how a cast recording takes shape. Some shows make the shift from stage to studio more seamlessly than others.

Since I generally approach a cast recording as though it's a radio broadcast of the show, including a bit of connective dialogue often helps smooth out areas with awkward transitions. Many contemporary musicals, such as those written by Stephen Sondheim, require a great deal of ingenuity to transform into a successful cast recording.

Sondheim wrote the lyrics to *West Side Story* (1957) and *Gypsy*

(1959) with Leonard Bernstein and Jule Styne, respectively, but it is shows such as *A Little Night Music, Company, Sweeney Todd, Sunday in the Park with George,* and *Into the Woods* that made him a legend.

As one who has produced several of Steve's cast recordings (*Passion,* 1994; *Company,* 1995; and *A Funny Thing Happened on the Way to the Forum,* 1996), I can assure you that the twists and turns he takes with rhyme and meter place great demands on the performer, engineer, and producer. Only Burt Bacharach's rhythmic complexities compare to Sondheim's.

But when Sondheim writes a show, he has a complete understanding of the plot, his music, and the voices and characters before him. Since the choreography and staging of a Sondheim show are as elaborate as the music, bringing his productions to life on a cast album demands ingenuity.

Passion was a complex show, and we agonized over how to transform its story and music so that the lead character—a tortured, unattractive woman—would be understood without visuals. I consulted with Steve and orchestrator Jonathan Tunick, and we decided that using orchestral sounds to heighten the sense of drama would be most effective.

A Funny Thing Happened on the Way to the Forum posed a different problem.

I'd always felt that Zero Mostel's performance on the original cast recording (Capitol Records, 1962) was too aloof for the salacious character he played. I'm sure that the thinking at the time was, "This is a show with a lot of absurd moments, but it won't play well on record because there aren't any visuals."

Audiences expected more from a cast recording in 1996, and I mentioned my feelings to Stephen Sondheim and Nathan Lane. I explained that I wanted to bring the zaniness and joviality that I saw on stage into the recording studio. "It's okay to be over-the-top—to be the same character you play on the stage," I told Nathan. "That's what the show is about, and that's what I want on the record." Sond-heim felt the same way, but there were times during the *Forum* sessions when Nathan thought he was playing it up *too* much, and Steve and I had to reassure him.

Because the pace of bringing a show to Broadway is frenetic (music and script changes are made and rehearsed right up until the hour of the first performance), actors in a show have very little time off—especially during the first few weeks of a run.

Since a cast recording must reflect those last-minute changes, it's usually made during the first week of the opening. And if the show is a runaway hit, you want the album to be on the shelves as quickly as possible.

That is why Broadway cast albums are usually recorded in a single day.

The practice dates to the late 1940s, when producer Goddard Lieberson (then president of Columbia Records) began recording shows like *South Pacific* and *My Fair Lady*. Back then, the cast would get a day off to record the entire album, for which they'd receive one week's salary.

The limited time allowed for recording can cause considerable pressure and anxiety. It's easy to fall behind when you're packing so much work into such a short amount of time, so I map out trouble spots before we begin and parcel our time out carefully.

I start by seeing the show.

If I'm scheduled to record a show, I try to watch as many previews as possible. I'll also try to see the play two or three times after opening night. It might sound excessive, but I've got to understand the author, composer, lyricist, and director's concept of the show before I can determine what portions of it will work for the recording.

Before I produced the off-Broadway cast recording of *Little Shop of Horrors* in 1982, I spent almost two months watching the play. At the time, the production was tiny: it was housed in a small theater on Second Avenue, and the pit "orchestra" consisted of only three musicians. During those preview sessions, Howard Ashman, Alan Menken and I sat and made judicious cuts for the recording. Making cuts is *always* difficult; the cooperation and consent of the writers, producer, and director are essential.

Since my production coordinator Jill Dell'Abate must painstakingly block out the entire day of recording segment by segment, she often joins me for the prerecording previews. With all of the singers, dancers, and actors involved in a Broadway production, the scheduling of meal breaks and such must occur so as to maximize the use of the talent we've got access to from eight in the morning to eleven at night.

When I record a show, I record the first run-through from start to finish. Then, I do at least two full takes on every number. I'm also a believer in playbacks; the actors should have the opportunity to feel the rhythm and hear the voice. I love getting the cast hyped up about what we're doing.

In addition to conceptual and interpretive changes, there are certain technical considerations that accompany the recording of a cast album.

First, the pit orchestra often needs expansion.

What sounds pleasing in the theater can sound thin in front of the microphones, and adding two cellos, two violas, and some extra woodwinds gives the recording a much richer sound. I often bring in a spare trumpet player for the long day of recording, too.

There's an art to physically arranging the cast in the studio, too.

Actors are accustomed to using their bodies while singing, and you can't restrain that. They have to be comfortable and feel as though they're on the performance stage.

For this reason, I like to put the whole cast in the back end of the studio so they can have a clear view of the conductor and the band. I'll put up some screens, but everyone should be able to see the conductor on the podium. If arranging the studio that way is impractical, we'll set up a video monitor to make him visible to the entire cast.

It's also important for me to remind the solo singers that singing into a microphone is much different than projecting their voice in the theater.

The seminal stage musicals of the 1940s and '50s (such as Rodgers and Hammerstein's *Oklahoma!, Carousel,* and *South Pacific*) contained songs that had simple inner rhythms. The lyrics weren't crowded together, which helped the actors articulate (and audiences hear) the words more clearly.

Today the lyrics come fast and furious.

Contemporary composers and lyricists such as Stephen Sondheim, Andrew Lloyd Webber, Stephen Schwartz (*Godspell, Pippin),* Jonathan Larson (*Rent*), Marc Shaiman *(Hairspray),* Robert Lopez and Jeff Marx (*Avenue Q*), and Elton John, Tim Rice, and Lee Hall (*Aida, Billy Elliot*) all write with far greater rhythmical and lyrical complexity than their predecessors. Singers and dancers, therefore, make enunciation and articulation a priority.

This is when striking a balance is imperative.

What point would it serve to rein in a dynamic actor like Hugh Jackman?

When he goes for the big notes, I want him to pull from the bottom of his body to reach them. I give the performer plenty of room to work, and set things technically to deal with the energy being directed at the microphone.

How does recording a cast album in the digital realm differ from the way we did it in the 1960s?

Not all that much. Digital is well suited to recording cast albums, because it gives us more room on the hard drive, and we can make far better edits. But we still record everything in one day.

As I mentioned, Broadway cast albums are recorded soon after opening night, and the cast has gone through a grueling month to reach that point.

It may look like they're fresh, but the truth is, when a show opens, the cast is usually worn out. When they come in to record they frequently have sore throats, colds, and other maladies that they've been able to prevent up to opening night.

It's frustrating that there isn't more time allotted to either break up the sessions or permit an actor to come back in for retakes. Why shouldn't they have a chance to fix small mistakes? A performance of the show is fleeting; the cast recording will stand for all time.

You'd be surprised at what a little breathing room can do.

In London, the producer of a cast recording has almost unlimited access to the cast and plenty of time to work. Recording isn't confined to a single day.

I recently recorded the London cast of Elton John's *Billy Elliot,* and the absence of time constraints made working on it a pleasure.

The first Broadway cast recording I produced was *Promises, Promises* in 1968. The show was a musical adaptation of Billy Wilder's *The Apartment,* starring Jill O'Hara and Jerry Orbach; Burt Bacharach and Hal David wrote the score. The show's best-known song, "I'll Never Fall In Love Again," helped immortalize the production, making it an indelible part of the Broadway firmament.

Although I won my second Grammy for the cast recording of *Promises, Promises*, the show has special meaning for me because of my work on its sound production.

As Burt and Hal discovered, the sound inside of a Broadway theater left much to be desired. After a few acoustically dismal rehearsals, they stopped by A&R with a proposal. "Can you help us give audiences inside of the Shubert Theater the kind of sound they're accustomed to hearing on a stereophonic record?"

As I'm sure you realize by now, I'm an inveterate problem solver, and I instantly took Burt and Hal up on their offer.

To meet the challenge Don Frey, Hank Cattaneo, Jim Scherer,

and I set out to do something for the theater that it long deserved: let the music enhance the visuals without overpowering them. "Why not swaddle the audience in sound, the way Walt Disney did with *Fantasia?*" we asked.

The goal was ambitious, and achieving it required us to do something that wasn't ordinarily done with theater acoustics: combine reverberation and direct sound.

Our approach was practical, rather than theatrical.

First, we analyzed the acoustics in the Shubert Theater using measuring devices and techniques that had never been used inside of a theater before. The process we used was called Acousti-Voicing.

The testing involved placing a microphone sixteenth row-center, where it picked up high and low frequency noise emitted by the test speakers. The sonic information captured by the microphone allowed us to chart the precise frequency response at each point in the room.

Then, we designed a system that relied on speaker placement to create the illusion that sound was coming at you (the audience member) from the stage. The system incorporated a set of graphic equalizers, twenty-four amplifiers, one hundred and eighty microphones, eighteen Altec speakers, a custom built Langevin broadcast board, and an EMT reverb plate.

A sound engineer manned the mixing board in the rear of the theater; he controlled the reverb and equalization, and fed the audio signal to the speakers scattered throughout the theater.

I designed a customized acoustic orchestra pit with a ceiling and sound baffles between sections of the orchestra—and added a vocal group in the pit. This was the first of its kind.

Any acoustician looking at the system we devised for *Promises, Promises* would have been perplexed, because the equipment employed wasn't designed for what we were doing. The techniques may have been radical for Broadway, but they worked. Soon, sound designers and audio technicians from the surrounding theaters came in, and when they heard how the system sounded, began adopting our methods in their own venues.

With ticket prices exceeding a hundred bucks apiece, theater patrons now demand that the sound they hear in the theater equals or bests the quality of the story, songs, and acting.

Today, theater soundboards rival those found in the studio, and each actor—as well as every instrument in the pit—has their own microphone. Where we once hid wired condenser microphones inside of sets and props, wireless mikes are now integrated into the actors' costumes, hair, and makeup, and are virtually invisible.

While sound historically took a back seat to the visuals in a stage production, sound design has become an integral part of the Broadway experience.

None of what we accomplished with *Promises, Promises* would have worked without the faith that David Merrick, Burt Bacharach, and Hal David had in us. I enjoyed the break that designing multimedia productions and theater sound gave me, and the opportunities it provided for me to prove my theory that no obstacle was too big to overcome.

With Liza Minnelli
Phil Ramone Collection

The Broadcast

I'm not ashamed to say that television has been my greatest teacher.

In the mid-1950s, I entered and won on Ted Mack's *Original Amateur Hour*—the *American Idol* of its day—and became a frequent guest on *Family Hour*, Mack's Sunday night television program. Back then I was billed as "Phil Ramone—the Velvet Tone."

Being involved with Ted Mack and his traveling show was invaluable for a kid like me. The old vaudevillians had learned all sorts of tricks, which they generously passed along.

"When you leave the stage, keep one foot outside the curtain so the audience knows that if they applaud enough you'll come back for an encore," they would say. Or, "You're stepping out of the spotlight when you deliver your punch line—don't do that!"

Whenever I produce a stage or television show, I still tell the performers, "Look directly at the audience, and don't forget the balcony. The camera will love it."

Sound has historically been given the short shrift on television productions. Twenty or thirty years ago the thinking was, "It's coming from a tiny monophonic speaker. How good does it have to be?"

Those days are over.

Home theater setups with big screens and surround sound have become the focal point of home entertainment, and people want high-quality music programming. Whether they're watching a sit-com, variety show, music special, or feature film, today's viewers have high expectations for the audio that accompanies the visual part of a program.

I never took the low road when it came to audio for video. Every television show to which I contributed became a new opportunity to elevate the quality of the sound.

Few artists appreciated my efforts more than Liza Minnelli.

Liza and I met in 1972, when she was preparing to do *Liza with a "Z"*—a legendary television special in which choreographer Bob Fosse had Liza sing and dance live. The show was filmed on 16mm film before an invited audience at Broadway's Lyceum Theater, but it was performed from start to finish with no breaks or editing.

I came into the production because some of Liza's dancing was strenuous, and Fosse wanted to prerecord several of the songs. He didn't want it to seem as though she were struggling to sing and dance at the same time, but he was adamant about not wanting it to appear that Liza was lip-synching, either.

I saw immediately how instinctive a performer Liza was, and it gave me an idea. Why not prerecord the songs, and use a combination of the prerecordings and Liza singing live? There were physically demanding moments—when Liza was dancing—where prerecording her vocals would be helpful. But when she wasn't dancing, she could sing live with ease. The difficulty in executing the plan was in finding a microphone that could be secreted inside Liza's provocative dress.

As Liza recalls, the weeks leading up to the filming were full of anxiety:

"Halston designed my costumes, and we weren't sure that the

standards and practices people would allow them to be seen on television. We rehearsed for seven or eight weeks, and Bob Fosse insisted on filming it live. He also insisted that no one—not NBC, or Singer [our sponsor]—would see anything before the night of the performance.

"Somehow, on the day of the show, a lady from the network censorship department got into the theater and saw the *Cabaret* sequence. 'Stop!' the censor lady said. 'You can't wear those costumes—you're practically naked.'

"My dress was cut rather low, and there wasn't a bra within fifty miles. Bob Fosse and Fred Ebb took her into an office, and when they returned I said, 'Is it all right for me to wear these costumes?' 'Yes—the censorship lady said it's fashion.'

"It was Phil's idea to use a wireless radio mike, but it required a cable and a transmitter to work. But the microphone, cable, and transmitter box all had to be hidden inside that skimpy red dress! Phil somehow figured out how to use a small transmitter, and how to run the wire up through my stockings and into the transmitter, which was in the small of my back. I kept it on through the whole show, but it was only turned on for the first dance set."

Bob Fosse was skeptical when I explained my plan to combine lip-synching with live performances. "Liza and I will practice," I said, "and then we'll run through the number with you. If you can tell the difference between when she's singing live and when I'm covering her with the prerecording, I'll agree that she should lip-synch the entire show."

We prerecorded the numbers, and I placed a microphone inside the chest of Liza's costume. She and I rehearsed so that when she was coasting she'd sing live, and when she was dancing full out I could fade up the prerecorded vocal track so she could lip-synch. I said, "When it comes to a part where you're singing live, slam the mike on your chest with your hand so it bangs—that way people will know it's live."

As Liza later said:

"Bob Fosse told me, 'Oh, I don't know if we can do this.' So we did a test: when Phil signaled me from the back, I would stop singing and my prerecorded voice would come on but my mouth would keep moving. Phil figured out how it went from playback to real voice and back again without the audience ever knowing it, and they were sitting right there. It had never been done before. Bob Fosse couldn't tell the difference. It was a time in our lives when Phil and I were both starting out, and were in top form."

Liza with a "Z" won four Emmys and a Peabody Award, but for years remained a cult classic—the kind of show that cabaret fans raved about but the mainstream audience forgot.

Then, in 2000, Liza's friend Michael Arick—a film editor and restoration expert—located the original film and multitrack audio tapes, and digitally restored them to reflect the vibrancy of the performance we saw in the theater on the night of May 31, 1972. Cleaned up and remixed for 5.1 surround, *Liza with a "Z"* looks and sounds more brilliant than ever.

Another close friend who I've worked frequently with on television productions is Elton John.

Elton and I met when I engineered and produced his first live broadcast in America, which aired on New York's WABC-FM

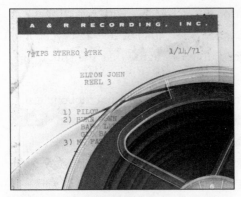

Original tape box and reel for Elton's
WABC Radio concert of 11-17-70
Phil Ramone Collection

(WPLJ) on November 17, 1970. The concert—hosted by Dave Herman—was part of a series that included performances by B.B. King, Aretha Franklin, Procol Harum, Don McLean, and the Allman Brothers.

We broadcast the shows from A&R Studio A1 on Seventh Avenue, in front of a small, invited audience. The concerts were informal, and I tried to create a casual atmosphere by putting up stage lights with colored gels, scattering overstuffed throw pillows on the floor, and passing around some wine. It was cozy, and the audience loved being part of it.

Stereo radio was in its infancy in 1970, but there was a small contingency of rock-and-roll loyalists who routinely taped FM stereo simulcasts at home on sophisticated reel-to-reel equipment. When bootleg albums of the Elton John show appeared shortly after the concert aired, Elton's record company (MCA) decided to release it officially as *11-17-70*.

While he admits to being impatient with recording live for broadcast, Elton understands the imperfection of taping a radio or television show:

"There's a hell of a lot to do behind the scenes when you're recording live," he explains. "You're conscious of the fact that you're being recorded. It's complicated enough doing a studio album, but

With Elton John
Phil Ramone Collection

getting everyone to sound good—and getting everything to come up through the [mixing] board for a live show—is a miracle. There are so many things that can go wrong at a live gig, but I don't have to worry about the recording, because I know that Phil has all of the technical problems under control."

I didn't think we'd ever get past the dress rehearsal for Elton's *One Night Only* concert, recorded at Madison Square Garden in 2000.

There was a lot of movement in the lights, and Elton wasn't pleased with the set design. But the lights and other details that Elton complained about were things he could see. What he *couldn't* see was the chaos unfolding in the recording truck: The computer on the mixing board had frozen in the middle of a song.

Once the computer crashed, we were unable to change anything in the mix. Fortunately, our mix—especially Elton's vocal— was in great shape, and the frozen board was still passing the audio signal through to the recorders. Because of the crew's quick response, nothing was lost—and a catastrophe was avoided.

No one expected what came next.

Halfway through the show, Elton made an announcement: *"This will be my last performance."*

We were stunned.

After completing the concert Elton went backstage, packed up, and left the Garden. I was in the recording truck, so I didn't get the chance to speak to him after the show. When I saw him later, I didn't mention my concern.

Moments like this create drama, and the crew was anxious.

"Are we here tomorrow?" they asked.

"Are you booked for tomorrow?" I sputtered. "You'll be here! And trust me: if Elton's not here, the show will be quite dull."

The next day, the lighting and set were redesigned, the tempos adjusted, and the audio problems corrected. Elton was placated, and the show went on without incident.

Somewhere in the middle of the concert—at roughly the same point as the night before—Elton again addressed the audience. "Last night I said I wasn't going to do this anymore," he said. "I was full of shit!"

Everyone was nervous because we had committed to delivering *One Night Only* within a week of the concert's recording. We did the run-through on Friday, taped on Saturday night, began mixing at eight o'clock Sunday morning, and did all of the editing and mastering between Monday and Thursday. We delivered the album at the end of the week; by the following Tuesday, it was in the stores.

If *One Night Only* tested our skill, we were pushed to the limit when we recorded Elton's shows at Radio City Music Hall in June 2004.

The Radio City gig wasn't a typical Elton John event.

Instead of a hits-packed concert, Elton tailored the engagement to include early songs that he rarely performed live. It was refreshing and indicative of the uncanny knack Elton has for reinventing his live shows.

The concerts had four separate musical components for our engineers to deal with: Elton (piano and vocals), his band, a sixty-voice gospel choir, and an eighty-piece symphony orchestra. Leakage is one thing; having all of these disparate musical groupings on one stage with Nigel Olsson and the band playing right next to them is quite another!

In all we had 104 channels of audio being fed via fiber-optic line from the stage to the two recording trucks parked near the stage door on Fifty-first Street. In one truck, engineer John Harris was receiving and mixing the choir and strings (each violin, viola, and cello was miked individually, under the instrument's tailpiece), and feeding his mix to the second truck.

Back in the second truck (the control center), Frank Filipetti was mixing Elton and the band, while adding in John Harris's orchestra and choir mix from the first truck. Balancing the strings

with piano and vocals—and a rock band on top of it all—was mon-
umental. If Audio-Technica hadn't generously sent over all the extra
microphones, we might not have heard the strings at all.

The beauty of mixing a show like Elton's Radio City concert in
5.1 surround sound is that it allows us to purposefully design the
mix to make the listener feel as though they're sitting in a certain
spot in the venue. I think it's cool to bring the listener onto the
stage, giving them the sense that he or she is standing right next to
Elton and his piano. There's something about that close proximity
that allows for a lot of detail to be heard—detail that you would
never hear if you were watching the concert in a big arena.

I'd be remiss if I didn't mention the satisfaction I've gotten from
working on the annual Grammy Awards telecast.

What began in the late 1950s as a small industry-only affair held
at a Los Angeles hotel has become a grand production enjoyed by
millions of people the world over.

Grammy producers Pierre Cossette, John Cossette, Ken
Ehrlich, and director/producer Walter Miller consistently produce
a program that's both entertaining and reflective of the Academy's
commitment to the musical arts and sciences, and I'm especially
proud of the Recording Academy's contribution to television sound
production. We were the first awards show to broadcast in high-
definition, and to present a 5.1 surround-sound program on network television.

When we began broadcasting the Grammys in 5.1, the response
was very positive. We've gotten to the point where we can receive
e-mails from viewers while the show is in progress. "The left side
sounds like it's a bit lower than the right. Should it be that way?"
and "The applause is coming from behind me—should it be that
way?"

It was thrilling to communicate with viewers who are mindful of
the technical feat behind what we've done. "Yes—the soundstage is
correct," I explain as they send in their questions. "We've set your

listening position at tenth row center, about fifty feet in the air. But you'll notice that we sometimes bring you closer to the stage, too."

We've come a long way from the mono sound of my youth, and it's hard to believe that while I'm standing amidst a full orchestra onstage at the Staples Center or Radio City that the multidimensional sound I'm enjoying is also being experienced by millions of people listening in the comfort of their homes.

When I began my career as a recording engineer, mixing in surround for television was considered space-age technology—and light-years ahead of its time. I'm ecstatic that it's become a reality, and that it's affordable for the average consumer. More than this, I'm thrilled to be using it to produce music programming that allows everyone—regardless of time, place, or financial means—to hear it in all of its full-dimensional glory.

What's New?

I'll do anything to make a record sound better.

As a young engineer, I vowed to fight the limits of the existing technology and break the recording traditions that everyone had gotten to know. My mind-set hasn't changed.

I'm *still* excited when I have the chance to test-drive an experimental format, or put a new piece of equipment through its paces. But the truth is that the equipment used to make a record isn't nearly as important as how the engineer and producer use it.

Today, we can do miraculous things digitally, with the click of a mouse—things that were difficult (if not impossible) to do in analog. I saw the potential in digital recording and embraced it from the start.

The earliest digital recordings I made were in 1980 for Billy Joel's *Songs in the Attic,* a collection of live recordings. The idea was to present a handful of tunes from Billy's first four albums—records that while less than perfect in their production contained some of his most expressive songs.

We recorded Billy in a variety of settings—from clubs to arenas—on an early 32-track 3M digital machine that I dubbed "the DC-10" (a notoriously unreliable airplane). We mixed some of the album at RPM Studios, and the rest in a mobile recording truck rented from Le Mobile, parked in the driveway of my home in Pound Ridge, New York.

It was only a matter of time before Hollywood went digital, and the format won a starring role when I supervised the final mixes for Barbra Streisand's *Yentl* in 1983.

The story (based on *Yentl, The Yeshiva Boy* by Isaac Bashevis Singer) is about a young Jewish girl in nineteenth-century Poland who has but one purpose: to attend religious school—a privilege that at the time was afforded only to Orthodox males.

The property couldn't have been better suited to Barbra's many talents, not the least of which were producing and directing. As lyricists Marilyn and Alan Bergman explain, "Barbra brings to anything she sings passion, intelligence, and vocal brilliance. In the case of *Yentl,* she performed with a total understanding of and immersion in the character."

The recording truck used to mix *Songs in the Attic,* "Camp Ramone," 1981. The Necam computer mainframe was run from the truck to the garage, where it could be kept cool in the summer heat.
Courtesy of Larry Franke

The complete score—instrumentals and vocals—was prerecorded on analog tape at Olympic Studios in London, with Michel Legrand conducting. Once the picture was shot, Barbra lip-synched to the tracks that had been prerecorded in London.

But after the film was edited, Barbra heard about the new twenty-four-track digital recorder (model PCM3324) that Sony had manufactured, and she wanted to try it.

Since the movie was finished (and had been shot to Barbra's analog vocal prerecordings), it was decided that Michel Legrand would go back to Olympic Studios and rerecord the instrumental score on digital tape, conducting to Barbra's existing analog vocal track. Remember: Vocals for film are usually sung to a prerecorded music track, if not live with the orchestra. What Michel was asked to do was very unusual—and difficult.

The rerecordings were made on an empty soundstage with only the musicians and technicians in the room; the digital rerecording of the orchestra was glorious. There was none of the noise of the previous version, and no analog tape hiss. But when Barbra listened to the new mix—a combination of her original analog vocals and Michel's new digital instrumental tracks—she wasn't pleased. "That's not how the orchestra phrased the score the first time," she said.

We put up the analog instrumental tracks from the first sessions, and compared them to the digital rerecordings. Barbra was right: at some points, the tempos in the digital rerecordings were slightly different than on the original analog recording, and I understood why.

Just as Barbra phrases differently from take to take, Michel Legrand feels a piece of music differently each time he conducts it. While his new score matched Barbra's vocal, the small (but perceptible) variations in tempo upset her.

"I want the *exact* orchestral note that we hear on the original analog recording to land in the *exact* same spot on the digital rerecording," she said.

When the session masters were delivered to me at M-G-M in Culver City, I received three different sources with which to make our mix: the twenty-four-track analog recording of the score, the twenty-four-track digital rerecording of the score, and the analog recording of Barbra's voice.

Accomplishing this in Pro Tools today would be a snap; we can easily move one section of the recording (a vocal) forward or backward until it precisely matches another (the orchestra).

But creating a hybrid mix from analog and digital sources at the beginning of the digital age was tedious.

We could edit the analog tape with a razor blade and splicing tape, but cutting digital tape could get you into deep trouble. The only way to accomplish digital editing was to use the same technique used for videotape editing, which involved making a copy of a copy to edit.

Integrating individual bars of music from the digital tape into the new analog master was time-consuming: It took nearly two hours to edit and capture sixteen bars of music. The master film for one particular song was shot at the incorrect frame rate, which affected the pitch of Barbra's vocal, and it took me a week to get that one song into acceptable shape.

The engineer who had done the original recordings at Olympic in London came to Los Angeles to assist us, but quit after two weeks. I don't think he anticipated the insanity of what we wanted him to do. "I can't do this," he complained. "I already did the job in London—I won't do it again."

I called Jim Boyer and asked him to fly in from New York.

As Jim remembers:

"Phil called, and said, 'I need you to come out here—now.' I went directly to the studio as soon as I arrived. We had a system: Phil worked in Culver City with Barbra, while I synchronized and edited the tapes at Lion Share Studio in Los Angeles.

"Engineering-wise I'd never seen anything like it," Boyer continues. "We were distilling both analog and digital media to a single analog master—for film and record. There was no time-code (the industry standard for linking multiple tracks together so they line up exactly), so we substituted a sixty-cycle tone to help synchronize the vocals to the music tracks.

"One of the pitfalls of the early digital technology was editing; they hadn't yet developed computerized digital editing, so we used a razor blade to make the edit. But you couldn't cut the tape or take it apart more than twice or it became unusable. We were constantly making safeties and backups so we could edit the digital tapes.

"I was blown away by Barbra's memory; we had dozens of tapes, and she could remember specific words and phrases that she wanted from each in the final take. It was awesome—scary, really. When we matched the vocals to the printed music score, the unfolded vocal take sheet was the size of the console. This was before automation—if you didn't write it down, it didn't get remembered. It was the beginning of the digital age and Barbra, Phil, and Columbia Records wanted to be in on it."

Here's how a typical *Yentl* day unfolded:

Barbra and I would work on remixing the film soundtrack at M-G-M in Culver City from eight a.m. to six p.m. We worked straight through with very few breaks. Then, we'd get in the car and drive to Lion Share Studio in Hollywood, where we'd meet Jim Boyer and the Bergmans to mix the songs for the soundtrack album.

Marilyn and Alan Bergman were our guardian angels—they practically lived at Lion Share from the beginning to the end. They'd written the songs for the film, but the reasons for their presence ran much deeper: They were two of Barbra's closest friends. She trusted them implicitly, and they were coproducers on the picture.

The mixing sessions at Lion Share ran until two a.m., and afterward I'd drive Barbra home. She'd unfailingly chide me for driving too slow. *"C'mon, c'mon—you can drive faster than this!"* she'd urge as the car wound its way toward Beverly Hills.

After dropping her off, I'd head back to my hotel, knowing that in a precious few hours we'd be off to Culver City and another eighteen-hour workday.

Once the mixes for the picture and album were done, we went to A&M to record studio versions of "The Way He Makes Me Feel" and "No Matter What Happens," which were arranged and conducted by Dave Grusin.

Yentl is as strong—theatrically, cinematically, and musically—as anyone could wish a movie to be. I won't soon forget the thrill of hearing Barbra hit and sustain a high D at the end of "A Piece of Sky" (the finale), or the elation I felt when she and I cut it to picture and watched it together.

Looking back, I'm not sure how Jim Boyer and I functioned— let alone survived. One night Jim left the studio and walked into the Beverly Hilton with a fifteen-foot piece of two-inch recording tape stuck to his shoe. He was so tired it took him a few minutes to realize why everyone was staring as he crossed the lobby.

Not long after I began working on *Yentl*, fellow producer Tom Dowd visited me. When he looped back through Hollywood a few months later, he was shocked to find that I was still at it. "Phil, you look green," he said. "I've made two albums in the last three months, and you're still sitting in the same damned chair!"

Although the original masters were analog, it was a real kick when CBS/Sony chose Billy Joel's *52nd Street* to be the very first commercial CD ever released.

When Sony asked me to remaster the album for that first CD, I insisted on replicating the original two-track mix that Jim Boyer and I had made for the original LP. I didn't want to use the LP assembly master that contained EQ and other processing; I wanted the first-generation multitrack mixdown tape, so I asked Columbia to give me the tape I'd originally handed in so we'd have prime sources for remastering. Even though Sony was their Japanese partner, CBS was reluctant to let the tape out, and agreed to do so only when I promised to carry it to and from Japan myself (it stayed on my lap the whole time).

52nd Street packed a solid punch, and the CD remaster we did in Japan sounded much better than the LP, with improved clarity and strikingly deep bass. People don't understand the physical limitations of vinyl, but we could never have translated the deep bottom end we heard on the master tape to an LP. Going from LP to CD was like going from black-and-white TV to color.

During my trip to Japan, I spent a lot of time with Sony executive Norio Ohga. Ohga gave me a CD player, and when I got back to the States I took the player and the *52nd Street* CD to WPLJ-FM in New York and asked if they'd listen to the new format. They played a couple of the CD tracks on the air, and the telephones started to ring.

"Why does what you are playing sound so much better?" callers asked. Even with all of the wires, antennae, compressors, and transmitters that an FM radio signal goes through, people could hear the difference.

Another example of how technology can be adapted to what we do in the studio is the EDNet fiber-optic system—a digital cable system that transmits high-fidelity sound from one studio to another using sophisticated telephone links, and Dolby encoders and decoders.

When I started talking about using fiber-optic phone lines to make Frank Sinatra's *Duets*, my colleagues thought I was crazy. My response was, "The technology is there to serve. Why not use it?" With EDNet, a producer can record an orchestra in New York, a vocalist in California, and background singers in Chicago—all at the same time. How could that be bad?

The question I debated when considering the use of EDNet on *Duets* was "Can I make it easier for Frank Sinatra to be in the studio, and have a good time?"

Don't forget: Practically everything Sinatra did in his career was live. Even his studio sessions were recorded live with the band, in front of a small, invited audience. In his prime, Sinatra was the guy who said, "If we can't get it within the first few takes, there's something wrong with us." His commitment to excellence taught me a valuable lesson about immediacy, and from the moment I met and worked with him in 1967 it became the core of my work ethic.

Recording Sinatra's *Duets* wasn't just about technology—it was about how to get the other performers attuned to *his* style of singing. I tried to make it as easy as possible for them to harmonize with Frank, even though he wasn't in the room.

I created lyric sheets that broke down every line, so we could map out which lines the duet partner would sing (it's something I do for all the duets I record). We adjusted the orchestrations in some spots, because when one vocalist sings to another vocalist's prerecorded track the keys don't always match. I remember Natalie Cole saying, "I thought I could just phrase with him so easily—it took me a half hour to figure it out." Sinatra did musical things that no one had ever thought to do.

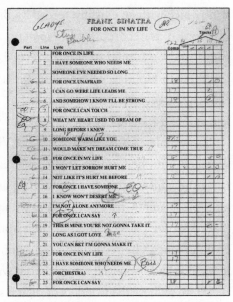

Original lyric leadsheet for Gladys Knight–Frank Sinatra recording, *Duets,* 1993
Phil Ramone Collection

When you tell someone, "You're going to sing a duet with Frank Sinatra," they say, "Wow! Thank you!" The magic moment was when they first heard his voice—the most incredible voice of any time—coming into their headphones. Imagine a twenty-two-year-old rookie ballplayer stepping out onto the field for the first time with one of their boyhood idols. No matter who you were, Sinatra made you feel like a rookie again.

I flew to Detroit to record Aretha Franklin, because she wanted to be looking at me when she sang to Sinatra's vocal. The first time I played his recording of the song it frightened her. "Can I do this?" she asked. "Of course you can," I assured her. Few artists respect talent as much as Aretha does, and that made it a beautiful affair. After she finished adding her part she said, "I need to write Frank a letter to let him know how much I love this." "Why don't you tell him on tape?" I suggested. "It'll mean so much more if he can hear it from you."

Taking the duets idea a step further, Danny Bennett—Tony's son and manager—called me in 1997 and asked if we could pair his dad's voice with an existing record by Billie Holiday.

Tony was recording *On Holiday*, a tribute album of Billie's songs, and he wanted to end the record by singing, "God Bless the Child" with Holiday, who had died in 1959. The problem was that Billie never recorded the song in stereo, so there was no way to isolate and extrapolate her vocal.

Columbia A&R man Don DeVito wasn't deterred, and searched until he found a 16mm film featuring Billie singing "God Bless the Child" from the 1940s. The arrangement was sparse (piano, bass, guitar, trumpet, and sax), and the rhythm section was placed so far back in the mix that you could barely hear Count Basie's piano. The recording's redeeming factor was the vocal: Billie's voice had been well miked, and it was clear.

Here's where the wonders of digital sound restoration came into play.

First, we cleaned the film's audio track by transferring it to digital and processing it through CEDAR and Sonic Solutions noise reduction systems. These computer programs miraculously remove the ticks, pops, hisses, and clicks from vintage discs, tapes, and films, and they worked wonders with the Billie Holiday soundtrack.

Then, I asked arranger Rob Mounsey to help identify and isolate as many of the instrumental notes in the original film performance as possible. Using digital equalization and phase controls, I found a way to reduce the frequencies of those notes so they were almost inaudible. What we were left with was Billie's voice with almost no music behind it.

Next, Rob transcribed the original arrangement, and we had a group of musicians play along with it in the studio. We followed the exact blueprint of the Basie chart, and rerecorded it honoring the integrity and tone of the film performance. We now had three separate elements to work with: Billie's cleaned vocal, the original Basie band performance, and the re-created (newly recorded) band performance.

The test was in mixing these three tracks together and overdubbing Tony's new vocal. In some spots we let Basie's piano dominate the mix, and in other spots (where the film had been damaged or the sound was distorted) we emphasized the new piano performance. In some places we removed Billie's voice to accommodate Tony's. We created a credible instrumental and vocal track using a monophonic film, a newly recorded band, and a live Tony Bennett vocal, enabling Tony to do something that he'd long dreamed of doing: sing a duet with Billie Holiday.

As with the Sinatra duets, I took some heat for the Bennett/Holiday recording. "Come and sing with your dead grandmother," someone joked. "Ramone will take care of you."

I stand by my assertion that restraining an artist or producer from using the technology creatively would be like telling George Lucas that using special effects in *Star Wars* was unacceptable because they weren't real.

Digital editing, mixing, and mastering systems like Pro Tools, Cue Base, and Nuendo have revolutionized the way records are made. Analog-to-digital conversion has become an art for some audio designers and manufacturers, and high-resolution (24-bit 96k) consoles like the Pro Tools ICON, Yamaha DM2000, or Euphonix System 5 with 166 inputs have supplanted our trusty forty-eight-track analog boards. A myriad of processing tools, and lightning-fast, high-capacity computers like the Apple G5 have helped computer hard drives replace analog and digital tape recorders.

One of the delights of working in the digital domain is the speed with which edits and fixes can be made. Recording and editing multiple takes on the spot gives the artist a very good idea of what the record will sound like before they leave the studio.

Fortunately, I've worked with many artists who developed their skills and work ethic before they had so many technological options. By and large, they're receptive to using technology to further their artistic vision—they don't lean on it to compensate for lack of preparation.

Tony Bennett—who began recording on monophonic analog tape—is an old-school performer who completely embraces new technology.

When we recorded *Playin' with My Friends: Bennett Sings the Blues*—a collection of duets with Diana Krall, B.B. King, Billy Joel, Kay Starr, Sheryl Crow, and a handful of others—Tony marveled at the swiftness with which we cut together a composite from multiple takes. The Sheryl Crow date stands out for me, because it illustrates how the technology makes recording more efficient.

Tony, Sheryl, and the accompanying jazz combo arrived at the Hit Factory in New York at six thirty on the appointed evening to record "Good Morning, Heartache," and from the first take it was apparent that Tony's and Sheryl's voices melded beautifully. As Sheryl caressed the melody, Tony sidled up to her at the mike;

their coziness made it sound like they'd been singing together for years.

As the takes progressed, I scribbled my impression of each performance on a legal pad. "The sax solo in takes three and six were the ones to remember," I told Joel Moss, the engineer. "And Tony's final verse sounded better in takes one, two, ten, and fourteen."

Sheryl's vocal became stronger as the evening wore on, but there was something special about her first few takes—the vocals were drenched with the pathos and vulnerability implied by the lyrics. These thoughts were duly noted.

By the fifteenth and final take, I had a definite idea of how I wanted to assemble the parts—a rough blueprint for editing and mixing the track. "So you're really going to sew all this together right now?" Tony asked when he came into the control room.

He'd learned the art of recording at the same time as I did—when we edited with a razor blade and splicing tape. But the wonders of digital make editing a snap, and within a few minutes Joel had a rough cut of "Good Morning Heartache" ready for Tony and Sheryl to hear.

Could I have accomplished the same thing by editing analog tape? Sure—I've done it thousands of times. The beauty of digital technology is that it enables me to edit faster and more precisely, and in this instance, let the artists leave the studio with a greater sense of satisfaction.

The advances in recording technology have been invaluable to artists, engineers, and producers, but what about the consumer?

Until recently, the record industry ignored Internet delivery because it was ill informed. I remember going to the labels with a group of fellow producers to convince them that the future of music was tied to the Internet, years before it took off. No one dreamed that the Internet could one day dominate the music market.

Some of us had enough faith in it.

In 1997, Larry Rosen, Jon Diamond, and Dave Grusin formed N2K Encoded Music—a company dedicated to bridging the gap between traditional (CD) and Internet delivery—and I was hired to head the music side of the company.

The goal of N2K was to link online technology to the music by encoding video material on the disc and allowing computer users to link directly to the N2K Web site, where they could download singles and hear exclusive concerts.

For the first few months, the video programming on N2K discs was encoded on CD-ROM, which was problematic because of glitches that arose on some computer platforms. After receiving hundreds of complaints from customers who couldn't access the CD-ROM material on our discs, it became clear that we needed a better format for encoding.

Knowing that DVD technology had been developed (and that the film studios were readying their catalogs for eventual DVD release), Larry and I approached the four major electronics manufacturers (Panasonic, Sony, Toshiba, and Mitsubishi), and asked them when they would have the technology to author and manufacture DVDs in place.

When they answered, "One year," we went off on our own to figure out how to author a glass master for DVD. This was a year before DVDs hit the market; there were no standards, and matching audio to video—and creating chapter titles and menu bars—was laborious and expensive. We ruined three glass masters (at a cost of $20,000 each) before we got it right.

The first N2K DVD music album was *Dave Grusin Presents West Side Story.* In addition to the two-track stereo mix, we included a 5.1 surround mix with video accompaniment.

N2K lasted only a short time, but during that time we were on the cusp of an audio-video revolution. We took a positive step forward at a time of technological uncertainty, and I'm proud to have been associated with it.

Audio and video technology continue to advance at a frightening pace; the changes we used to see over the course of a year now come within three to six months. It took years for the CD to replace the LP as the playback medium of choice, and now that it's so widely accepted, mainstream record buyers are hesitant to upgrade to a higher-resolution format. Will they someday replace their CD collections with high-resolution discs, chips, or memory sticks? And with the success of iPods and numerous downloadable music sites, will there even be a need for hard audio media in the future?

The future is here.

Digital streaming, computer downloading, and high-resolution A/V are the next wave in audio technology. While the DVD-Audio and Super Audio CD formats didn't catch on as expected, other high definition video formats like HD-DVD and Sony's Blu-ray Disc systems are beginning to hit the market.

In the last fifty years we've gone from mono to stereo to 5.1 surround sound, and even that is poised to change; soon, we may have 6.1, 7.1, and 8.1 home theaters.

Audio, video, and video gaming have all become part of the "family entertainment system," and each medium is racing to integrate technology from the others in an effort to create the definitive entertainment product. Sophisticated sound has even gone mobile: Recording engineer Elliott Scheiner recently developed a 5.1 surround system for Acura, and it's successful because the car is the place where many people are listening—and watching.

When I produce television or concert specials, I record them in surround—even if the initial product isn't planned as a 5.1 release.

For example, not long ago, Frank Filipetti and I taped Elton John's *Red Piano* show at Caesar's Palace in Las Vegas, and it was cut live to fifty separate tracks. In addition to the standard microphone setup, Frank used a Holophonic microphone: a large ball containing capsules on the top, bottom, and sides (three capsules in front for left, center, and right channel information; two capsules in the rear for left and right rear surround information; and one capsule each for the top and center rear channels).

Where does it end?

Just as the finest-grain film, the best lenses, and the most expensive camera can't condense the subtlest gradation of color seen by the eye into a photograph, a sound recording—analog or digital—can't give you a flawless reproduction of what you'd hear if you were seated tenth row center at the performance. It can, however, proffer an approximation that's damned close—better, in some respects—and I'm glad to be living at a time when the technology to create the ultimate listening experience is seeking a new peak.

With Ray Charles, 1986
Courtesy of Sam Emerson/Redbox

Back to the Artist: Ray Charles
Genius Loves Company

As I said at the start, making records is all about the artist.

My life has been graced by a series of musical bookends, and I'm pleasantly surprised at how people from my past seemed to wend their way back into my life. I first engineered for Frank Sinatra in 1967, and produced his last two albums in 1993 and 1994. Elton John and I met during a live radio broadcast in 1970 and we're still at it, recording live shows in New York, London, and Las Vegas. Then, there's a man who's influenced more styles of music than any other artist I know—Ray Charles.

When Atlantic Records released *The Genius of Ray Charles* in 1959, people stopped to listen. It wasn't an R&B album, nor a jazz album, or even rock and roll. It was a mercurial blend of all three, and with it Ray Charles annihilated tradition.

I felt special, because I'd witnessed the fury he unleashed

on "Alexander's Ragtime Band," "Don't Let the Sun Catch You Cryin'," and "Let the Good Times Roll" firsthand in the studio, before anyone else heard the full thrust of musicians from the Basie and Ellington bands, plus Ray's own powerhouse rhythm section.

Ray's impeccable musicality was impressive; he could hear mistakes in the arrangement that no one else would ever pick up on. "No—I want dotted eighth notes there," he'd say, or, "Hold on! That second trumpet should be B-flat at the start of the verse, and Mr. Tenor Man—your note should be a G. The chord is a G-seventh." All of us marveled at his aural acuity.

The sessions for *The Genius of Ray Charles* were one of the first times I'd seen a real audience in the recording studio. Normally, Ray and his piano would have been positioned in the center of the room, with his band behind him. On these dates, he was pressed right up against the control-room window glass—that's how many people were crammed into the studio. Until that night, I'd admired Ray, and thought of him as a fine R&B singer in the tradition of Big Joe Turner and the other luminaries recording for Atlantic. That album turned my head, and my admiration into love.

Ray and I met briefly again in 1987 when Ray and Billy Joel recorded "Baby Grand," but other than seeing each other at some awards show or charity event, our paths hadn't crossed in years.

Then in June 2003, I produced the Songwriter's Hall of Fame show and one of the honorees was Van Morrison. When I called Van and told him the news, he said, "I won't come all the way from Ireland unless you get me the one guy I've wanted to meet in my life, and that's Ray Charles." I knew that it would be an electrifying collaboration.

It took a bit of juggling to get Ray to New York, and their meeting is one of the most tender things I can ever recall happening at eight thirty in the morning! That night they sang "Crazy Love" on the show, and dazzled the audience.

The success of Ray and Van's performance prompted a conversation with John Burk and Hal Gaba at Concord Records, who'd been talking to Ray about the possibility of doing an album of duets. That started us rolling toward *Genius Loves Company*, Ray's final studio album, and the biggest-selling record of his career.

When John Burk and I met, he told me he'd made a conscientious decision to not make this an "electronic duets" album as I'd done with Sinatra *Duets*. "I have a definite mind-set for this project," John explained. "You really can't get that intangible quality when they're not singing together in the room. I want to get the guests in the room with Ray, partly because from a fan's perspective I just want to see what will happen."

Ray was frail.

Shortly before the project began, he was diagnosed with advanced liver disease, and the treatments he received were draining. Despite his weakness, Ray thrust himself into selecting the songs and musicians he wished to include on the album. We began with a list of potential partners, and whittled it down slowly.

In the beginning, we waited to see who Ray's people might be able to get, and I offered to troll for other artists. Once we had a list of guest artists and the songs they wished to sing, John Burk went back to Ray and said, "This artist would like to do this song with you."

It's been said that "the tree has many branches, and Ray controlled them all." He was truly all encompassing, and it was imperative that each guest artist be someone who made sense, and represented each of the genres that Ray was noted for. We didn't want the project to be gimmicky; we were looking for mutual respect.

We began with artists who had command over multiple genres, because Ray's attitude toward music was "There are no walls or limits," and the same principle applied to his guests. As Ray said, "I thought it was time to have some of the friends that I love and the artists I admire come into my studio to sing with me live, the way we did in the old days."

More than a year after first kicking the idea around I found myself sitting in Ray's studio at 2107 West Washington Boulevard in Los Angeles.

The place hadn't been touched since being completed in 1964; Peg-Board panels backed with fiberglass lined the walls, and the floor was made of old-fashioned asphalt tile—the kind that produces a funny "slap" echo. It was a nostalgic throwback to the studios of my youth.

It was Ray's favorite room. As he said, "This studio has given me twice as much pleasure as my house in Baldwin Hills."

He began building the studio in 1962.

"I liked the location," Ray explained. "People were trying to tell me to move to fancier areas like Beverly Hills, but why would I want to do that? What was wrong with a working-class black neighborhood? Why not put some money back into the community? Besides, the location was great. [It was] close to downtown, close to Hollywood, and a straight shot to the airport. The land was reasonable and because I'd designed the building myself, I knew it would fit me to a T."

The studio was especially comfortable for Ray because it was built with his disability in mind: He could manage the staircases and easily navigate through the rooms. He could walk in at any time, sit down at his keyboard, and get the sound he wanted. The main studio is forty-five by twenty-eight by twelve feet, and while the control room was tiny, it suited him. He loved to get in there and mix the records himself.

While I understood the sixties vibe, I knew I needed to modify the sound of the room the moment I walked in.

One of the first things I discovered was that the drum sounds were uncontrollable, so I sent out for a big, old-fashioned beach umbrella, lined it with acoustic foam, and positioned it directly over the drums (like you'd do if you were selling hot dogs at the beach). I also put some small screens around the front of the drum kit to keep leakage to a minimum. These things helped cut down on the reflection, and gave the drum sound better definition.

The room was dotted with the freestanding gobos—movable partitions—that acousticians of the sixties used to isolate one section of the studio from another. They were big and heavy, and they obstructed the musicians' view of each other. They didn't do much for me acoustically, so we removed them.

Since Ray's duet partners would be in the room recording alongside of him, we conformed our setup around Ray's. I was interested in having Ray play without headphones, so he'd hear the detail of the drums without a lot of reflection off the walls.

The first thing Ray said when I went out to say hello was, "How far is the drummer from me?" "He's in his usual place," I explained. "I moved him over a little bit, and put in an umbrella up to cut the reflection from the ceiling. It won't cut it down from a live point of view, but it'll keep the drummer out of the guitar and acoustic bass mikes."

A lot of people misunderstood Ray, and wrongly accused him of being a tyrant. "Impatient" would be a better way to describe Ray Charles. Most gifted people who've lost one of their senses (Ray, Stevie Wonder, singer Diane Schurr) move at a frightening pace—they can't sit around and wait. Part of their frustration is that when they hear a wrong note, they want it fixed immediately. With Ray, his musicians feared that he'd hear a wrong note and chastise them on the bandstand. It was true; he'd admonish someone in front of an audience if they weren't paying attention—he just wouldn't tolerate it.

While he was a stickler, Ray could be also quite flexible.

We were doing several songs that had long been associated with him, and at one point during the sessions he said to me, "You know I like to pull these tempos around." I said, "I've been meaning to ask you why you move the tempo around. You don't always play a song in the same tempo as we're accustomed to." "Listen to Count Basie," he explained. "He's the king."

When it came to recording *Genius Loves Company*, Ray was Mr. Charm.

The sessions weren't very long. We'd get Ray for an hour or two in the morning—maybe. Afterward, he'd leave for his treatment and physical therapy, have some lunch, and rest for an hour or two. A few times we rehearsed in the morning, and if he was feeling well enough, he'd come back to record in the afternoon.

Ray was decisive about who he chose to sing each song with him.

He was, for example, hesitant to include "You Don't Know Me" on the album. He wanted to be sure that whoever sang it with him hadn't had the song shoved down their throat.

"I'd love to have Diana Krall sing it with me," he said.

Since "You Don't Know Me" was on Diana's wish list, she got the honor.

In addition to being a singer, Diana Krall is a fine jazz pianist, and I wasn't sure whether she'd want to play as well as sing. She did not. That honor fell to Randy Waldman, and I remember that when he played some striking chords, Ray complimented him. "Wow— that's a great change. That's really clever."

When Ray and Diana Krall did their first run-through, he started singing and said, "Why don't you sing right here, daawl- ing?" Diana began, and in that inimitable voice Ray said, "Oh, that's so sweet!" When the run-through was over, she started apologizing for the sound of her voice. "I hope you understand—I'm not warmed up yet."

"Now stop worrying! That's not why we're here," Ray said, putting her at ease. The sweetness and courage he exuded didn't allow us to become overly intense. He had a way of shakin' it that said, "These are the good times." When Diana walked into the room, it was all about the two of them.

For "Fever" we didn't want to cut it like the Peggy Lee version, but some of the bass and drum breaks on Peggy's definitive record are practically part of the arrangement.

"Fever" is a playful song with sexual overtones, and it was well suited to Ray and Natalie Cole. It was the one song where we didn't have a man and woman singing toward each other in typical love-ballad fashion; it was more like the duets that Ray had done in the sixties with Betty Carter. "Fever" was coy and sassy, but it had humor—and both Ray and Natalie understood the humor of relationships.

I'm not going to tell you that the artists weren't nervous—we were all nervous. Why wouldn't we be? I'm used to that anxiety being a part of the process. When we were recording "Do I Ever Cross Your Mind," I said to Bonnie Raitt, "If you don't mind, this would be the time to play your guitar." I knew that Bonnie had loved the song since hearing it on Ray's *Modern Sounds in Country and Western Music.* She said, "Oh, well I'd rather overdub."

Bonnie told me that making a record with Ray had been a lifelong dream, and I sensed that she wasn't comfortable playing in front of him. "Bonnie, he's not going to criticize you. He's going to welcome the collaboration."

Ray was so excited about "Do I Ever Cross Your Mind" that he later said that Bonnie proved something he'd long believed: "Country and blues ain't just first cousins, they're blood brothers."

"Here We Go Again" was a treat. Norah Jones had burst onto the scene a couple of years before, and in a sense, she represented the "new guard." She had mentioned Ray's influence in several interviews, and you can hear it in her style.

As John Burk recalls, it was Norah who got a full taste of the real Ray Charles.

"The first time they met, I brought Norah up to Ray's office, and Ray went to the upright piano to show her how to approach the song," Burk explains. "He wanted her to do something different, and it was not at all what she was expecting. And she just took to it. It was heartening to see the master and the student, side by side, going into this collaboration on a song that was very different from what she and I both expected."

For me, the most riveting track on the album is Ray's duet with Elton John on "Sorry Seems to Be the Hardest Word." Both Elton and I had heard Ray perform the song at the NAMM tribute to Elton the year before, and we were floored. I wasn't surprised when Ray said it was the only song he wanted to do with Elton.

I made a cassette from the NAMM show and played it for Ray to remind him of how he'd played it then. He liked the arrangement, but he didn't like his vocal performance. "Let's get Elton in and we'll just sing to the instrumental track [from the show]." "No, no," I said. "We need fresh legs for this one. We'll cut it live from start to finish."

Arranger Victor Vanacore worked with Ray on the chart. When he was finished, Victor made a simple demo at his house so Ray would have an idea of the tempo, feel, and string parts. Ray had already given us tacit approval, which meant there didn't have to be a lot of discussion about the arrangement.

The instrumental track for "Sorry Seems to Be the Hardest Word" was recorded in two parts: a rhythm session and a string overdub session. Because I needed a large space for recording the strings, we went to Henson Studios for the tracking. The sound at

Henson has a lot of character. It's the old A&M Studio on La Brea, and hundreds of well-known records from the 1960s and '70s were made there.

It took all day to make the instrumental track, and Ray popped in during the afternoon. When I saw him, I never expected that he'd make it to the vocal session the next day. It was apparent that his health had plummeted in two weeks: He was fragile, and I suspected that the vocal date would be canceled.

I knew he was still on the ball when he listened to the playback and said, "That tempo's not 106." I told him that I was running the tempo at 105, 106, and 107 beats per minute. "Why are you doing that?" he asked. "I'm running it at all three tempos in case you change your mind about the tempo tomorrow," I explained. I saw his energy return. "There ain't gonna be no change of mind. Just let me hear it at 106."

The tempo was reset.

Ray listened and said, "That's it. I'll see you tomorrow."

Then he snuck out.

It was sad to see him leave, and I was uncertain that we'd ever see him again. I knew that Ray wanted it to happen, but there was clearly a chance that he wouldn't make the vocal date. When Ray started listening and getting fussy about the tempo, I thought we might still have a chance. I knew he wasn't going to let this one go.

The vocal session started at ten.

We were told that it was better to record Ray before noon, because of his physical therapy schedule. If all went well and he was able to rest after noontime, he might be able to come back at three. We were gambling. Would the ten- to one o'clock session give us enough time, or should we schedule the session for three? If we made it three and it didn't work, we might lose the song entirely. Both Elton and Ray then were in prime shape musically, but Ray wasn't in prime shape healthwise.

When Ray arrived and they led him into the Record Plant, I

gave the signal to begin recording. As I glanced at the console, I noticed that one of the assistants was fiddling with the balance, and I said to engineer Joel Moss, "Let's put the no-touch rule into effect. Hit the computer so it's recording, and just let it run. We might find out later that what we've got is awful, but it might be perfect." I wanted to catch everything that transpired between Elton and Ray; I didn't need anyone missing those magic moments.

Elton had arrived at eight thirty, and when Ray came in they sat and had tea, chatting for a while. It was Elton's way of preparing; he wanted Ray to walk into the room and feel the love and respect, and that's exactly what happened.

It was time to record.

I arranged it so that Elton and Ray would be three or four feet away from each other, face-to-face, because I wanted Ray to hear Elton acoustically and not through his headphones. They began their first run-through, discussing who was going to sing which line. "You sing this line . . ." "No, no, no—I think you should sing it, and I'll come back in here . . ."

Elton was being very careful. He looked at the lead sheets I had prepared and gingerly said, "Well, it says here . . ."

Ray pounced on that immediately. "Who said that?"

"I did, Ray," I interjected.

"Well how do you know that's what I want to do?" he asked, somewhat indignantly. I chuckled. "They're only suggestions—we can do whatever you'd like. Instead of us fishing for ideas, this is what I do. I start by suggesting certain vocal solos on some lines, harmonies on others."

Everyone in the room got the message right away: Getting the vocals laid down would be a one-shot deal. Ray said, "I'm ready to roll one." "Okay Ray, here we go." We rolled it, got a nearly flawless take, and then did one more for insurance. The final record is an edit of those two takes, and the wistful, melancholy tone of the recording speaks for itself.

By the end of the second take, all of us were in tears, but we wouldn't let Ray catch us crying. It was a bittersweet time in all of our lives—especially mine. After we were done, Ray waved to me, and I walked out to the studio and hugged him. He said, "I'm sorry—I'm really not feeling well today." They wheeled him down the hall and out into the warmth of the sun.

I never saw Ray again, but he heard the finished mix of the album. We recorded "Sorry Seems to Be the Hardest Word" on March 3; Ray died three months later, on June 10, 2004.

Recording with Ray deeply affected Elton, who took a CD of the entire session home so he could savor the conversation they'd shared. "When people mention Ray Charles, I just smile," Elton explained. "That grin, that voice, and his music are so joyous. It was amazing to sit in the studio and sing with him. It's incredibly impressive to be with someone whose music had meant so much to me.

Original track sheet for "Sorry Seems to Be the Hardest Word"
Phil Ramone Collection

He had a prodigious effect on my career, so it was a very emotional experience."

When Elton heard the first mix of the song, he noticed that one of the Pro Tools editors had eliminated a breath—a little gasp—and he said, "No, no, no. You don't take those things out. You may want it cleaner for some technical reason, but that's not what Ray and I want." When he heard the next mix, you could tell he was moved. Halfway through the song, I saw tears well up in his eyes. He turned to John Burk and me and quietly said, "This is one of the most meaningful moments of my recording career." For all of us, "Sorry Seems to Be the Hardest Word" became the ultimate metaphor, even though Bernie Taupin didn't write the lyric to reflect the end of someone's life. No one predicted that it would be the last thing that Ray would ever sing.

Genius Loves Company may have started out as a duets project, but it turned into something with far more intrinsic value. "All of these artists are friends of mine," Ray said. "It's been great, man, really great to be able to take these classic songs and get behind them in different ways. It's taken me back to my roots."

I'm not sure who first called Ray Charles a genius. It may have been Tom Dowd, or a marketing person at Atlantic Records. It could be argued that whoever chose the title *The* Genius *of Ray Charles* for the album of that name in 1958 was a tad overenthusiastic, and that Ray hadn't quite earned that status yet—at least with the public.

We insiders knew he was a genius the moment we saw him work. We knew he was a "musician's musician," and that his eclectic musical taste and fastidious approach were something quite special.

Being immersed in his musicality gave one a chance to learn; in this regard, he set the pace for us all. As I reflect on everything that accompanied *Genius Loves Company*, I think of something that Ray said once: "I've been makin' music since I was three. You hear about people saying they're gonna retire, but retire to what? I don't wanna do nothing but what I'm doing."

To be continued . . .

Kindred Spirits

With Charles L. Granata, NYC, 1999
Charles L. Granata Collection

I met Phil Ramone in 1998, when we appeared together on a speaking panel to discuss the music of Frank Sinatra.

Although *he* didn't know it, I felt like I'd known Phil for years.

At the time, I was writing and lecturing on the way Sinatra recorded his music; Phil was my subject's greatest living exponent. After one such discussion, I asked Phil if he would consider writing the foreword for a book I was writing on Sinatra's recording methodology. "Absolutely," he said. "Here's my number—call me, and we'll talk."

I called, we talked, and Phil's warm recollections helped get my Sinatra story off to a very good start. It was the beginning of a pleasant friendship.

Our collaboration on the Sinatra piece in September 1999 brought me to the Shire, the ten-acre farm in Bedford, New York, that was (until recently) the Ramone family's home. The visit offered my first glimpse of Phil's superb taste, and the tasteful way in which he lives his life.

Despite being a relative stranger, I was treated with warmth and graciousness.

It was pouring outside, and there was a fire burning in the main parlor. As I set up my tape recorder, a friendly woman with a thick Irish accent came in and asked if she could make me some lunch. Soon, a sandwich and a Coke appeared. So did Andre Previn's son, who was a houseguest—and, like me, hungry.

The Shire, I learned, was a spacious, cozy place where family, friends, and business associates were always welcome.

Phil and I sat in a corner near the fireplace and chatted for the better part of two hours. He spoke fondly of his love for Sinatra and his music.

He recalled the first time he'd watched Sinatra record in May of 1961, when Bill Putnam snuck him into a recording session at United-Western Studios in Hollywood. Frank was recording "Granada" and a few other songs with Billy May's big band; as a fellow engineer and Phil's mentor, Putnam knew that "the kid" revered Frank, and thought he'd get a kick out of running the tape recorder.

Then, Phil talked about the Sinatra sessions he'd engineered at A&R in 1967. They were Frank's first New York sessions in more than a decade; for the occasion Phil literally rolled out a red carpet. The sessions wrought the Sinatra favorite, "(Over and Over) The World We Knew."

But it was Phil's recent projects with Frank Sinatra—*L.A. Is My Lady* in 1984, and *Duets* and *Duets II* in 1993–94—that we dwelled on. The former was Sinatra's last all-star jazz record; the latter two were million-selling, Grammy Award–winning efforts that became the biggest-selling records of the singer's career.

The stories of Phil's days and nights in the studio with Mr. S. delighted me, and I was sorry when our interview drew to a close. As I packed up my microphones, I casually asked Phil what had turned him on to Frank Sinatra.

"I grew up with his music," he explained. "And I loved his album covers—especially the ones that show him standing in the studio, with the orchestra crowded around him in a semicircle. I studied those pictures to see what kind of microphones they used, and what instruments they were used on . . ."

In that moment, I realized that Phil and I were kindred spirits.

As a youngster I was obsessed with records. Anything having to do with sound recording, actually: LPs, seventy-eights, reel-to-reel tapes and tape recorders, turntables, amplifiers, and microphones all made their way into my bedroom—and my life. The best place for a kid to find records in those days was the old-fashioned, neighborhood yard sale.

It was at such a sale, circa 1973 or '74, that I bought my first copy of *Getz/Gilberto*. I had no idea who Getz or Gilberto were, nor did I care. The album cost me a dime, and I fell in love with the cover and the cool Verve label. It was the first time I saw the name Phil Ramone on a record jacket.

Not long after, another Saturday afternoon record-hunting expedition yielded a stack of Frank Sinatra's Capitol and Reprise records—including *Sinatra's Swingin' Session!!!* and *The Concert Sinatra*—two albums with covers depicting the singer standing in the studio, with the orchestra crowded around him in a semicircle.

I, like Phil, studied those covers.

Kindred spirits.

I was fourteen years old when Billy Joel's *The Stranger* was released in 1977, and I spent hours blasting the album through a pair of old Sony headphones. The record packed a mean wallop.

As an amateur drummer, I was drawn to Liberty DeVitto's solid beat, and the unrelenting drive of Doug Stegmeyer's bass. The sound was crystal clear; the bass tones throbbed with a focus that I'd rarely heard before. To my ears, the punchy, resonant quality of the drums was the way drums should *always* sound on a record. Best of all, every song on *The Stranger* was great.

The Stranger solidified my love for Billy Joel, and his producer—Phil Ramone.

Thereafter, I relished each new Billy Joel release—*52nd Street,*

Glass Houses, Songs in the Attic, An Innocent Man, The Nylon Curtain, and *The Bridge*—not as a Johnny-come-lately, but as a young musician and audiophile who bought them the minute they came out. I can mark each moment of my adolescence through those individual Billy Joel albums, and the landmark songs that sprang from them.

It seemed that everywhere I turned in those days, Phil Ramone was there, an omnipotent and omnipresent figure on the record scene, simultaneously producing soundtracks, jazz records, and pop albums by the likes of Paul Simon, Billy Joel, Phoebe Snow, and a plethora of other great artists.

I was thrilled to learn that it was Phil who engineered Ben E. King's "Spanish Harlem," "Raindrops Keep Falling on My Head" from *Butch Cassidy and the Sundance Kid,* Simon and Garfunkel's "My Little Town"—even the Starland Vocal Band's "Afternoon Delight." All were Top 40 pop songs that were in heavy rotation on WABC-AM radio in New York, and they piqued my pre-teen interest. I simply wanted to hear them over and over; even then I recognized the sophistication of their production.

But Sinatra was our nexus.

When Frank recorded at A&R with Quincy Jones in 1984, it was Phil behind the board. They filmed the recording sessions and made a documentary showing Sinatra at work in the studio. I watched the tape with rapt attention, and there, to my delight, was Phil Ramone. It was the first time I put a face to the name.

I was in a meeting at Sony Music's New York headquarters in early 1993 when I first heard of Frank Sinatra's *Duets* project.

My colleagues and I were planning a massive reissue of the nearly three hundred sides that Frank Sinatra had made while at Columbia Records in the 1940s, and Frank's business manager, Nathan "Sonny" Golden, was conferring with our team. During a break, I asked Sonny about The Man:

Me: How's Mr. Sinatra doing?

Sonny: He's fine. He's getting ready to do the *Duets* album.

ME: He's going to sing face-to-face with the rock and rollers?

SONNY: They're using some kind of fiber-optic line to let his
         partners sing from remote locations.

ME: Really? Who's producing?

SONNY: Phil Ramone.

I was not surprised.

While a bit controversial in its day, *Duets* represented cutting-edge technology and reflected the progressive thinking of its producer.

Before I left the Shire on that wet September day in 1999, I told Phil that he should write a book. "I'd love to work with you on it," I said naively. He was a world-famous record producer, and I was a first-time author.

Phil and I crossed paths a few times after that.

Joe D'Ambrosio, his assistant at the time, kept in touch and helped arrange for me to interview Phil again for my second book, on Brian Wilson's *Pet Sounds*. I bumped into him at the Grammy Awards in Los Angeles in 2002—the year that Carlos Santana's album *Supernatural* won big.

Through the years, the idea of writing a book with Phil was always in the back of my mind.

And so, I was flattered to receive a call to meet with Phil and his (now our) literary agent, Lisa Queen, in April 2003. They outlined an idea they had for Phil's book, and I jumped at the chance to help write it. After all, Phil is a kindred spirit.

It has been my privilege to collaborate with Phil, and to help turn his recollections into this volume. It's been three years in the making; during that time I've spent hundreds of hours with Phil, talking about music, recording, life, art, politics, and just about every other topic imaginable.

I was again welcomed to the Shire—this time as a frequent

guest, many times overnight. The warmth I had experienced on my first visit several years before had only offered a taste of the lively spirit of the household.

During the course of our work, I've spoken at length with dozens of Phil's friends, artists and colleagues—including Quincy Jones, Billy Joel, and Tony Bennett. To a person, the admiration and respect that artists, arrangers, engineers, record company executives, and friends have for Phil Ramone is evident in their words, their hugs, and most of all, in the music they create under his watchful eye.

More than anything, I'm fortunate to have had the rare chance to watch Phil as he recorded (on separate occasions) Carole King and Elton John, and as he mixed albums for Olivia Newton-John (with engineer Joel Moss) and Elton John and Ray Charles (with engineer Frank Filippetti).

To illustrate the surety of Phil's direction, I'll reconstruct (from my hastily scribbled notes) a bit of the magic I saw in the studio as Phil recorded Carole King at Right Track Studios on West Forty-Eighth Street in June 2004:

Phil greets Carole at the door, and kindly introduces me. Once her coat is off, he walks Carole into the control room so she can meet the crew. Then, it's into the studio where a music stand and boom-mounted microphone await her.

CK: Oh, Phil! You have my lovely Neumann mike . . .

PR: Naturally.

[He returns to the booth.]

PR: We're ready when you are.

[Carole runs through the song—"Ton Nom"]

CK: I'm trying that first line two or three different ways,
       but it's all coming out the same.

PR: That's okay—experiment all you want.

[Carole sings again]

PR: It's fine, but there's one line where it's a little phlegmy.
      One more for me would be great.
[Two more takes—still a little rough]

There's a short break. The song has some difficult changes, and
Phil asks if Carole is comfortable with the tempo. She returns to the
studio, and does another take—her fifth.

PR: Let's try one more. The only way to play it is softer,
      but then we might lose the emotionality of it.
CK: Do you want me to try it a bit softer?
*[She sings a few lines to give Phil an idea of the level she's
thinking of]*
PR: Yes! That's great. You're still in the range—
      you're still breaking our hearts!
[On the sixth take Carole nails the vocal]
PR: It's a beauty! I love you for that . . .

At the mike, Carole thinks like a producer. She knows exactly
which words from which take work best, and she mentions them as
she goes along. Phil, following the lyric sheet, makes small notes in
the margin.

When she comes back into the control room, Phil suggests a tea
break.

Carole and I sit in the green room, talking about politics and
current events. The Iraq War is foremost on everyone's mind, and
Carole isn't shy about expressing her views. She breaks me up when
she grabs a yellow Post-it note and "sketches" her impression of the
current administration. The drawing—a musical lyre—is as meta-
phoric and pointed as one of her songs.

Those songs—"Up on the Roof," "You've Got A Friend," "I
Feel the Earth Move," "So Far Away," and "(You Make Me Feel
Like A) Natural Woman" have been part of my life since childhood.

They moved me then, and they move me now—in the somewhat inexplicable way that great songs should.

As we chat, Phil is in the studio, cutting together a rough edit of Carole's best vocal takes. He dashes in and out of the green room, asking if there's anything he can get for her. When he's finished editing, he calls her in.

Before playing the rough edit of "Ton Nom," Phil mentions that Peter Cincotti, a young artist he's been working with, has just recorded "Up on the Roof."

"Would you like to hear it?" he asks.

"Of course," she answers.

Cincotti's rendition of Carole's "Up on the Roof" is exceptional. Its tenderness of spirit embodies all of the sentiment that Carole surely thought of when writing the song.

After the preview, Carole beams.

"I love it!" she exclaims. "Please tell Peter how beautiful it is, and how much I love his voice," she says.

"Would you like to tell him yourself? I've got his cell number right here—I can call him," Phil ventures.

The call is placed. The conversation between King and Cincotti is warm and natural. "It's *wonderful*, Peter," she says. Phil sits quietly, watching like a proud papa.

After the respite, Carole listens to the playback of "Ton Nom." As Phil explains how he'll smooth out the edits, Carole nods affirmatively. "I trust you so much, Phil—I know that whatever you do will be fine."

Those words say it all.

Everyone trusts Phil Ramone, and that trust is well placed. With Phil at the board, one knows that the music is in good hands.

What can I tell you about Phil Ramone that hasn't been said?

That he isn't simply a musician, a recording engineer, or the preeminent record producer of his time. Phil Ramone is a true Renaissance man.

He's in tune with the arts, well versed in politics, and has a deep understanding of social issues. He can compare the coaching strategies of the Yankees and Mets, explain the history of French advertising art, and point out the merits of using rare sea salt instead of regular on your food—all in the same conversation.

Phil is also an inveterate thinker.

As the stories in this book amply demonstrate, Phil Ramone is one of the music industry's great problem solvers; a person who would be as comfortable working in a think tank or science lab as in the recording studio. He studies people and situations like an efficiency expert, constantly devising ways to improve the way things work.

Then too, Phil handles every aspect of his personal and professional life with meticulous care—a quality that rings true in the plethora of great music he's had a hand in creating. He's organized, fastidious, and loathes unpreparedness.

But more important than any of these things is the human, altruistic side of Phil Ramone. Although his work often takes him from his family, he's never really far—spiritually or emotionally. Genuine concern for others is one of Phil's most endearing personal qualities.

So are modesty and humility.

Phil would never tell you that he was a child prodigy, or that he played a Royal Command Performance for the Queen when he was just ten years old. But I will.

He would never admit that he had a major role in helping Billy Joel craft some of his best-known songs, but I'll tell you that, too. "Phil Ramone was as responsible for writing many of those songs as I was," Billy told me at the start of our first conversation. "He helped me sort out my ideas and bring structure to them."

Phil's style is elegant and simple, his approach to life unpretentious.

The accolades of a lifetime spent at the forefront of American pop culture—the coveted Grammy Awards (fourteen and counting)—

aren't prominently displayed in Phil's home. Neither are the hundreds of photos of Phil with every major figure in the history of music, film, art, and politics. They're there, of course: the Grammys are elegantly tucked into nooks in the library, the photos carefully filed away in the office. But these are places where few people get to roam.

My life has taken twists and turns; the road that led me to music and writing has been rather unconventional. Had I known as a teenager what I know today, I would have fulfilled my passion for the recording arts by calling Phil Ramone, and volunteering to sweep the floors at A&R.

Though I could kick myself for not doing so, I can honestly say that collaborating with him on this book was the next best thing. Thank you, Phil—for sticking to it and seeing this book through. Love you, man!

Charles L. Granata
Livingston, New Jersey
April 2007

I owe a special nod to all of those in the A&R Recording Studios family who gave so much of themselves to the artists, musicians, and me, and who helped make A&R one of the greatest recording studios in the world: Roberta Ash, Laura Loncteaux Benn, "Reverend Bob," Janet Boyd, Jim Boyer, Jacquie Buchanan, Diane "Foxy" Charlap, Sherry Day, Nick DeMinno, Laura Doty, Dolly Drum, Larry Franke, Don Fry, Carol Peters Gadd, Michelle Galfas, Muriel Gellis, Maria Hein, Patty Ido, Bradshaw Leigh, Jay Messina, Georgie Ofrel, Elliot Scheiner, Al Schmitt, Bob Schwartz, Michele Slater, Bernie Teitel-baum, Ken Topolsky, Art Ward, and Mary Wood.

And for those I'll never forget: Jack Arnold, Milton Brooks, Tom Dowd, Ahmet and Neshui Ertegun, Arif Mardin, Bill Schwartau, and David Smith.

As in the making of a record, the creation of a memoir requires the assistance of many people. The authors are deeply indebted to the following friends, colleagues, and family members who gener-ously offered us their time and talent during the preparation of this manuscript:

Jeff Abraham, Chuck Ainly, Steve Albin, C. Scott Amann, Den-nis Arfa, Kerry Aylward, Karen and Russel Barling, John Barry, Barry Beckett, Tony Bennett, Danny Bennett, Alan and Marilyn Bergman, Steve Berkowitz, Adam Block, James Bordino, Jim Boyer, Betsy and Frank Bresnick, Joshua Bresnick, Alan Bronstein, Hugh Brown, Buddy Cage, Greg Calbi, Gerard Campanella, Richie Cannata, Hank Cattaneo, Amedeo Ciminnisi, Jill Cooperman and Dylan Camche, Elvis Costello, Diana D'Angelo, Jill Dell'Abate, Didier C. Deutsch, Don DeVito, Liberty DeVitto, Laura Doty, Maureen Droney, Marty Ehrlichman, Michael Feinstein, Frank Filipetti, Robert Finkelstein, Larry Franke, Don Fry, Steve Friedman, Will Friedwald, Josh Getlin, Astrud Gilberto, Neil Gilles, Joann and Wayne Goldberg, Nathan "Sonny" Golden, Burton Goldstein, Joyce Gore, Adrienne & Guido Granata, John and Mary Beth

Granata, Randy Haecker, Roy Halee, Jane Hecht, George Helmy, Bob Irwin, Ted Jensen, Billy Joel, Elton John, Jeff Jones, Quincy Jones, John Kelly, Matthew Kelly, Carole King, Marc Kirkeby, Jamie Krents, Bradshaw Leigh, Karen Lemquist, Tommy LiPuma, Roosevelt Louis, Meaghan Lyons, George Massenburg, Andreas Meyer, Joel Moss, Liza Minnelli, Rob Mathes, Rob Mounsey, Dan Palmere, Charles Pignone, Darcy Proper, Felix Ramirez, Andrew, David, Lauren, and Walter Reinfeld, Clarke Rigsby, Mark Rupp, Philipe Saisse, Rob Santos, David Sarser, Elliot Scheiner, Eric Schilling, Al Schmitt, Wynn Schwartau, Walter Sear, Bernard Searle, Paul Simon, Nancy Sinatra, David Smith, Kip Smith, Jude Spatola, Rani, Mark, and Matt "Bean Dean" Steinberg, Barbra Streisand, Steve Sussman, Creed Taylor, Bob Waldmann, Sylvia Weiner, and Mark Wilder.

We are also indebted to Lisa Queen & Jonah Cardillo at Queen Literary; Will Schwalbe, Emily Gould, Zareen Jaffery, Karen Minster, and David Lott at Hyperion; Nancy Munoz, Lisa Perez, and Ananda Kritsky at Phil Ramone, Inc.; Nancy and Martin Reinfeld, and Lulu for the gift of their support, guidance, and assistance during the three years we spent writing this book.

We are especially grateful for the participation of Greg Brunswick, whose exceptional research skills added immeasurably to the final manuscript.

Special thanks to the family members who have always been there: Andi, Kelly, and Rick Freedman, Doreen Kerner, Rick, Elizabeth, and Seth Kerner, Joseph Ichiuji, Sue Ichiuji, Stacy and Julie Ichiuji, Doug and Melissa Ichiuji, Kim and Neil Uppal.

Most of all, we owe our love and gratitude to BJ, Karen, Matt, Simon, Ann, and Maxwell Ramone, and Barbara, Kate, and Alex Granata. Your love, patience, and understanding have truly made this endeavor possible!

Photo Research: Helen Ashford (Michael Ochs Archive), Hugh Brown, Richie Cannata, Alan Dahl, Sam Emerson, Larry Franke,

Charles L. Granata, Dina Greenberg (WireImage), KEG Productions, Inc., Ananda Kritsky, Glen Korman and Che Williams (Sony/BMG Photo Archive), Nancy Munoz, Lisa Perez, Clarke Rigsby, and Jan Press Photomedia.

Lyric permissions: Neil Gilles

RECORDING ENGINEER

All titles are for albums unless otherwise noted
(*) indicates Coproducer or Producer credit in addition to engineering

1958

David "Fathead" Newman: *It's Mister Fathead* (Atlantic)

1959

Billy Taylor: *Billy Taylor with Four Flutes* (Riverside)

1960

Buck Clayton: *Goin' to Kansas City* (Riverside)

1961

John Coltrane: *Olé Coltrane* (Atlantic)

1962

Michel Legrand: *Plays Richard Rodgers* (Philips)
Quincy Jones: *Quincy Plays for Pussycats* (Mercury)
Quincy Jones: *Big Band Bossa Nova* (Mercury)
David "Fathead" Newman: *Fathead Comes On* (Atlantic)

1963

Kai Winding: *Mondo Cane #2* (Verve)
Quincy Jones: *Plays Hip Hits* (Mercury)
Gil Evans: *The Individualism of Gil Evans* (Verve)
Stan Getz & Luiz Bonta: *Jazz Samba Encore!* (Verve)
Count Basie: *Lil' Ol' Groovemaker . . . Basie!* (Verve)
Antonio Carlos Jobim: *The Composer of Desafinado, Plays* (Verve)
Lesley Gore: *I'll Cry If I Want To* (Mercury)
Stan Getz/João Gilberto: *Getz/Gilberto* (Verve)
Stan Getz: *Reflections* (Verve)

1964

Quincy Jones: *The Pawnbroker* (Soundtrack) (Mercury)
Quincy Jones: *Explores the Music of Henry Mancini* (Mercury)
Neal Hefti: *Li'l Darlin'* (20th Century)
Wes Montgomery: *Movin' Wes* (Verve)
Lesley Gore: "You Don't Own Me" (single) (Mercury)
Quincy Jones: *Golden Boy* (Mercury)

1965

Oscar Peterson Trio: *With Respect to Nat* (Limelight)
Quincy Jones: *Quincy's Got a Brand New Bag* (Mercury)
Lesley Gore: "Sunshine Lollipops and Rainbows" (single) (Mercury)
Broadway Cast Album: *I Had a Ball* (Decca)

1966

Joe Williams: *Presenting Joe Williams and the Thad Jones–
    Mel Lewis Jazz Orchestra* (Solid State)
Jimmy McGriff: *Tribute to Count Basie* (Delta)
Manny Albam: *Brass on Fire* (Solid State)
Manny Albam: *The Soul of the City* (Solid State)*
Jimmy McGriff: *The Big Band: A Tribute to Basie* (Solid State)*
Jimmy McGriff: *Cherry* (Solid State)
Jimmy McGriff: *A Bag Full of Soul* (Solid State)
Thad Jones/Mel Lewis: *Presenting Thad Jones & Mel Lewis*
    (Solid State)

1967

Neil Diamond: *Just for You* (Bang)
Neil Diamond: "Solitary Man"/ "Girl, You'll Be a Woman Soon"
    (Bang)
Dionne Warwick: "Alfie"/ "The Beginning of Loneliness"
    (Scepter)
Nelson Riddle: *Music for Wives & Lovers* (Solid State)

Frank Sinatra: *Frank Sinatra and the World We Knew* (Reprise)

Peter, Paul and Mary: *Album 1700* (Warner Bros.)

Peter, Paul and Mary: "Leaving on a Jet Plane" (Warner Bros.)

Janis Ian: *The Secret Life of J. Eddy Fink* (Verve Forecast)

Film Soundtrack: *Casino Royale* (Colgem)*

1968

Luiz Bonfá: *Bonfa* (Dot)

David "Fathead" Newman: *Bigger & Better* (Atlantic)

Jimmy Smith: *Stay Loose . . . Jimmy Smith Sings Again* (Verve)

Barbra Streisand: *A Happening in Central Park* (TV broadcast)
   (Columbia)

Dionne Warwick: "(Theme from) Valley of the Dolls"/"I Say A
   Little Prayer" (Scepter)

Dionne Warwick: "Let Me Be Lonely" (Scepter)

Dionne Warwick: "Do You Know the Way to San Jose" (Scepter)

The 5th Dimension: *Stoned Soul Picnic* (Soul City)

Peter, Paul and Mary: *Late Again* (Warner Bros.)

Dionne Warwick: *Promises, Promises* (Scepter)

Film Soundtrack: *You Are What You Eat* (Columbia)*

1969

Procol Harum: *A Salty Dog* (A&M)

The Winter Consort: *Road* (A&M)

Broadway Cast Album: *Promises, Promises* (United Artists)*

B.B. King: *Live & Well* (ABC)

Film Soundtrack: *Butch Cassidy and the Sundance Kid* (A&M)

Burt Bacharach: *Make It Easy on Yourself* (A&M)

Peter, Paul & Mary: *Peter, Paul & Mommy* (Warner Bros.)*

Film Soundtrack: *Midnight Cowboy* (United Artists)*

Film Soundtrack: *On Her Majesty's Secret Service* (United Artists)*

Louis Armstrong: "We Have All the Time in the World" (single)
   (Capitol)*

1970

Gordon Lightfoot: *Sit Down Young Stranger* (Reprise)

B.J. Thomas: "Raindrops Keep Falling on My Head" (single) (Scepter)

1971

Paul McCartney: *Ram* (Apple)

Quincy Jones: *Smackwater Jack* (A&M)*

Elton John: *11-17-70* (MCA)

Burt Bacharach: *Burt Bacharach* (A&M)

1972

Broadway Cast Album: *Pippin* (Motown)

James Taylor: *One Man Dog* (Warner Bros.)

Liza Minnelli: *Liza with a "Z"* (Columbia)

The Band: *Rock of Ages* (Capitol)

Paul Simon: *Paul Simon* (Columbia)

1973

Alice Cooper: *Muscle of Love* (Warner Bros.)

Chuck Mangione: *Land of Make Believe* (Phonogram/Mercury)

Chicago: *Chicago VI* (Columbia)

Paul Simon: *There Goes Rhymin' Simon* (Columbia)*

1974

Aretha Franklin: *Let Me Into Your Life* (Atlantic)

Duane Allman: *An Anthology, Volume II* (Capricorn)*

Paul Simon: *In Concert Live Rhymin'* (Warner Bros.)

Phoebe Snow: *Phoebe Snow* (Shelter/Capitol)*

Bob Dylan and the Band: *Before the Flood* (Asylum)

Burt Bacharach: *Greatest Hits* (A&M)*

1975

Broadway Cast Album: *The Wiz* (Atlantic)

Alice Cooper: *Welcome to My Nightmare* (Atlantic)

Stephanie Mills: *For the First Time* (Motown)*

Broadway Cast Album: *Chicago* (Arista)*

Simon & Garfunkel: "My Little Town" (single) (Columbia)*

Bob Dylan: *Blood on the Tracks* (Columbia)

Judy Collins: *Judith* (Elektra)

Paul Simon: *Still Crazy After All These Years* (Warner Bros.)*

1976

Barbra Streisand: *A Star Is Born* (Columbia)*

Barbra Streisand: "Evergreen" (single) (Columbia)*

Starland Vocal Band: *Starland Vocal Band* (Windsong)*

Starland Vocal Band: "Afternoon Delight" (single) (Windsong)*

Paul Anka: "The Times of Your Life"/"Water Runs Deep" (single)
   (United Artists)

David Sanborn: *David Sanborn* (Warner Bros.)*

1977

Paul Simon: *Greatest Hits, Etc.* (Columbia)*

1988

B.B. King: *The Electric B.B. "His Best"* (MCA)

1989

Gloria Estefan: "Here We Are"/"Cut Both Ways" (remixed) (Epic)

1991

Gloria Estefan: *Into the Light* (remixed) (Epic)

PRODUCER

1966

Harry Belafonte: *Calypso in Brass* (RCA Victor)

1977

Jimmy Carter: *The Presidential Inaugural Album* (Columbia)

Phoebe Snow: *Never Letting Go* (Columbia)

Kenny Loggins: *Celebrate Me Home* (Columbia)

Burt Bacharach: *Futures* (A&M)

Billy Joel: *The Stranger* (Columbia)

1978

Phoebe Snow: *Against the Grain* (Columbia)

Chicago: *Hot Streets* (Columbia)

Billy Joel: *52nd Street* (Columbia)

1979

Chicago: *Chicago XIII* (Columbia)

1980

Paul Simon: *One-Trick Pony* (Warner Bros.)

Billy Joel: *Glass Houses* (Columbia)

1981

Paul Simon: *On the Concert Stage* (video)

Billy Joel: *Songs in the Attic* (Columbia)

1982

Simon and Garfunkel: *The Concert in Central Park*
    (Warner Bros.)

Karen Kamon: "Da Doo Ron Ron"/"You Can Do Better
    Than That" (single) (Columbia)

Broadway Cast Album: *Little Shop of Horrors* (Geffen)
Billy Joel: *The Nylon Curtain* (Columbia)

1983
Barbra Streisand: *Yentl* (Columbia)
Barbra Streisand: "The Way He Makes Me Feel" (single) (Columbia)
Michael Sembello: *Bossa Nova Hotel* (Warner Bros.)
Billy Joel: *An Innocent Man* (Columbia)
Film Soundtrack: *Flashdance* (Casablanca)
Michael Sembello: "Maniac" (single) (Casablanca)

1984
Karen Kamon: *Heart of You* (CBS/Sony)
Film Soundtrack: *Ghostbusters* (Arista)
Julian Lennon: *Valotte* (Atlantic)
Karen Kamon: *Voices* (Atlantic)

1985
Paul McCartney: "Spies Like Us" (Capitol/Parlophone)
Film Soundtrack: *White Nights* (Atlantic)
Billy Joel: *Greatest Hits Volume 1 and Volume II* (Columbia)

1986
Julian Lennon: *The Secret Value of Daydreaming* (Atlantic)
Eddie Rabbitt: *Rabbitt Trax* (RCA)
Paul McCartney: "Only Love Remains" (single) (EMI)
Marilyn Martin: "Night Moves" (single) (Atlantic)
Billy Joel: *The Bridge* (Columbia)

1987
Paul McCartney: "Once Upon a Long Ago"/"Back on My Feet"
    (single) (EMI)
Broadway Cast Album: *Starlight Express* (MCA)

1988

Barbra Streisand: "Till I Loved You"/"All I Ask of You"
(single) (Columbia)

Paul McCartney: "Figure of Eight" (single) (Parlophone)

1989

Film Soundtrack: *Goya . . . A Life in Song* (Columbia)

Cyndi Lauper: "A Night to Remember"/"I Don't Want to Be
Your Friend" (Columbia)

Karen Carpenter: *Lovelines* (A&M)

Paul McCartney: "P.S. I Love You"/"Love Me Do" (single) (EMI)

1990

Paul Simon: *The Rhythm of the Saints* (Warner Bros.)

1991

Billy Joel: *Leningrad* (video) (CBS/Sony Music Video)

1992

Sinéad O'Connor: "I Believe in You" (A&M)

Ringo Starr: *Time Takes Time* (Private Music)

Sinéad O'Connor: *Am I Not Your Girl?* (Chrysalis)

Liza Minnelli: *Live from Radio City Music Hall* (Sony Music)

1993

Gloria Estefan: *Christmas Through Your Eyes* (Epic)

Frank Sinatra: *Duets* (Capitol)

André Previn: *What Headphones?* (Angel)

1994

Sylvia McNair and André Previn: *Sure Thing—
The Jerome Kern Songbook* (Polygram)

Frank Sinatra: *Duets II* (Capitol)

Diane Schuur & B.B. King: *Heart to Heart* (GRP)
Barry Manilow: *Singin' with the Big Bands* (Arista)
Broadway Cast Album: *Passion* (Angel)

1995

Frank Sinatra: *Sinatra 80th Live in Concert* (Capitol)

1996

Pavarotti & Friends: *For War Child* (Decca/London)
Film Soundtrack: *Jingle All the Way* (TVT)
Brian Setzer Orchestra: "Honky Tonk" (Interscope)
André Previn: *Ballads* (Angel)
Broadway Cast Album: *A Funny Thing Happened on the Way to the Forum* (Angel)
Brian Setzer Orchestra: *Guitar Slinger* (Interscope)
Gerry Mulligan: *Legacy* (N2K Encoded Music)
Johnny Mathis: *All About Love* (Columbia)
Natalie Cole: *Stardust* (Elektra)
Broadway Cast Album: *Company* (Angel)
Broadway Cast Album: *Big: The Musical* (Universal)
Patricia Kaas: *Café Noir* (Sony Music)

1997

Paul McCartney: "Love Come Tumbling Down"/ "Beautiful Night" (EMI)
Paul McCartney: "Atlantic Ocean"/"Love Mix"/"Same Love" (EMI)
Tony Bennett/Billie Holiday: "God Bless the Child" (Columbia)
Clint Eastwood: *Eastwood After Hours: Live at Carnegie Hall* (Warner Bros.)
Patricia Kaas: *Dans Ma Chair* (Sony Music)
Dave Grusin: *Dave Grusin Presents West Side Story* (N2K Encoded Music)

Billy Joel: *Greatest Hits Volume III* (Columbia)

T. S. Monk: *T. S. Monk on Monk* (N2K Encoded Music)

1998

The Three Tenors: "You'll Never Walk Alone" (single)
    (Polygram)

The Brian Setzer Orchestra: "Hollywood Nocturne" (Interscope)

Aretha Franklin: "Here We Go Again"/"In the Morning"/
    "Nessun Dorma" (Arista)

Pavarotti & Friends: *For the Children of Liberia* (Decca/London)

Barry Manilow: *Manilow Sings Sinatra* (Arista)

1999

Elton John: *Elton John and Tim Rice's Aida* (Disney/Hollywood)

Luciano Pavarotti & Friends: *For Guatemala & Kosovo*
    (Decca/London)

Natalie Cole: *Snowfall on the Sahara* (Elektra)

Michael Bolton: *Timeless/The Classics Vol. 2* (Columbia)

George Michael: *Songs from the Last Century* (Virgin)

2000

Pavarotti & Friends: *For Cambodia and Tibet* (Decca/London)

Diane Schuur: *Friends for Schuur* (Concord Jazz)

Liza Minnelli: *Minnelli on Minnelli: Live at the Palace* (Angel)

Broadway Cast Album: *The Wild Party* (Decca Broadway)

2001

Elton John: *One Night Only/The Greatest Hits* (Universal)

Pavarotti & Friends: *For Afghanistan* (Decca/London)

Various: *An All-Star Tribute to Brian Wilson* (TV broadcast/
    DVD, Image Entertainment)

Tony Bennett: *Playin' with My Friends: Bennett Sings the Blues*
    (Columbia/RPM)

Diane Schuur: *Swingin' for Schuur* (Concord Jazz)
Michael Amante: *Michael Amante* (Medalist)
Broadway Cast Album: *Seussical: The Musical* (Decca Broadway)

2002
Elton John and Alessandro Safina "Your Song" (single) (Mercury)
Rod Stewart: *It Had to Be You . . . The Great American Songbook*
    (J Records)
Liza Minnelli: *Liza's Back* (J Records)
Bono: "That's Life" (Mercury)
Various: *Party at the Palace/The Queen's Jubilee Concert*
    (BBC/Opus Arts)

2003
Chicago: *Chicago XXV—Christmas* (Warner Bros.)
Michael Amante: *Tell Her I Love Her* (Medalist/RCA)
Rod Stewart: *As Time Goes By . . . The Great American Songbook*
    Volume II (J Records)
Peter Cincotti: *Peter Cincotti* (Concord)
Broadway Cast Album: *The Boy from Oz* (Decca/Broadway)

2004
Film Soundtrack: *Beyond the Sea* (Rhino)
Ray Charles: *Genius Loves Company* (Concord)
Peter Cincotti: *On the Moon* (Concord)
Olivia Newton-John: *Indigo: Women of Song* (Universal—
    Australia issue only)
Barry Manilow: *Scores: Songs from Copacabana and Harmony*
    (Concord)
Tony Bennett: *The Art of Romance* (Columbia)
Clay Aiken: *Merry Christmas with Love* (RCA)
Elton John: *Dream Ticket* (DVD—Live from NYC & London)
    (Universal)

2005

Ray Charles: *Genius & Friends* (Warner Bros./Rhino)

London Cast: *Billy Elliot* (Universal International)

2006

Tony Bennett: *Duets: An American Classic* (Columbia/RPM)

Gladys Knight: *Before Me* (Verve)

Billy Joel: "All My Life" (single) (Columbia)

2007

Various Artists: *We All Love Ella: Celebrating the First Lady of Song* (Verve)

AWARDS, HONORS, AND DEGREES
Grammy Awards

1964   Stan Getz/Gilberto: *Getz/Gilberto* (Best Engineered Recording)

1969   Broadway Cast: *Promises, Promises* (Best Score)

1975   Paul Simon: *Still Crazy After All These Years* (Album of the Year)

1978   Billy Joel: "Just the Way You Are" (Record of the Year)

1979   Billy Joel: *52nd Street* (Album of the Year)

1980   Producer of the Year (nonclassical)

1983   Film Soundtrack: *Flashdance* (Best Album—Original Score/Motion Picture)

1994   Broadway Cast: *Passion* (Best Musical Show Album)

2002   Tony Bennett: *Playin' with My Friends:*
Bennett Sings the Blues
(Best Traditional Pop Vocal Album)

2004   Ray Charles: *Genius Loves Company*
(Album of the Year)

2004   Ray Charles: *Genius Loves Company*
(Best Surround Sound Album)

2004   Outstanding Technical Significance
to the Recording Field

2005   Tony Bennett: *The Art of Romance*
(Best Traditional Pop Vocal Album)

2006   Tony Bennett: *Duets: An American Classic*
(Best Traditional Pop Vocal Album)

**Other National Academy of Recording Arts and Sciences
(NARAS) Honors**

1965   National Trustee Award, Engineering
1984   Governors Award: Honor Roll for A&R/Producers
2000   New York Heroes Award
2001   National Trustees Award

Other Honors and Awards
1992   TEC Hall of Fame Award
1994   Rock Walk Award
1998   National Mentoring Partnership:
National Recognition Award

Honorary Degrees
Doctor of Musicology, Berklee College of Music, Boston, MA
Doctor of Musicology, Five Towns College, Dix Hills, NY
Doctor of Humane Letters, Skidmore College, Saratoga Springs, NY